GANGS, DRUGS AND (DIS)ORGANISED CRIME

Robert McLean

BRISTOL
UNIVERSITY
PRESS

First published in Great Britain in 2019 by

Bristol University Press
University of Bristol
1-9 Old Park Hill
Bristol
BS2 8BB
UK
t: +44 (0)117 954 5940
www.bristoluniversitypress.co.uk

North America office:
Policy Press
c/o The University of Chicago Press
1427 East 60th Street
Chicago, IL 60637, USA
t: +1 773 702 7700
f: +1 773-702-9756
sales@press.uchicago.edu
www.press.uchicago.edu

British Library Cataloguing in Publication Data
A catalogue record for this book is available from the British Library

Library of Congress Cataloging-in-Publication Data
A catalog record for this book has been requested

ISBN 978-1-5292-0302-8 hardcover
ISBN 978-1-5292-0304-2 ePub
ISBN 978-1-5292-0305-9 ePdf

Cover design by Blu Inc
Front cover image: www.alamy.com
Printed and bound in Great Britain by CPI Group (UK) Ltd,
Croydon, CR0 4YY
Bristol University Press uses environmentally responsible print partners

Contents

List of Tables and Figures

Table

Figures

Acknowledgements

This book is dedicated to my mum. I love her so much and miss her every day. There is not a day that goes past where I do not think of her. Sadly, she passed before I completed my honours degree, but I know she would have been proud to have seen my graduation earlier this year. I know she would also have loved meeting her grandchildren Clair and Faith, and my beautiful wife Nicola. She is the bravest person I have ever met, and a hero in every sense of the word. I would also like to thank my step-dad Allan, my brothers William, Lenny and Graeme, and my extended family. Of course, I would also like to take this opportunity to do an old-school Glasgow 'shout-out' to my childhood friends, some of whom I sadly have no idea where they have ended up, but they played a big part in my life nonetheless: the boys from Hutton, including Goffer, Mick, Price, Spice, Algie and Andy; the YBM from fifth year, including Haddow, Donny H., Pea, Rab Mac, Billy and Big Del Curry; the other Govan lads, including Steg, Denzo and Del boy; the Erskine mob, including Moe, Chewy, Gaz, Dooltz, Fuzzy, Purdy, Gordy, Wullie, Kenny, Wade, Fraser and Geo, and all the rest (far too many to include); the Glen St boys, including Gav, Shearer, Don and Jack, as well as Steve, Frazer and Shand (I miss you every day mate); the footy lads from the Croft and Bridge; and the rest from everywhere else. I would also like to thank my colleagues who have been beyond supportive. In particular, Dr Irene Rafanell, Associate Professor James Densley, Associate Professor Simon Harding, Professor Chris Holligan and, most of all, Professor Ross Deuchar, my PhD supervisor, mentor, Christian brother and close friend. Last of all, I would like to thank the participants without whom this research would not have been made possible.

About the Author

Dr Robert McLean is a lecturer at Northumbria University. The original research that provides the foundation for this book was carried out during his time at the University of the West of Scotland (UWS), where he was a PhD student from 2012 to 2017 and also an Associate Lecturer from 2015 to 2018. Ethical approval for the ongoing research was granted by his then home institution at UWS. Robert has a produced a considerable amount of scholarly literature on the main topics in the book, as well as in related areas such as prisons, desistance and spirituality.

Preface

About the book

The book provides a systematic overview of gang organisation as a means for gang business. While most books on gangs tend to provide descriptive accounts of gang behaviour, or analyse certain aspects of gang structure, or even locate gangs within the broader context of the social world in which they operate or originate, this book goes a step further in that the structural process that both influences and is itself influenced by gang activity is examined. Likewise, either consciously doing so or not, most books on gangs tend to focus on a particular gang type when discussing 'gangs'[1] or address the gang as though it were a whole. This is often to the detriment of other typologies, namely, those labelled with overly narrow definitions, such as peer groups or organised crime groups. Yet, this book accounts for the structural processes and activities carried out by gangs at various stages of evolution, beyond those group formations typically labelled 'gang', and makes considerable effort to discuss how the gang at one stage evolves into, or has some degree of relationship with, the gang at the next developmental stage.

Furthermore, when British gang scholars carry out gang research in one location (for example, London) they tend to discuss their findings in one of two ways. The first way tends to present the findings – regardless of where the actual research has been conducted (for example, London) – as though they are representative of gangs across the country, with variations being slight or non-existent. The second way is very much the opposite, with some gang researchers (particularly in Scotland) isolating their studies in the given context so much so that findings are thought to be completely incompatible with other gang studies from further afield, for example, Manchester. Therefore, this book looks to bridge this gap by providing an account of gangs in a very specific context while, at the same time, analysing how they are both unique and yet very much still the same (and thus comparable). By highlighting both differences and similarities, more effective policy can emerge.

Lastly, books on gangs also tend to be written by those at opposite ends of the authorship spectrum, with ex- or reformed offenders writing subjectively at one end, and academics taking an objective approach at the other. This book, however, adopts a hybrid approach to the gang phenomenon. Therefore, in summary, it is fair to say that adopting an authorship stance in the middle aids the book in its effort to give a full systematic account of gang organisation as a means for gang business in a specific context and yet still have far-reaching implications regarding the broader UK landscape.

Why Glasgow and why gangs?

Before proceeding, though, it is important to justify my reason, and process of thought, as to why I decided to study gangs, how I identified existing gaps in literature and, basically, why this research should be given attention, particularly given that I originate from anything but an academic background. To do so, I must – albeit reluctantly – give a brief narrative piece to demonstrate the unique insight that can be brought about by practical experience, as well as theoretical knowledge, and how one supports the other and vice versa. While some researchers stress that true scientific analysis can only be achieved with the removal of researcher subjectivity, others equally highlight that not only is this an impossibility in qualitative research, but having the ability to call upon personal experience to understand the socially constructed world is also invaluable (Mruck and Breuer, 2003). Likewise, in relation to the research that was undertaken for this book, being able to reflect upon personal experience and intertwine this with the findings that emerged from the field and knowledge of literature enabled the research to move beyond contemporary gang narratives and the conventional wisdom of gang research (this will be explained more clearly later). Please note that although some of the following section is perhaps presented in a vague manner, this is largely because it must be substantially censored for a variety of reasons.

Having grown up in one of Glasgow's most deprived housing estates that has a long and synonymous history with gangs and gang violence, I was aware of the local 'Young Team' from an early age. In Glasgow, the Young Team is often an abbreviated term used to describe a group of young teenage boys who engage in territorial violence against other youths of similar age who stay outside the area of residence. These areas, or schemes as they are often known, vary significantly in size and can range from being literally a few tenement blocks, as with 'Young Kimbo

Kill'[2] located in Glasgow's Govan district, to an entire town or housing estate, such as 'Young Garren' (Erskine) or 'Linwood Paka' (Linwood) (see Figure 1).

Also, given that gangs are territorial-based outfits, membership itself is often ascribed through residence and peer association (predominantly male), as opposed to one having a willingness to join; you join simply through hanging around. Like many youths in the scheme, I had elder family members, and knew older teens in the area, who would frequently discuss their own gang experiences (past or present) with myself and friends. This was often done so in a way that glorified violence – the chase and thrill of fighting. Intertwined with Scottish banter, it was typically done so in a humorous way. In many ways, by the age of 12, I was more acutely aware of Glasgow gangs, membership and territoriality than the average academic. Miller (2015), drawing upon North American gang literature, incorporates Vigil's (1988a, 1988b) conceptualisation that youths are socialised into gangs and gang membership via local cultures in Glasgow. This was very true for us, particularly as the group began to solidify in response to external threats – perceived or real – as we explored and narrated others' stories with our own (see Klein, 1971; Sandberg 2010; Presser and Sandberg, 2015). It was a process of territorial othering (see Hallsworth and Brotherton, 2011). Essentially, by the age of 12, I was not a gang member who had undergone consensual ascription into the gang; rather, like every male in my scheme who hung around in large groups in certain locations, we became a visual reference point for other youths outwith the scheme who identified us as rivals – potential or otherwise. Even for those who did not hang around, rival outfits would say of them 'They come from [area X or Y]' and, at times, this would be enough to warrant an assault.

Figure 1: Teucharhill scheme, home to local gang Young Kimbo Kill (YKK)

Source: Historic Environment Scotland, © HES.

Now seen as a gang by others outside and within the scheme, this regenerative process would also see us being labelled with the local estate or neighbourhood name, for example, 'Young Govan Team' from Govan, 'Young Priesty' from Priesthill or 'Young Shortroods' from Shortroods. Yet, rather than shy away from this label, we ascribed to it and adopted it as our own. When you lack economic and social capital and are similarly socially excluded from mainstream leisure activities deemed to be legitimate (primarily due to reasons related to poverty), then gang fighting breaks the boredom. Likewise, it can bring a sense of status, masculinity, honour, friendship and social bonding among youths – the latter points are, at times, all too regularly overlooked. A reputation, often acquired through the display of those masculine traits strongly associated with a working-class value system (such as being tough, aggressive and physically strong), means status among peers, and higher status means more recognition and social standing. Ultimately, in many ways, we simply imitated and sought that which wider society already ascribed to. The only difference is that we attained it, or attempted to do so, via different means, adhering to those social scripts most available to us (Varese, 2010). In our Young Team, we would fight everyone from our age range from all locations and even go to underage nightclubs[3] in the city centre like Archaos to: (1) meet females; and (2) fight other Young Teams from the wider Glasgow league table, if you will, and spread our reputation beyond the local, if possible. At times, it was spread for the wrong reasons, though, that is, getting battered as opposed to doing the battering. Yet, come my mid- to late adolescent years, like many, I had matured out of territorialism. Yet, there remains an important distinction between the gang and territorialism. For those who (1) retained delinquency, and what was developing into criminality, as an integral feature of their identity, and (2) could access illegal markets by way of kinship and local reputation, the gang grew to serve a different purpose.

Fast-forward a decade or more and my life had changed rapidly. For reasons that I keep to myself and those I love most dearly, I had gone wayward and become involved in a substantial amount of trouble over the years. However, by age 21, I had become a born-again Christian and had ceased to partake in behaviour that was deemed 'unlawful', albeit, at times, fluctuating in and out of the desistance process, which, in reality, is lengthy. As part of this process, I had also begun to seek a legitimate career path. As such, I attended local voluntary courses to help improve my spelling and counting capabilities prior to attending college and subsequently university in the years to come. As part of my honours degree, I had to complete a dissertation that focused on Glasgow gangs, and with the help of my then lecturer Dr John Roger, I was eventually accepted for a doctoral study under the tutelage of Professor Ross Deuchar – a leading, if not the leading, contemporary scholar regarding gangs in Scotland. Nurturing my academic studies, Ross encouraged me to read up on gang literature, which I duly did. Yet, as I did so, I noticed that a large section of gang life went by unnoticed in a Scottish context. What happened to all the gang members once they moved beyond their mid-adolescent years? Why were gangs assumed to cease existence once territoriality ended? How about gangs involved in organised crime? The literature just went cold. I quickly realised that what Scottish gang literature had come to examine was not, in fact, the gang per se, but rather predominantly territorialism along with territorial othering, as well as working-class idiosyncrasy regarding protest masculinities, to which the gang was duly part of but not recognised as also existing externally from. Existing literature analysed in a very detailed manner the gang life that echoed so much of my own – as well as my gang peers' – lifeworld, but only till approximately our mid-adolescent years, when territoriality no longer seemed important. For this reason, the gang as discussed by contemporary Scottish literature is referred to as the Young Street Gang (YSG). The literature failed to account for what happened afterwards and failed to progress beyond the YSG and towards other evolving gang forms. Where was the transition away from territorialism and towards those other social arenas described most regularly by Police Scotland as organised crime?

While the literature traditionally spoke of maturing out of territorial fighting in YSGs – with which I agree totally – this was a process for the many as opposed to the few (see Miller, 2015; Windle and Briggs, 2015). The YSGs that I had fought for (there were several throughout Strathclyde due to parental relocation) had predominantly consisted of a few individuals who were essentially core members, with the rest being the outer layer of the gang. For the core members, delinquency served as an integral feature to both their identity and that of overall YSG cohesion and purpose (see Hallsworth and Young, 2004, 2006, 2008). Often, for this few, offending had begun before YSG membership and would continue long after. Yet, most others, in many ways, drifted in and out of YSG association (see Matza, 1964). For the latter, outer layer, once territorialism ceased to be considered important – often coinciding with the ability to legally enter the world of work at 16 – then gang membership did end to all intents and purposes. Offending was rare and when it did occur, it was typically done so in relation to peer group delinquency. Delinquency was therefore only ever evident throughout young adolescent years, where street socialisation was most prominent. Yet, this was by no means the case for the few core individuals who were, in fact, the gang per se; without their presence no gang would exist, and no point of reference would be there for other associates to drift to and from.

Vigil (1988a, 1988b) writes about how youths are simply absorbed into street gangs via street socialisation; yet, a point that is all too often overlooked, particularly in the Scottish context, is that once there, some individuals will solidify into a gang core to which others will duly attach themselves. Thus, the YSG may be part of street socialisation and wider violent street worlds (see Hallsworth, 2013), but from this process emerges a proper gang that goes beyond territoriality (see Harding, 2012). Essentially, the YSG evolves as earlier loose associates drift away from it and the remaining core members solidify, age and become exposed to external threats beyond other YSGs, such as financial pressures, responsibilities to provide for family, pressures to work and so on. Thus, while most individuals cease gang offending during their mid- to late adolescence, for the few core members, the gang holds the potential to evolve and adapt in response to these new pressures (see Densley, 2012, 2013, 2014).

Having undergone this process and seen close family, extended kinship and friends (most unknown to each other and in various schemes) undergo similar processes, I felt that the current literature was lacking something significant. For this reason, I felt compelled to explore and detail those relationships that gangs and criminal trajectories, as well as the role that other gang typologies, may play in this process. The gangs discussed in contemporary Scottish gang literature are, by all accounts, territorial-based fighting outfits that have no leadership or hierarchical cohesion, nor are they involved in any crime-for-profit activities (see Patrick, 1973; Miller, 2015). As mentioned earlier, it is for this reason that I term them 'YSGs' as opposed to simply using the word 'gang' or 'street gang' (given that the drug-dealing gangs within the English literature are, at times, also referred to as 'street gangs', I thus wanted to be as clear as possible on what can be a confusing subject). However, this understanding and perception of gangs simply did not fit with my experiences growing up, and I believed the gang to be considerably more complex than it was being made out to be. For myself, there was more to the gang than just examining the initial YSG formation. Thus, I wanted to undertake research that explored the possibility of gang evolution in Scotland, particularly given that, in many respects, Glasgow is like those English cities of Manchester, Liverpool and Birmingham that have all seen their own street gangs becoming ever-more involved in aspects of organised crime such as drug dealing. Therefore, prior to conducting the research, I felt that it was arguable that YSGs in Glasgow also retained the ability, or potential at least, to evolve into something more than territorial peer groups. Likewise, given that little is actually known about the activities that gangs get up to beyond recreational violence, I wanted to explore such things and shed light on them. This is what led to the study of gang organisation as a means for gang business.

Notes

1 (Serious) Organised crime groups are discussed under the umbrella term 'gang' in this book.
2 Only the cottage housing (at the bottom of the photo in Figure 1) remains at present. Kimbo Kill members predominantly have residence in the neighbouring Drumoyne scheme, where many were relocated following demolition.
3 An underage nightclub is a nightclub that only allows those under 18 years of age to enter. Often, these venues will run an underage nightclub during a particular time frame (say, 5 pm till 9 pm) and then an overage nightclub for those over 18 years of age (say, 10 pm till 3 am).

Introduction: Book's Purpose, Content and Structure

Book purpose

Broadly speaking, there are two intended purposes of the book:

1. to shed light on gang organisation as a means for gang business by exploring the interplay between structure and activity, and how this evolves in conjunction with, and as a consequence of, gang evolvement; and
2. to re-engage Scottish scholarly gang literature back into the wider revisiting of the British gang by providing a more holistic analysis of gang evolvement and typology beyond the gang in its embryo stage of development, and by also exploring some of those reasons why Scottish gang research has stagnated in the first place.

Considering these two purposes in more detail, the first and main purpose of the book is somewhat generic in that it is broad and seeks to shed light on gang organisation as a means for gang business. This means that the gang is viewed from what could be considered an almost totalising viewpoint in that the gang, in a specific context, is analysed at every stage of development – although, of course, some boundaries have to be established in order to not cover everything, ranging from drug-dealing gangs, to paedophile networks, to motorcycle gangs and so on, given that the scope of the book can only be so wide. Therefore, it is all gangs that engage in, or look to engage in, organised crime in the physical (not cyberspace) realm that this book primary explores. To achieve this first aim, the book will look to reveal how gangs should be thought of as existing on a continuum along which they can move back and forth, or evolve. Loose peer groups are at one end of the scale and hierarchical purpose-driven criminal organisations are at the other. The interplay that exists between activity, the individuals and the group, as well as with other groups, will also be explored in the book. Essentially, this is achieved by looking at two key features: gang *structure* and gang *activity*. However, given that activity can be a broad concept, certain aspects of delinquency and criminal behaviour that are deemed to be particularly harmful or prevalent in gang behaviour will be given significant attention at the expense of other forms of activity, including violence, drug supply and the use of weapons to achieve objectives. The audience that the first objective is aimed at is wide in that it is primarily for undergraduate and postgraduate students, academics interested in gang behaviour and structure, practitioners who work with gangs at various stages of development, practitioners involved in tackling drug harms or weapon use/carrying, law enforcement, and anyone within the general public who has a general interest in all things related to gangs.

The second purpose of the book is more complex, and perhaps more specific with regard to the intended audience; yet, it is one that I feel strongly about and believe needs to be addressed if gang research in Scotland is to cease this period of stagnation, which has gone on for far too long. This second purpose is to re-engage Scottish scholarly gang literature back into the wider scholarly gang discourse in the British context. I believe that while gangs have been significantly researched by scholars in the UK context, with some identifying gang activity and others not so much (if at all), this has not been the case in Scotland. Rather, while scholars throughout the rest of the UK, like Simon Hallsworth, James Densley, Tara Young, Simon Harding, John Pitts, Grace Robinson, Dev Maitra and James Windle, to name but a few, have been exploring whether or not gangs resembling those found in the US context really do now exist in contemporary Britain or not, in Scotland, there has been a tendency to become overly fixated upon the gang at the embryo stage of development. This has been to the detriment of identifying other gang typologies. Consequently, it is widely believed in academia, and even among the general public, that gangs in Scotland are almost incomparable with those in England, never mind the US. Yet, I argue that this is not the case and seek to first explain why, and also to reveal why this view has come about. As the intended audience is quite diverse, the general style of writing will be tailored to suit.

Book content and structure

Given that the purpose of the book is twofold, and that the audience is wide, there are several issues to overcome when structuring the book. One of the problems, of course, as with all books, is what to include and what not to include. As this is a book on gangs aimed at a broad audience, there must be certain parts included that might be more applicable to one segment of the audience. The first purpose of the book means that a lot of descriptive material must be included to aid practitioners and students alike to help them grasp a firm understanding of the very nature of some activities that gangs and gang members get involved in – to help link theoretical conceptualisation with everyday realities. To do this, the book will move beyond an academic analysis of structure and activity alone and dedicate several chapters to looking specifically, in detail, at those activities that gangs are most often associated with and present them in a somewhat descriptive manner. This includes topics such as what gang activity looks like.

Equally, though, because the book is also aimed at an academic audience, there are several issues that will automatically arise in the academic mindset and thus need to be addressed for the second objective to be achieved. Given that the secondary purpose of the book is to re-engage Scottish scholarly gang literature back into the wider British gang discourse, a critical review of the gang literature is required.

Another issue, though, is that what the general public, media and political establishment may argue is a gang, those in academia may argue is not. Yet, even in academia, the argument between the use of broad or narrow definitions has dichotomised. Therefore, to get around this, and to make the book applicable to a broad audience, the term 'gang' is applied here as an umbrella term to describe *any group of two or more who offend together consistently and over a period of duration, and either see themselves as a gang or are seen by others as a gang*. Such broad terminology draws upon certain premises used in the majority of gang literature. Yet, this broad definition brings with it problems of its own, particularly when analysing gang evolvement and the interplay that may exist between structure and activity during this process. This means that the term 'activity' can be applied broadly to groups at either end of the spectrum. Thus, to help aid the intended audience and address both objectives of the book, the literature review is extended to include a critical review of the term 'organised crime'.

To aid the flow of the book, it is structured into four distinct parts. Part I of the book consists of just one chapter – Chapter 1 – which contains several themes: 'Introduction', as the heading suggests, introduces the reader to gangs, gang activity and how gangs are perceived in various arenas. It also locates the gaps in literature and knowledge that this book looks to fill. Next, 'Glasgow: the backdrop' sets the context of the study and this is followed up with 'Meet the participants', introducing the reader to the participant sample.

Part II of the book contains two chapters that are both essentially reviews of existing scholarly literature. Chapter 2 is a literature review of gangs. The first half of this chapter looks quite generically at gangs in, first, the US context and, second, the UK context. The second half of this chapter looks at organised crime and discusses how gang literature has become increasingly entwined with discussions of organised crime, particularly as the drug trade has now become a global phenomenon. Chapter 3 is a critical literature review of Scottish gang literature specifically, drawing attention to the key pieces of research before discussing how certain practices have led to an overly fixative gaze being placed upon the gang at one stage of development. The chapters within this part of the book present the reader with background knowledge of gangs and organised crime, and give detailed insight into gangs and the existing literature that has emerged as a result within the Scottish context.

Part III of the book looks at the key stages of gang development and examines the interplay and relationship between structure and activity. The chapters present gang organisation through the voices of the participants themselves. Chapter 4 bridges the literature review and the findings by drawing upon my own evolving gang model. This model is used hereafter to analyse the gang at its various stages of development. The model is essentially an evolving continuum on which gangs exist. Three key stages are identified as existing on the continuum, but, in reality, some variation does exist in each stage of development. However, the typology helps aid conceptualisations and understandings of the gang and how each stage of development is linked. Much of the discussion in this chapter refers to labelling and how this impacts upon the naming of groups. Chapter 5 then looks at the activities of gangs and gives a largely descriptive account of offending behaviour. This chapter is useful in helping the broad audience understand the range of activities that gangs are involved in, particularly as, in the given, context gangs are typically thought of as being primarily based around violence and lacking the ability to engage in market-based criminal activities. Chapter 6 then looks more specifically at gangs and drug supply. This focused approach on gang activity allows for a critical analysis, as opposed to a merely descriptive review, of structure and activity to take place. Given that all gang typologies identified in the research are involved in drug supply to some extent, this activity carries a fair degree of constancy and allows for a coherent analysis of structure and activity, and the interplay between them, within a *glocal* context (see Hobbs and Dunningham, 1998), whereby a global phenomenon penetrates the local arena.

Part IV of the book consists of only one chapter. Chapter 7 seeks to summarise the book in two ways. The first and second objective of the book – to shed light on gang organisation and re-engage Scottish gang literature back into the wider UK gang discourse, respectively – will be addressed by providing both a general summary that brings together some of the wider literature, and findings that emerged from the original, and ongoing, data. This section outlines how a gap in knowledge has been filled and advises as to which areas of interest future research should explore, as well as how this might best affect practice and policy. Yet, note that a report (see McLean, forthcoming), written in conjunction with this book, contains a substantial discussion on practice, policy and research implications. This chapter also offers up some research limitations. Before proceeding with the main text of the book, however, included next is a section on 'terminology', which acts as a point of reference for the reader.

Terminology

This section brings together some of the complex terms and definitions used within this book. Yet, given that a full discussion is not possible here, and as entire chapters and major headings within the book are dedicated to their description and analysis, this section should only be treated as a general summary for those terms used throughout and to provide definitions. Definitions that are specific to me and this book are placed in *italics*. I also provide a glossary for readers to help translate some of the local lingo used by the participants in the quotes (see Table 1 in the Appendix at the end of this section).

Gangs

The term 'gang' is applied here as an umbrella term and is used quite loosely to provide some consistency to the reader, particularly given the wide audience. While the boundaries set here are by no means concrete, the term draws largely upon workable and descriptive gang definitions used by a range of academics, law enforcement and media outlets to describe the phenomenon *whereby two or more individuals who commonly associate with one another carry out acts of delinquency and/or criminality over a sustained duration, and often see themselves or are seen by others to be a gang.* The term 'gang' applies to everything from peer groups to organised criminal groups, with all the variations contained within.

Young Street Gang

Within the confines of the umbrella term 'gang', I apply the term 'Young Street Gang' (YSG) throughout to indicate the gang type that I believe to have been predominantly studied and researched by scholars analysing contemporary gangs in the Scottish context. The YSG is a gang in the recreational stage of development, prior to evolvement to a stage whereby criminality becomes intrinsically embedded into both group and group member identity and behaviour. I consider a YSG to be *a regenerating, self-aware group of young people (primarily male) aged from early to mid-adolescence that emerges from playgroups and street socialisation and that engages in acts of delinquency, primarily in the form of territorial violence.*

YSGs have attachment to territory and often self-designate with a gang label that reflects their area of origin. Given that scheme identity is generally intertwined with YSG identity, YSGs are typically large in number. Yet, in an effort to be more precise, I also apply the term 'core member' to refer to those within a YSG's inner circle and the term 'outer layer' to refer to those loose associates and affiliations who drift to and from a YSG. Core members are *those who consider criminality to be an integral feature of their identity and are typically persistent offenders who are responsible for disproportionate rates of crime in their community.* The YSG outer layer generally comprises *loose associates and affiliations who will regularly drift in and out of recreational offending behaviour and socialisation with core members.*

With maturity, age and access to the world of work, offending will typically either cease completely or decline significantly for members in the outer layer. These points are further discussed in the following under the subheading 'intrinsic criminality'. How individuals are categorised is also explained further.

Young Criminal Gang

Like the YSG, the Young Criminal Gang[1] (YCG) is within the umbrella term 'gang'. The YCG is generally situated at the midpoint on the gang continuum between those loose recreational gangs and more organised gangs. YCGs are generally small and comprise of former YSG core members. While most YCGs evolve out of YSG formations, some do come about without prior involvement in YSGs. Likewise, it is not uncommon for a YCG to come into being as the result of gang members from two or more YSGs merging. The YCG is a:

> *cohesive group of two or more close-knit individuals – age range from mid-adolescence to mid-20s – for whom criminality is intrinsic to their own identity and – as a consequence of close socialising – group behaviour. While relationship purpose is primarily centred on social aspects, in response to a criminal identity, maturity and external pressures, such individuals refine and organise prior street-based gang structures – affiliated with territorial violence – as a means for business and participate in criminal activities, predominantly involving drug distribution.*

The YCG is essentially a remnant of core YSG members, and while age range and activities are generally consistent across findings, these are only approximate indicators given that gangs exist on an evolutionary continuum as opposed to having an either/or status. In distinguishing gang evolution, YCGs differ from YSGs in several ways; yet, a key distinction is that YCGs veer away from territorial conflict and instead refocus attention on tangible financial profit. However, it is important to note that the majority of YSGs do not evolve beyond this stage. Thus, not all YSGs become YCGs (for further discussion of YCGs, see McLean, 2017).

Organised Crime Group

The National Crime Agency, Police Scotland and numerous other variations of British law enforcement, as well as those scholars of organised crime, typically refer to Organised Crime Groups (OCGs) or Serious Organised Crime Groups (SOCGs) as: *(1) involving more than one person; (2) being organised, meaning that they involve the control, planning and use of specialist resources; (3) causing, or having the potential to cause, significant harm; and (4) benefiting involved individuals, particularly with financial gain.*

OCGs are also included under the umbrella term 'gang'. The word 'group' is only used to indicate the typical older age, maturity and professionalism of those involved. It is common for the behaviour of YCGs to mirror those of OCGs, with the main difference being that with experience comes greater efficiency.

Organised crime and organised efforts of crime

Definitions of what exactly constitutes organised crime can vary significantly depending on who is applying the term and where it is being applied (see Hobbs, 2012; Sproat, 2012; Hobbs and Antonopoulos, 2013; Carrapico et al, 2014). Within a Scottish context, no unified, across-the-board definition of what exactly constitutes organised crime exists either, although, drawing upon European Union (EU) criteria, Police Scotland highlight certain traits to provide a workable definition (see Scottish Government, 2009a, 2015, 2016), which is also the same definition for OCGs seen earlier. Law enforcement makes no distinction. Essentially, organised crime is categorised as group/gang behaviour. However, similarly to both Morselli (2009) and Varese (2010), I argue that many definitions of organised crime, workable or otherwise, all too often prove to be inadequate, either in that they can potentially be both net-widening and mesh-thinning. I therefore add a fifth point to the earlier definition: *(5) as a group, members' activity seeks to illegally govern the sphere in which they operate.*

Thus, only activities that include all five points can be termed 'organised crime' in this book (for greater analysis, see the discussion on organised crime in Chapter 2). Behaviour that simply retains the four points outlined earlier is considered 'organised efforts of crime'. I add the prefix 'effort' to indicate behaviour that is on the trajectory towards being organised crime but not quite there because it fails on illegal governance. I do not believe all gang behaviour to fall in either the 'not organised' or the 'organised' category of crime; thus, I occasionally use the term 'organised efforts of crime' to better indicate the type of behaviour that some of the gangs are involved in, often where social as opposed to economic intent is the main motivator behind the commission of crime. This is primarily in relation to discussions of YCGs, who typically blur the organised–non-organised, structured–non-structured, planned–unplanned, and so on, dichotomies.

Intrinsic criminality

Although the distinction between core YSG members and members in the outer layer can, at times, be substantially blurred, in relation to this study (in seeking a workable definition), those who displayed intrinsic criminality were defined as core members, while those who did not were defined as in the outer layer. Defining a participant as displaying intrinsic criminality centred upon two key factors. The first factor used for defining whether or not an individual was considered to be intrinsically criminal was with regard to their offending patterns in order to establish whether offending is a lifelong pattern or only an event. Typically, offending patterns were examined in a manner similar to that used by Farrington et al (2006) to define persistent offenders. This meant looking at offending patterns in three ways: (1) when offending began; (2) the duration of offending; and (3) the type of offending. The second factor refers to how individuals perceive criminality. This was done by asking participants to discuss whether they considered their predisposition towards crime (if offending patterns were evident) as being an innate or an intrinsic feature of their very being, although acknowledgement was given that such features may become accentuated under certain life experiences and socialisation. Thus, participants who engaged with YSGs and who displayed intrinsic criminality were defined as core YSG members, while participants who engaged with YSGs but did not display intrinsic criminality were defined as in the YSG outer layer.

Both factors had to be met before a participant could be deemed to be a core YSG member.

First, concerning offending patterns, if participants (1) had an early onset of offending prior to adolescence and (2) continued to offend throughout childhood, adolescence and into adulthood (where applicable), and if (3) the seriousness of offending had increased over time, then they were considered to have met the first factor for displaying intrinsic criminality. This was measured against the second factor of perceiving crime as being innate to their being or identity. If participants meeting the first factor also considered themselves to be predisposed towards criminal participation due to innate or intrinsic features (such as their characteristics, morality, traits and belief system), then participants were perceived to be core YSG members. Results proved remarkably distinct and consistent. In the original study, of the 35 participants meeting the set criteria for participation in the study, 33 had met the first factor for identifying intrinsic criminality, whereby they engaged in early offending (often something as minor as vandalism, for example, smashing windows) that then persisted into adulthood (where applicable). Likewise, offending typically increased in seriousness with age prior to involvement in OC. Of the 33 participants who met the first factor for identifying intrinsic criminality, 30 met the second factor and believed that their criminality or criminal participation was due to an innate predisposition towards crime based upon their intrinsic being (though seven felt that certain innate characteristics that predisposed them towards criminality were perhaps influenced significantly over other aspects of their being by their external environment, such as family socialisation). However, it should be noted that this distinction between core members and those of the outer layer was made in order to explicitly distinguish between levels of YSG involvement (as no contemporary Scottish model explicitly did so, although some earlier works by the likes of Davies [2008], studying razor gangs, highlights similar levels of gang distinction). Thus, the distinction may not be as clear-cut as is being presented. Rather, the binary distinction of YSG involvement was made to reduce the criminalising aspects of the YSG as a whole, and also to provide a workable definition that is applicable to this study's purpose. Undoubtedly, a greater and more detailed study would be needed to fully determine the exact levels of YSG involvement beyond the binary model presented here.

Note

[1]   In my previously published journal articles and thesis, Young Criminal Gangs were called 'Young Crime Gangs'. I have simply extended the term 'crime' to 'criminal' for the purpose of the book. This is the term that will be used hereinafter, even in future journal articles.

Appendix

Table 1: Glossary of Glasgow slang terminology

Slang Glasgow term	Term meaning (note subject to change with time and space)
Aye	Yes.
Banter	Humorous verbal interaction.
Batter	Attack violently.
Blade	Knife.
Bottle	Can refer to a glass bottle but can also mean to strike a person over the head with a glass bottle.
Chib	A weapon other than a knife.
Chico	Refers to the purity level of cocaine. This is mixed only somewhat (typically perceived as half) with mixing agents.
Crap	Rubbish.
Crapped it	Scared.
Council	Refers to the purity level of cocaine. It has been heavily mixed with other agents and has little purity
Doing	Attack violently.
Eccie	Ecstasy tablet.
Gear	In this study typically relates to cocaine but can also mean heroin.
Get me	Do you understand?
Grassed	To inform (typically) police on another's criminal behaviour.
Greet	To cry.
Hanging around	Socialise.
Hard man	Someone who is accepted as being a tough person and good fighter.
Hun	Derogatory word for a protestant/Rangers supporter.
'Insert name' boys/team	YCG.
Junkie	Drug addict; typically, heroin user.
Know what I mean	Do you understand?
Krew	YSG.
Mental	While it can mean someone has a psychologically defect or is perhaps unbalanced, it can also be used to refer to someone being brave or gallus.
Patsey	Giving someone a line of (typically) cocaine free of charge.

(continued)

Slang Glasgow term	Term meaning (note subject to change with time and space)
Pure	In reference to cocaine it means that the product is unmixed. In reference to simply linguistic usage, it is used as a prefix to emphasise the word which follows, for example 'pure mental'.
Rikimaru	In reference to the name of a computer character who is a ninja warrior and is heavily armed with an array of knifes, swords, and daggers. The term is applied to an individual who is heavily armed with similar weaponry.
Rough	Being tough, hard, or having the ability to fight well. Can also mean feeling unwell from being intoxicated.
Scheme	A housing estate.
Slash	To cut someone's face open with a knife.
Tim	Derogatory word for a catholic/Celtic supporter.
Toke	Consume cannabis.
Wee	Little or young person. May be in reference to the self or others.
Weed	Cannabis.
Young Team	YSG.

PART I

1

Background

The purpose of this book is twofold: the first, and main, purpose is to shed light on gang organisation as a means for gang business; the second is to re-engage Scottish scholarly gang literature back into the wider British gang discourse, where scholars have been revisiting the gang in recent decades. This chapter of the book introduces the reader to both points by first discussing, in the section titled 'Introduction', how there has been a drastic increase since the turn of the century in the perception that US-style street gangs are now being found on UK soil. These gangs consist of individuals who are organising themselves into gang or gang-like structures/networks to conduct gang business, whatever that may be – although it is often viewed as being linked to illegal drug supply chains. Therefore, the main point of the book is to shed light on what is still a largely hidden and poorly understood phenomenon in the British context.

Second, the introduction then proceeds to highlight how, during this process, UK scholars have sought to revisit the gang in the contemporary era. However, while there has been a scurry of activity south of the border in England, where gang researchers are looking to discover whether or not UK gangs are really now beginning to resemble their US counterparts in that they are, indeed, organising as a means for gang business, this has not been the case in Scotland, where gang research has instead become stagnant, focusing on only one type of gang formation: essentially, the gang in its embryo stage of development. This, of course, has simultaneously been detrimental to the researching and identification of other gang typologies.

Drawing upon the earlier narrative, the chapter then moves to the context of the study. The section titled 'Glasgow: the backdrop' provides some generic socio-economic, cultural and political information on the background of the location where the research was carried out, and likewise contains some of the participants' thoughts and perceptions of the communities in which they were raised. This is followed by the section titled 'Meet the participants', in which I then formally introduce the reader to the research participants and outline the areas with which they strongly affiliate themselves. The chapter is then concluded with a summary.

Introduction

Shedding light on gang organisation

Despite some occasional lulls, over the last 25 years, there has been a continual and growing vocalised concern that youth offending has been on the increase across Britain. Deficit views of young people and disadvantaged communities have been combined with a punitive turn within criminal justice systems, emerging against the backdrop of young people's behaviour continually being viewed as problematic and alarming. Most commonly, this has been generated by the media, and has predominantly focused on gang culture and gang-related violence and criminality. David Lammy (2018) even refers to 'McMafia Britain', where criminal networks are increasingly exploiting young people and sending them out as foot soldiers to fight gang wars:

> Across Britain there has been a surge in violent knife crime. More than 37,000 knife offences in England and Wales were recorded last year alone, a 21% increase from the previous 12 months. In the capital, Metropolitan police files show that half of all deaths involving knives are directly linked to the drugs trade and gang turf wars. Many other deaths are a result of the culture of violence that gang activity fosters. And gun crime is soaring too, with more than 6,500 offences in the past 12 months – a 20% increase. The media and political focus is on the youths – knife arches in schools, stop and search, public awareness campaigns and tougher, mandatory prison sentences for minors found carrying a knife. But while the rhetoric may be reassuring, we are now trapped in an endless cycle of tough-on-crime headlines that will do very little to stop the infanticide before us. This rhetoric implores single mothers, teachers, social workers and communities to do more; but knife crime is not being driven by youths. It is being driven by a sophisticated network of veteran organised criminals. (Lammy, 2018)

Ultimately, although somewhat sensationalised, these headlines nonetheless capture the general mood among the British public, whereby there has been a fearful rise in recent decades in the public perception that US-style gangs are increasingly being extrapolated onto and proliferating across UK soil (Pitts, 2008; Deuchar, 2009; Harding, 2014). This is a process that is thought to have been significantly aided by complex processes apropos globalisation, which has impacted upon the social, cultural, economic and political realms of British society (see Pitts, 2008). Consequently, contemporary gangs in Britain are now being viewed as quite different from their predecessors that existed throughout much of the 20th century (McLean, 2018b). British gangs are now being presented as increasingly organised, criminally intent and ever-more violent (see Deuchar, 2009; Densley, 2013; Harding, 2014). Densley (2012: 2) summarises this phenomenon in what is essentially a change to gang structure and gang activity by adopting the term 'gang organisation'. Gang organisation simply refers to the process whereby certain individuals pull together resources, skill sets and various types of capital with other like-minded individuals to make concentrated efforts in achieving individual and group goals via primarily illegal means of business. For this process to be successful, these individuals will often have pre-existing criminal familial and/or delinquent/criminal networks (NCA, 2013). Thus, this phenomenon is, of course, one that typically favours those already adhering to or operating within gang or gang-like structures/networks (Harding, 2012, 2014).

However, as a consequence of sensationalising events, media outlets are also guilty of typically oversimplifying those objects that are involved in this dramatisation. This is because while there is a need for media to make an event newsworthy, there is perhaps more importantly a need to also make that which is being discussed conceptually acceptable and accessible to the intended audience so that it is understood. Thus, while media headlines may have a tendency to simplify a range of complex group types and variations that are engaged in offending behaviour under the umbrella term 'gang', their reporting nonetheless highlights a deeper and often overlooked issue[1] in that group offending, regardless of how it is labelled, has gradually become ever-more prevalent in contemporary Britain, along with the range of activities in which such groups are now engaged – more often than not, reported to be related to violence, drug supply and various forms of trafficking (McLean et al, 2017). Drug supply, in particular, has been highlighted both in and outside the media as being a particularly acute problem in relation to increased gang activity (see NCA, 2013; Scottish Government, 2013). Therefore, this rise – or, to some at least, perceived rise – in gang activity is a story that cannot be told without also considering the growth of the illegal drugs trade on the global scale.

Globally, the illegal drugs trade is now a multibillion-dollar industry (Gootenburg, 2007, 2011). Aided significantly by complex global processes, the accessibility and demand for illegal drugs has expanded at an unprecedented rate, from which the UK, and Scotland more specifically, is by no means immune. The growth of the UK illegal drug market[2] has coincided with the voids left behind in the legitimate market following large-scale overnight deindustrialisation followed by subsequent inadequate replacement for many, what could be considered, traditionally working-class populations (Moore, 1991; Wacquant, 2001, 2009; Roger, 2008; Holligan, 2013). The proliferation of gangs is a perceived consequence of this process as they seek to profit from peddling such commodities in these ever-expanding voids in the market (see also Anderson, 1999; Levitt and Venkatesh, 2001; Levitt and Dubner, 2006, Venkatesh, 2008). Consequently, following such trends, the UK government has responded with a range of initiatives, strategies and other approaches aimed at reducing the drug supply and resultant gang activity. Similarly, in Scotland more specifically, the Scottish Government (2009a, 2009b, 2013, 2015, 2016) has also introduced numerous initiatives and publications aimed at tackling Scotland's drug/gang problem. To help eradicate the growing number of those criminal gangs involved in drug supply, initiatives like the Scottish Government's (2015) Serious Organised Crime Strategy (SSOCS), more specifically, entail police tactics to dismantle criminal networks. Yet, missing from such strategic planning is: a recognition of how different gang types may be involved in drug supply to various degrees; any clear insight as to how supply processes actually work and may often incorporate and criminalise non-gang, fringe and vulnerable populations; the changing nature of the drugs market; the blur in overlap between the legitimate and illegitimate sphere; and the variation of (dis)organised crime that takes place. Despite considerable gaps remaining in both the literature and understanding of gangs and illicit activities, particularly in relation to illegal drug markets, both 'gang talk' and 'drug talking' discourses have steadily been brought ever closer together (Hallsworth and Young, 2008; McPhee, 2013; McLean et al, 2017).

In summary, there is a populist belief that group offending is on the rise in contemporary Britain. These groups are typically termed 'gangs' despite much debate existing around the use of labelling in the academic realm. These gangs are seen to increasingly resemble those in the US and are thought to be primarily involved in drug supply. Yet, despite widespread media reporting, considerable police attention and significant academic investigation, there remains a lot that is largely unknown about gang organisation: the media often simplify complex processes and would benefit from a clear conceptual framework; police strategic planning could benefit from empirical-based research acquired outside law-enforcement networks; and the academic community become somewhat less dichotomised with insights that bridge gang theory and lived reality. Often, when gang research is carried out, it is from the perspective of gang activity or from the perspective of gang structure. Yet, this book looks to bring both together and present them as one given that each is substantially intertwined with the other, and that both are influenced by, and a consequence of, one another. Therefore, the first, and main, purpose of the book is to shed light on this phenomenon of gang organisation as a means of gang business, with particular emphasis given to the activity of drug supply.

Re-engaging Scottish scholarly gang literature

The second purpose of the book is to re-engage Scottish scholarly gang literature back into the wider gang revisiting by UK academics, as outlined earlier. The widespread belief that contemporary British gangs are, indeed, increasingly now beginning to replicate their US counterparts, in that they are now more inclined to organise as a means for gang business, has become a popular discourse. In addition, this process has also been seen to have aided gang proliferation. Yet, this discourse is one that has primarily been driven by the political establishment, media and law enforcement, as opposed to the academic community, where there remains a fair degree of scepticism (see Hallsworth and Young, 2004, 2006, 2008). In the academic community, there is still little consensus as to what exactly constitutes being a gang and whether, or not, criminal behaviour is even to be included as an intrinsic feature of gang definitions. This lack of unity has meant that gang research in Britain has essentially become split between those who believe that UK gangs are now organising as a means for business and proliferating across the country, and those who argue that they are not (see Pitts, 2012; Hallsworth, 2014). This has meant that the academic community has not moved along at the same pace as other 'gang talkers' operating in the professional realm. Consequently, most of what the general British public know or believe to know about gangs is based upon stereotypes, media representations, assumptions and whichever agenda certain agencies may favour at that time, as opposed to actual empirical research from the ground level (Deuchar, 2009, 2013). Lammy's earlier quote perfectly captures the very issue that has plagued British gang researchers, and split opinion down the middle, in that there is much debate as to which type of groups should be labelled gangs and which should not.

While media outlets tend to categorise a range of complex and inherently different groupings under the singular label 'gang', academics operate from an almost opposite modus operandi. Instead, academics tend to dispute and disseminate as far as possible to obtain 'truth'. Yet, the other side of the coin regarding the dismantlement of things to the very point to which they can be dismantled is that this exercise often ceases to become relevant, or useful, to those beyond the realm of academia. For example, in relation to gangs, it has become almost impossible in British academia to discuss two or three gangs from different studies, areas or context under the one topic as disputes and critical review always arise around the argument 'Is this a gang per se or something else?' – for which there has literally become countless variations, ranging from peer groups, to urban collectives, to street gangs, to criminal groups, to (Serious) OCGs (Deuchar, 2009, 2013; Hallsworth and Young, 2004, 2006; NCA, 2013; Scottish Government, 2009b, 2015, 2016).

Ultimately, as mentioned previously, this has resulted in a dichotomised position in academia, where some believe that contemporary gangs in Britain are increasingly adopting US gang style, purpose and behaviour, while others dispute even the very existence of gangs altogether (Hallsworth and Young, 2004, 2008; Densley, 2012). Ultimately, though, when we simplify the matter to its most common denominators, what all 'gangs' share in common is that they are all essentially classified as groups of two or more commonly associating individuals who tend to engage in offending – or at least what is widely perceived to be offending – behaviour on a regular or persistent basis (see Harding, 2014; McHugh, 2016, 2017).[3] Thus, while this book will look at the differences between gangs, urban collectives, peer groups, OCGs and so forth, for the sake of simplicity, consistency and the reader's sanity, as well as my own, all such groups will be referred to hereinafter using the umbrella term 'gang', with any differences being located within the term itself.

So, then, where do we stand in relation to the contemporary British gang debate? While the initial response to gang organisation in Britain was slow, there is now a considerable degree of momentum behind this 'revisiting' of the British gang by academics (see Hallsworth and Young, 2006), despite opinion remaining somewhat split (see Densley, 2013). Yet, while UK gang scholars sought to revisit gangs during this time in order to identify to what extent these groups were, or were becoming, 'typical', and whether or not they resembled those being reported in media and political circles, this process has not been as coherent and consistently spread throughout the UK as one might expect. By this, I mean that when I say that UK gang scholars have undertaken a revisiting of the British gang, this is not quite true; rather, owing to numerous contributing factors, which will be explored later, gangs have only been analysed in isolated pockets or across specific regions of the country. Consequently, this has meant that Scottish gang literature, in particular, has failed to properly engage itself in this process of revisiting the British gang in the contemporary era (see McLean, 2017, 2018a, 2018b, 2018c). Scottish gang literature had, and still has, become stagnant throughout. Ultimately, Scottish gang literature has failed to move beyond an overly fixative gaze placed upon what is essentially youth groups involved in recreational violence.

If one places gang organisation or evolution along a continuum, this gang type is essentially the gang in its most embryonic stage of development. I term the gang in this stage the 'Young Street Gang' (YSG) (see McLean, 2017). The unwillingness of Scottish academics to move beyond exploring the YSG has seen all other gang types being neglected. Although this unwillingness is one that is largely subconscious and due to many contributing factors, it is also nonetheless due to a culture of academic stuffiness to some degree, whereby many researchers draw their 'expertise' from books and second-hand data alone at the expense of empirical research, especially that which pushes boundaries and looks to explore links between serious organised crime and gang offending. As one reviewer stated to me recently: "gang literature in Scotland has become saturated, so why bother studying them at all.... Everything there is to know, we already know". Yet, it is here that this book excels in that it draws upon cutting-edge empirical research while also critically reviewing that which we think we know or assume to be true.

The reluctance to fully engage with gang research in Scotland is bewildering to say the least. Rather than taking a back seat, one would think that Scotland would lead the way in the revisiting of the gang, particularly given that the country's most populous region, the West Coast, and the largest city within, Glasgow, has a somewhat chronic and historically persistent gang culture, which has seen the city coined 'the Scottish Chicago', 'the city of gangs' and, more recently 'Europe's knife capital' (Mceachran, 2003; Johnson, 2010; Davies, 2013; McLean, 2017). While the two former titles refer to the infamous razor gangs of the 1930s, the latter title is largely attributed or affiliated with those YSGs that have received the bulk of academic attention in recent decades (McLean, 2018b). This lack of interest in the academic realm is even more startling when one considers the emergence of what could be considered almost a new trend in gang activity: in not more than 10 years, we have gradually witnessed greater mergers between gang activity and organised crime. Gang activity has become steadily ever-more intertwined with particular aspects of organised crime, in particular, drug supply. This has been evidenced by the National Crime Agency (NCA, 2013) and Police Scotland alike. The latter have acknowledged this process and even identified over 300 criminal gangs thought to be engaged in such activities throughout Scotland, with the majority thought to reside in and around the Glasgow conurbation (Scottish Government, 2009a, 2009b, 2015). Yet, Scottish academics remain staunch and steadfast in their approach. Therefore, it has been left to our English counterparts to take up the cause.

While English gang research has led the way in British gang revisiting, Scotland's lack of willingness to engage has resulted in a skewed and distorted perception of gangs in Scotland. This has had a detrimental effect as there is now an inability to compare gangs in the Scottish context with those in the English context, and more so when considering those gangs beyond the YSG or urban collective stage of development. For example, it is taken for granted by much of the public that gangs in London cannot be compared with gangs in Scotland as the former are organised and involved in drugs while the latter are disjointed, loose and involved in recreational violence (Squires et al, 2008; VRU, 2011; Deuchar, 2013; McLean, 2018a, 2018b). Yet, this is simply not true, and this book aims to demonstrate why. Therefore, this book will look to help re-engage Scotland back into the wider UK gang discourse and bring the country up to speed in British gang revisiting by uncovering the various gang typologies involved in disorganised and organised criminal activity that exist in Scotland, and thus make them comparable with those in the English context, in order to assist academics, practitioners, police and the political establishment alike.

However, it is important to note that while, at a glance, some may believe that this is a book applicable only, or primarily, to Scotland, given the effort to re-engage Scotland back into the wider gang literature, and that gang organisation is examined in the Scottish context, this is not the case. To suggest that would be comparable to suggesting that Harding's (2014) book *Street casino*, or Densley's (2013) book *How gangs work*, are only applicable to gangs in London and thus only worth being read by those in that context. We must acknowledge here that even English gang literature is also somewhat skewed, although less so than that in Scotland, and is by no means totally collegiate, given that most gang research even in England has been disproportionately carried out in only a handful of major cities, including the likes of Birmingham, Derby, Manchester, Liverpool and London (for example, Ward and Pearson, 1997; Mares, 1999, 2001; Shropshire and McFarquhar, 2002; Aldridge et al, 2008; Cox, 2011; Rahman, 2016). Rather, such books and research are shown to have broader implications. This book must be considered likewise. It would be short-sighted to consider the book as a Scottish book per se, as opposed to a book on UK gangs that happened to be carried out in and around the city of Glasgow. Thus, the re-engaging of Scotland back into wider gang revisiting is more of a personal mission, with the wider purpose of the book being to demonstrate how gangs operate more generally and how subsequent behaviour is often a consequence of gang organisation.

Therefore, in seeking to, first, shed light on gang organisation and, second, re-engage Scottish scholarly gang literature back into the wider UK revisiting of the gang, this book draws upon the unique position of myself as researcher, and upon empirical data gathered from what is now six years of fieldwork. This fieldwork consists of formal interviews with 10 practitioners, 12 ex-offenders and 47 active offenders,[4] as well as countless informal discussions and field notes. This allows the book to present data in the voices of high-profile (ex-)offenders and expert practitioners as to how (dis)organised crime, namely, illegal drug supply, is carried out by a variety of criminal gangs within hierarchical and vertical criminal networks.

Glasgow: the backdrop

Deprivation, marginalisation and social exclusion

It is important to outline the background of the location in which the study took place in order to allow the reader to grasp the concept and identity of the region and circumstances in which the research was carried out. It also brings the research more to life for the reader. While Glasgow is not Scotland's capital, it was nonetheless at one time known as the second city of the British Empire (see Gray, 1989). The industrialisation of the city saw Glasgow become the country's largest and most populated urban area. Only several decades ago, the population stood at over 1 million, and at over 2 million if the conurbation is considered. Yet, in recent decades, as part of an aggressive overspill policy,[5] boundary reconstruction along with population resettlement programmes relocating families into newly built surrounding towns have all significantly contributed to a reduction in the overall population, which now stands at approximately 599,700 (see Robertson, 1984). The city is endowed with a rich history, and in addition to having recently held the 2014 Commonwealth Games, it was also recognised in 1990 as the European City of Culture (Centre for Social Justice, 2008). Like most cities, though, Glasgow is a city of two tales. One side is economically vibrant, being popular among tourists and shoppers alike (Law et al, 2010). Similarly, it has proved popular among partygoers, with an active nightlife and club scene. This night-time economy (see also Hobbs et al, 2003) has coincided with increased security, cumulating in over 500 surveillance cameras across the city and a highly visible police and law-enforcement presence, in efforts to keep violence down and tourism high (Community Safety Glasgow, 2015). Yet, there is another side to Glasgow for which it is equally known. As Tiny (male, ex-offender/practitioner) states: "Visitors only see what they [local authorities] want them to see.... in the schemes [working-class communities], it's a different story." High rates of inequality, deprivation, violence and poor lifestyles have accumulated in a process known as the 'The Glasgow Effect', which is a term used to describe the analysis of various combined variables in an effort to identify why Glaswegians have such high rates of mortality and ill health when compared to the rest of the UK (Robertson, 1984).

The affluent West End is widely regarded as the cultural centre of Glasgow, yet it is also typical of a recurring enigma that operates throughout the city. Literally a street apart, no better location captures this image than Drumchapel and Bearsden.[6] In a 10-year period between 1981 and 1991, male mortality for those aged 15–46 increased by 9 per cent in Drumchapel but fell by 14 per cent in Bearsden. Similarly, young men living in the Drumchapel housing estate were found to be at twice the risk of death than their Bearsden counterparts (Peakin, 2014). Living in a scheme not too far from Bearsden, Jay (male, offender) states: "Chalk and cheese man really ... we have nothing in this scheme. Has just been left to rot ... five minutes up the road but you're in one of the [wealthiest regions] of [Scotland]."

Gaps between the 'haves' and 'have-nots' grew more significantly following the industrial collapse of heavy industry in Scotland (see Robertson, 1984). With deindustrialisation, Glasgow began a downward trend that saw deprivation and inequality rapidly increase, most notably, among working-class communities (Peakin, 2014). Findings from the Scottish Index of Multiple Deprivation (SIMD) reveal that in 2004, 69.5 per cent of Scotland's most deprived communities were in Glasgow. This percentage is significantly higher when considering Glasgow as the continuous urban expanse as opposed to alternating council boundaries (Scottish Government, 2012). Yet, while this trend has declined in recent years, almost half of the city's residents still live within the country's 20 per cent most deprived communities. Furthermore, 30 per cent of this population are economically inactive. These conditions invariably impact upon the well-being of the city's future generation. Currently, over one fifth of Glasgow's children live in workless households. In addition,

33 per cent of the city's children were thought to be living in poverty, and in some of the city's most deprived areas, up to 55 per cent of children could be described as living in poverty (Glasgow Indicators Project, 2015):

> "It is bad [in the west of Scotland]. I have worked for a few [local authorities across Scotland] ... I do believe the levels of poverty experienced in these communities is outrageous ... I've dealt with lots of families who literally have to make the choice to pay bills or purchase food for their children. Investment is desperately needed."
> (Clair, female, practitioner)

All in all, time and again, such statistics prove to be substantially greater than both the Scottish and wider UK national average (NOMIS, 2015). Such disproportionate rates of deprivation and inequality have been a continuous feature of Glasgow since the late 19th century as the city continues to experience the greatest levels of socio-economic deprivation in Scotland (Glasgow Indicators Project, 2015). The disproportionate levels of deprivation in Glasgow are clear when compared with other major Scottish cities (see Figure 2).

Figure 2: SIMD graph showing the 20 per cent most (dark grey) and 20 per cent least (light grey) deprived data zones (2012)

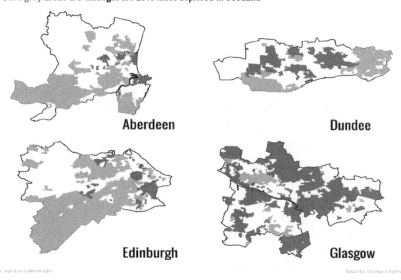

Deprivation in Scottish Cities
Source: Scottish Index of Multiple Deprivation 2012

Light grey areas are amongst the 20% least deprived in Scotland
Dark grey areas are amongst the 20% most deprived in Scotland

Aberdeen   Dundee

Edinburgh   Glasgow

Alongside increasing levels of austerity and welfare reductions, deprivation has continued to deepen over recent decades in Scotland, and specifically in Glasgow. It is important to draw attention to the levels of deprivation, marginalisation and social exclusion that occur within Glasgow given that most of the population are traditionally from working-class backgrounds and thus overwhelmingly affected by market fluctuations and social policies that impact negatively upon heavy industry and class-relevant demeanours. Furthermore, welfare reductions and population management strategies also have a significant impact upon a population heavily reliant upon the public sector and public services following the overnight deindustrialisation that assigned much of the population to the economic scrapheap. In addition, criminological research beyond that carried out in Scotland has established high correlations between socio-economic deprivation and crime (see Agnew et al, 2008; Young, 2007), both of which being prominent features of Glasgow's historical landscape. Although this correlation alone can in no way account solely for the historically high rates of gang violence, knife culture and organised crime found in the region, it may go some way to explaining an underlying problem that has remained inherent in the city since the late 19th century (see Davies, 2007).

Crime, gangs and drug harms

Against this backdrop of deprivation is crime or, as criminological research tends to focus more specifically on, highly visible and violent crimes against the person. Glasgow has become synonymous with crime, and violent crimes. In 2011/12, violent crimes in the city were double that of the national average (Glasgow Indicators Project, 2013). Even in the late 1920s/30s the city was dubbed 'The Scottish Chicago' in reference to its numerous gangs who often fought over issues related to sectarianism (Davies, 2013). These early razor gangs[7] were infamous throughout the country and helped breed a knife culture that culminated in the city being dubbed the 'Knife Capital of Europe' throughout the 1990s and 2000s. Although Glasgow has more gangs than London, not all knife crime is specifically related to this deeply embedded gang culture. Furthermore, while Glasgow has continued to produce disproportionately high rates of crime over the past century when compared to the national average, in 2014, recorded crime was actually at its lowest point in over 30 years (Scottish Government, 2014). However, when this research was initially conducted in 2013, Glasgow continued to display the highest number of recorded crimes per 10,000 of the population (Scottish Government,

2014). This trend has once again begun to spike in the past few years across the UK (Lammy, 2018).

While much of the gang research in Glasgow has been in relation to youth gangs and violence, in particular, knife violence, the more recent concern, beyond Glasgow alone, has been the growth of organised crime in the country (see NCA, 2013; Scottish Government, 2009a, 2015, 2016). An advanced capitalist system generates the growth not only of legal goods and services, but also of illegal goods and services (Gootenburg, 2011). Yet, this awareness of growing organised criminality is not confined to Scotland alone, but indicative of wider European Union (EU) recognition (see UNODC, 2004). The majority of organised crime is committed by what Police Scotland term 'Serious Organised Crime Groups' (SOCGs). Yet, as mentioned, any group that is engaged in persistent offending will be classified under the gang label for the purposes of this book. In 2009, Police Scotland identified that 70 per cent of these criminal groups were in and around the Glasgow conurbation, with 65 per cent being engaged directly in the illegal supply of drugs. Yet, most groups that participate in one form of organised crime also partake in other forms, for example, drugs supply means that illegal money and income is produced and therefore money-laundering activities generally ensue, and for those at the top of the hierarchy, so too does weapon acquirement. For example, Scotland's most sophisticated OCG not only moved £2 million worth of drugs per month across the central belt, but also had access to an unprecedented number of firearms, and was involved in numerous other activities beyond drug supply that could be deemed organised crime (see BBC, 2018).

Typically, though, the rise in crime that revolves around drug-dealing criminal gangs goes hand in hand with an increase in Scotland's drug problem. Scotland has a particularly acute drug problem (McArdle, 2010), both in relation to drug usage and supply (Scottish Government 2009a, 2015). In Scotland, 'levels of problematic drug use ... and drugs crime are among the highest in the world' (McCarron, 2014: 17). There are also an estimated 200,000 problematic drug users and 600,000 recreational drug users in the country, with anywhere between 40,000–60,000 children affected by parental drug misuse (Casey et al, 2009). Drug harms are thought to cost the Scottish economy around £3.5 billion annually (Scottish Government, 2009a) Unsurprisingly, therefore, the Scottish National Party (SNP) pledged to make Scotland 'drug free' by 2019 (Scottish Government, 2008). Thus, while the Scottish Government's (2015) Serious Organised Crime Strategy (SSOCS) is focused on prosecuting suppliers, users are to be 'treated'.

Meet the participants

Research location

While this book is aimed at a wide audience, most of those who read it will perhaps be involved in academia, including postgraduate students, researchers and established academics. Thus, it is important, particularly given the second objective of the book, to introduce the research participants, whose voices will be represented in this book, to the reader. Yet, before looking at the participants themselves, I shall carry on from the previous section that looked at Glasgow in a generic way and look more specifically at those locations within the Glasgow conurbation in which the participants were either raised or lived in at the time of the interviews. This section, though, will also include the locations that participants from the follow-up and ongoing research most affiliate themselves with. This is important as it shows that effort has been made to widen the scope of the research to the outer reaches of the Scottish West Coast more generally.[8]

Given that Glasgow has a long and synonymous history with gangs, and contemporary figures show that organised crime is disproportionately retained within this region, it was the perfect location to explore gang organisation. Most of the gang research carried out in Glasgow primarily focuses on the city's East End (Deuchar, 2009; VRU, 2011, Fraser, 2013). Similarly, the north of the city has also seen a substantial amount of attention, notably, including the work of Patrick (1973). Therefore, at times, this has proved detrimental to the south and west of the city. Although Davies (2008) does outline the case of the Beehive Boys who originated from the Gorbals housing estate, locals generally refer to this area as belonging more to the city centre rather than to the Southside. Most participants in my original study held residence in, or originated from, the city's Southside. This included the areas of Govan, Cardonald, Kinning Park, Pollok, Nitshill, Arden, Thornliebank, Paisley Road West, Barrhead and the continuous urban expanse of Renfrew, Paisley and Johnstone. Likewise, I also originated from Glasgow's Southside.

The participants who were included in the follow-up study were also primarily raised in Glasgow, although many had since relocated to other neighbouring towns and villages throughout the West Coast. Even those participants who had never lived in Glasgow nonetheless tended to have strong ties to the city and surrounding vicinity for various reasons, including kinship, friendships, employment, relationships and for partaking in illegal activity. The areas that participants in the follow-up study came from included areas as far west as Port Glasgow, Greenock and Gourock, as far south as the Ayrshire towns of Ardrosson, Stevenson and

Saltcoats, as well as Irvine, and as far east as Carluke and Airdrie (although the latter is still in the Glasgow conurbation).

Participant sample

The participants in this study came from two related studies. The initial study was officially carried out between 2012 and 2016 as part of my PhD. The follow-up study began in 2018 and is expected to run well into 2019. Given that this study is essentially the findings from two studies, albeit closely related as the second was simply the follow-up of existing outstanding leads, we shall approach it in two parts. We shall first look at the initial study. The initial study saw five practitioners, 12 ex-offenders and 23 active offenders interviewed. The data used in the original thesis were from this sample group. However, an additional seven interviews were carried out thereafter with female offenders in an attempt to address the gender-skewed sample, although, due to time constraints, the transcriptions of these seven additional interviews were not included in the original thesis. The criteria set for the offending interviewees were that they had to have been involved in or still be involved in activities that Police Scotland define as serious and organised criminal activity. Participants had to have been involved in group offending at some stage. The participants had to be over 16 years of age, simply to avoid ethical pitfalls given that I was still an inexperienced researcher at that stage. This allowed participants to look back upon their criminal trajectory and provide valuable insights into gang evolution. Therefore, I was interested in looking not so much at fringe offenders, but rather at core offenders. Also, as the study was in the Scottish context and due to travel limitations, I only interviewed participants who had grown up or lived in the Glasgow conurbation for the majority of their lives.

Now that the criteria had been set, I sought to initially access participants through outreach centres. This proved difficult due to both ethical considerations and the fact that offenders who have carried out serious and organised crime were not likely to engage with official state organisations – even if they had desisted from crime – due to fears of being prosecuted for illegal actions by the state (more so those still committing offences). Therefore, drawing upon personal experience, I contacted a church-based organisation that sought to help serious offenders to desist from crime. Within this organisation, the crimes were not the focus of attention; rather, forgiveness, citizenship and spirituality were concentrated on. Thus, offenders who could not seek help in desisting from crime through state-funded or state-run organisations could do so here through a faith-based organisation. Many of the activities carried out by this organisation simply sought to help offenders desist by way of helping grow their own personal spirituality in bible-reading groups and mainstream socialisation through participation in sporting activities. Offenders ranged in age from mid-adolescence to early adulthood. Not all offenders had engaged in the same range of offences, nor to the same degree. Rather, offences varied considerably as well as in severity. It should be noted that both the church denomination and organisations – along with the external partnerships in question – cannot be named due to issues of confidentiality. Many of these offenders feared not only state prosecution should their offences be made known, but also persecution from rivals, enemies, other criminal figures and so on should their participation in such organisations be made known. This would hinder their efforts to continue to desist from crime.

Workers within the church-based organisation were not paid for work carried out with offenders, although some may have been for other pastoral duties and responsibilities within the church itself. Work was voluntary, and workers' roles were often in line with their occupation. Thus, if a worker was a social worker, then their contribution may be in the same form, or if a worker was a sports coach, then their contribution may be in coaching. Initially, these workers were used as gatekeepers. They would recommend participants who I could then approach to be a potential sample member. Often, the workers had intimate and close relationships with offenders and had known them for several years or prior to their involvement in such organisations. I attended a range of the activities on offer. This helped build rapport with potential sample members. After a good relationship had been established, I would ask potential sample members if they would be willing to participate in interviews. This produced mixed results. Yet, after several participants were interviewed, I would use voluntary workers' knowledge regarding certain events as a method of triangulation. However, a few participants freely produced media articles (typically on mobile devices), regarding events without myself requesting that they do so. They did so not in a boasting manner, but rather simply as a way of bringing the author up to date with the events and narratives discussed. However, the sample yield was small and perhaps overly representative of known associates; thus, I decided to apply an additional snowballing sampling technique to expand the sample size and increase the likelihood of the sample being representative of wider Glasgow.

Several participants brought forward individuals or recommended others who could be approached as potential interviewees. Due to connections and shared history, a few of the potential interviewees had existing knowledge of me. Although this knowledge was limited to little more than knowing of my existence or shared acquaintances, this nonetheless helped establish some degree of trust. Similarly, this knowledge enabled me to verify those narratives that were being discussed. Applying a snowballing sample technique with a hard-to-reach group, though, took considerable time and effort to build trustworthy relationships that could entice potential sample members to give interviews. In total, this process took over three years. Much of the rapport between myself and the sample group was built through participation in sports, such as five-a-side football, MMA (mixed martial arts) or weightlifting.

The process of building rapport was also quite complex. Rapport had to be negotiated with each individual and tailored to suit the given context and setting. It would be impractical, unethical and beyond this thesis alone to outline the process with everyone; yet, an example is given in the following to show how such rapport building generally took place. Having taken part in one of the football programmes run by one of the partnerships who worked in conjunction with the church-based organisation, I met Henderson. Henderson was a particularly gifted footballer and proved popular on the football programme. Although much younger than myself, I immediately recognised Henderson, having played against him several times at numerous five-a-side football tournaments held at various locations across Glasgow. Henderson likewise recognised me and began to speak with me. While we had been football rivals in previous circumstances, in this situation, we were placed in the same team. As I had been an able player in my younger years, Henderson and I played well together, and this helped provide the building blocks for cementing a decent relationship. I made my intentions clear as to why I was attending the football programme from the start. I did not do this via a public declaration or statement, but rather did so casually when speaking with individuals. After several weeks of playing on this football programme, I approached the gatekeepers and asked if I could ask Henderson for an interview given that he met the set criteria, and also due to the good relationship that we had established. Once this was approved, following a verbal discussion among voluntary workers, I approached Henderson and asked him. He declined. However, after several weeks, Henderson approached me and asked if I would play for his own seven-a-side team who competed in one of the amateur leagues in Glasgow South. I agreed. While this was initially only meant to be a temporary arrangement, as one of the regular players had to cease playing due to an ongoing injury, it eventually proceeded to continue until the end of the league season. Once this arrangement ceased, I again approached Henderson and asked for an interview. This time he agreed. He attributed the change of mind to the fact that he now trusted me, and felt that an interview at this stage of his development would no longer hinder his efforts towards criminal desistance (previously, he felt that if he had spoken about his crimes, he may again be enticed to engage in such behaviour).

Among those 'undisputed facts' in criminological research is the gender gap in offending (Lauritsen et al, 2009: 362). Although females do offend, males tend to engage in criminal activity more frequently and at a greater intensity, and get involved in more serious types of offending (Esbensen et al, 2010). Likewise, the gender gap in offending undoubtedly influenced the gendered sample in this study, particularly given that drug dealing also tends to be a male-dominated sphere of activity (Denton and O'Malley, 1999; Hutton, 2005). Regarding drug supply, the severity and commodities distributed varied significantly. It was found that all 42 respondents from the original study who met the criteria had been involved in retail-level drug supply at some time. Despite variation in the quantity/bulk that participants purchased and distributed, 26 males and three females had engaged in wholesale practices. Seven participants had gone on to be involved in the importation and trafficking of drugs into the country. As lower-level retailers may not be as well informed about wholesaling and trafficking, voices from within each market level are prioritised. In terms of product, all study participants had sold cannabis at some time. Heroin, cocaine and, to a lesser extent, ecstasy were the most common Class A drugs sold, with over 80 per cent of the sample doing so. Cannabis was the most popular Class B drug, but amphetamines, barbiturates and other drugs were also discussed (see also Densley et al, 2018a, 2018b). Yet, while much of the data discussed criminal participation, it nonetheless still lacked an outsider's point of view; therefore, the decision was taken to request interviews from a number of those workers within the church-based organisations who had acted as initial gatekeepers. These totalled four male workers and one female worker. The contribution that these workers made in terms of relating organisation activities to their own occupation varied considerably. These included a youth worker, a sports coach, a social worker, a psychologist and a chef who was also a charity worker. All the workers had pastoral responsibilities. In addition, three of the male workers had also come from criminal backgrounds.

Thus, participants could be split into two groups. The first group is comprised of participants who met the set criteria and had been either approached in the church-based organisations – with the help of initial gatekeepers – or accessed through the snowball sampling technique. Several of the participants knew each other as some were part of the same YCG. Similarly, some participants mentioned others who had figured in the sample, although they were unaware of their participation.

Unfortunately, little detail can be given of participants, particularly as some participants may prove immediately recognisable from media reports, social media reports or even as mentioned figures in autobiographical accounts. Participants' ages were typically confined between the mid-teenage years to the late 20s, with outreach workers tending to be much older. Names provided are pseudonyms.

The second study was the result of several outstanding leads remaining from the first study. I therefore sought to carry out interviews to gather more data. I kept the criteria the same as before but placed more emphasis upon weapon-carrying and weapon-distributing practices. Also, this time, when applying a snowball sample, I simply broadened the distance that I was willing to travel to interview participants, mostly due to having more flexibility on alternative work-related time constraints. Some interviews were conducted using emails (with practitioners) and others using encrypted mobile devices such as Whatsapp messenger, Viber and the recorded voice messenger option. At time of book draft submission, the second interview schedule had resulted in interviews with five practitioners and 24 active offenders, although several were making real attempts to desist from crime. The participant ages in this data set ranged from 14 years old to 55 years of age. As mentioned earlier, interviews were ongoing at the time of draft submission and thus any interviews that have taken place thereafter have not been included here.

Chapter summary

In this chapter, I have outlined the two purposes of the book: first, to shed light on gang organisation as a means for gang business; and, second, to re-engage Scottish scholarly gang literature back into the wider UK gang discourse. The first section in the chapter was essentially split into two main themes, each in response to the specific book purposes. The first subsection draws attention to the fact that group offending in contemporary Britain is, or is at least widely perceived to be, on the rise. Media sources are used to capture this phenomenon. It was then pointed out that these groups are often not all the same and consist of a complex range of variations; yet, it was explained that they are often coined 'gangs'. Attention was drawn to the fact that gang activity is typically affiliated with organised crime and illegal drug supply. The section then proceeded to address the second purpose. Again, the media was used primarily to show how the gang label is one that is the main point of dispute in the academic community, which has resulted in a split between those who believe gang organisation and proliferation to be occurring in contemporary Britain, and those who argue that this is not the case. Yet, attention was drawn to a workable definition that is applied throughout this book.

The chapter continued and set the scene by outlining the background to the study. First, this was done by looking at demographics within the Glasgow conurbation. This was followed by the next section that then introduced the reader to the participants. The 'Meet the participants' section outlines how the participants were accessed for both the original research and the follow-up, ongoing research. I shall now proceed to Part II of the book, comprising Chapters 2 and 3, which provide the necessary and relevant literature reviews in relation to understanding the development of research on gang structures and gang activity.

Notes

[1] In British academia, there has been a much greater emphasis placed upon the manner in which various group typologies are labelled 'gangs' at the expense of recognising the considerable increase in reporting from various sources, not only the media, that group offending, however it is labelled, is on the rise. Sometimes, it can be similar to the saying 'One cannot see the forest for the trees in the way'.

[2] Note that there is no singular drug market; rather, the variation between national, regional and local, along with the huge variety of drugs and prescription medicines that are sold, means that there are, in fact, many different drug markets with regard to the drugs sold and areas of distribution. However, again, for the sake of simplicity and to make the book accessible to those outside academia, the umbrella term 'illegal drug market' will be used with all variations contained within (see terminology section in Preface, pp xxi).

[3] When such groups name themselves, it has been common practice to prefix the label 'gang', and when they do not, they are typically called 'groups'. This terminology is often also used in the UK arena to signal differences in offenders' ages.

[4] The original thesis comprised of five practitioners, 12 ex-offenders, 23 active offenders and a subsequent follow-up study of seven female offenders to balance the skewed male sample. The additional interviewees have all been part of an ongoing study from April 2018. The additional research was still ongoing as of January 2019. Final interviews were to take place in April 2019. Yet, due to incomplete transcriptions, deadlines, reviews and publication dates, all interviews carried out after the first draft submission in the autumn of 2018 have been excluded as inclusion would not accurately reflect the data set.

[5] The overspill policy sought to reduce population overcrowding with the construction of peripheral towns outside the Glasgow boundary. In addition, four huge housing developments would also be created within the city boundary. The housing estates of Castlemilk, Drumchapel, Easterhouse and Pollok were intended to function as almost independent townships.

[6] While many consider areas like Bearsden to be part of Glasgow, they are, in fact, part of the immediate conurbation and lie just outside the city's boundaries even though no green belt separates the area from the city itself.

[7] The prefix 'razor' was applied to the term 'gang' in reference to the gangs' willingness to both carry and use an open barber's razor for inflicting wounds on rivals.

8 Note that much of the populations of those towns that are not immediately attached to the Glasgow conurbation nonetheless have strong family ties to the city due to overspill and relocation policies, and that many of the towns were built to further aid the city's thriving heavy industry. Thus, populations moved from Glasgow to these new-build towns, for example, Port Glasgow and Greenock.

PART II

2

A Review of Gang Literature

Having outlined the purpose of the book in Part I, I set aside Part II of the book to help the reader understand the gang phenomenon. Part II of the book is split into two chapters. This chapter reviews existing US and British gang literature. Here, I make considerable effort to break the gang down and analyse literature from three perspectives: the environment; the structure; and activities. This is done to present the gang in a holistic manner, taking into account book constraints with regard to scope and audience. The chapter then summarises how research has gradually brought the gang and drug discourses closer in that drug distribution has become a central feature when conducting gang research. Chapter 3 then looks at Scottish gang literature, which is excluded from this chapter so that a more detailed analysis of the Scottish dimension can be given. This helps to justify the need for the second aim of the book, that is, to re-engage Scottish scholarly gang research back into the UK revisiting of the gang phenomenon. After briefly outlining key pieces of Scottish gang literature, Chapter 3 then focuses on those contributory factors that have seen such research stagnate and become overly fixated upon YSGs, to the detriment of other typologies and potential evolving capabilities.

Producing gangs

While early theorists like French sociologist Emile Durkheim (see Thompson, 2002) paved the way for studies concerning the normality of deviance, it was not until the early 20th century that the systematic study of juvenile delinquency and youth gangs emerged with Chicago School theorists like Park and Burgess (1924), Thrasher (1927), Wirth (1928), Shaw (1930) and Whyte (1942). Centred on 'urban ecology', such studies hypothesised human behaviour as being a product of external social environments. Drawing upon Park and Burgess's (1924) concentric zone model, Thrasher (1927) postulated that second-generation migrant youths often formed delinquent street gangs and that like the social disorganisation that characterised the inner-city neighbourhoods, gangs were temporary and would self-remedy by way of assimilation given time. Deducing that stable organised environments among settled homogeneous populations produce law-abiding citizenship, by contrast, disorganised environments characterised by diverse and unstable ethnic populations result in delinquency. Ultimately, socially diverse and disorganised communities led to conflict in which anxious youths congregated in gangs to socialise. Gangs offered status and recognition for individuals who were initiating their search for economic and political independence. Building upon such insights, Shaw and McKay (1942) found that zones of transition had particularly high rates of delinquency and proposed that environmental disorganisation led to social disorganisation, thus somewhat normalising deviant values. Edwin Sutherland (1939, 1947) similarly argued crime to be multi-factored, and argued that within the urban environmental context, differential association allowed deviant value systems to become more transmittable in such communities. In effect, criminality could be learned.

Adopting a somewhat different perspective to crime, Robert Merton (1938) argued that it was the organisation of capitalist American society that generated criminality. For Merton, crime was related not so much to the direct urban ecology of neighbourhoods, but rather those wider structural blockages that restrict or deny opportunity for achieving social goals related to the American Dream. The resulting strain could lead to deviant behaviour in various forms. Albert Cohen (1955) would later extend this concept and argue that in certain social stratifications, such as those occupied by the working class, deviant subcultures could emerge that would, in effect, become self-perpetuating. Cohen's work strengthened the idea that crime was largely a product of class status. Cloward and Ohlin (1960) similarly suggested delinquency to be a product of working-class communities. Drawing upon Sutherland's differential association, Cloward and Ohlin present working-class boys as rationally organising themselves into subcultural gangs where criminal learning processes are refined. While 'organised slums' produce criminal gangs, 'disorganised slums' are more likely to produce fighting gangs. However, David Matza (1964) attempted to address the growing tendency to criminalise working-class youths and argued that through narratives and 'techniques of neutralisation', working-class adolescents living mundane lifestyles regularly drift in and out of delinquency and delinquent association. By expressing 'subterranean values' that emphasise tough masculinities, delinquency allows working-class youths to break from the boring routine consistent with daily life in socially disorganised communities. For Matza, delinquency is largely age related and, as such, most youths simply mature out of offending.

As outlined earlier, when viewed holistically, the classic American studies brought about the idea that gangs are largely the product of the immediate social-economic environment in which primarily working-class communities produce delinquent youth groups. However, this view would change dramatically in the coming years, and by the 1990s, there had been a radical shift in perspective. Government officials, state authorities and the wider public were no longer unaware of the acute gang problem, and between 1970 and 1998, the number of US counties reporting gang problems had increased 1000 per cent (Miller, 2000: 2). Gangs were no longer to be considered mere delinquent outfits partaking in anti-social behaviour, but rather viewed as having become intrinsically criminal. So, what happened? While Miller's (2000) 30-year report *The growth of young gang problems in the United States: 1970–98* is primarily concerned with providing statistical information on gang proliferation, it offers up some explanations as to why this happened. Miller puts forth seven points of possible causality: drugs, immigration, gang names, migration, government policies, female-headed households and gang subculture. Yet, Miller notes increased access to drugs as particularly influential. A significant proportion of scholars concur and view drugs, in particular crack cocaine, as the primary cause for aiding gang proliferation, organisation and violence. When situated against the backdrop of overnight deindustrialisation throughout the 1970s–90s, profound economic restructuring meant that significant voids in the economic marketplace appeared. Drugs would fill this and acted as a tradable commodity to be distributed among marginalised communities now confined to the economic scrapheap (Wacquant, 2008, 2010). Controlling turf meant that gangs were able to monopolise power and, as such, become the shop floor for drug distribution (see Spergel and Curry, 1993; Anderson, 1999; Decker and Curry, 2002; Alonso, 2004; Levitt and Dubner, 2006; Venkatesh, 2008). However, this combined process of globalisation and overnight deindustrialisation was by no means confined to the US, but indicative of wider processes throughout the Western world. As such, gang proliferation was also no longer to be viewed as simply being a US phenomenon, but rather one that could potentially be extrapolated across Western society.

Gangland Britain

Traditionally, the British perspective concerning gangs had been very different from that of the US. Only in recent decades have gangs begun to be 'rediscovered' in Britain (see Hallsworth and Young, 2006). Traditionally, British scholars adhered to a sociological, as opposed to criminological, approach to explaining youth delinquency and, as such, subcultures, as opposed to gangs, were emphasised. Downes (1966) helped to pioneer this movement, and after attempting to apply US theories to the UK context, concluded that gangs did not exist in Britain. Rather, working-class youth simply tended to express their subcultural 'freedom' and 'difference', and, in doing so, occasionally engaged in behaviour that was deemed to be somewhat criminal. Willis (1977) similarly examined those factors that saw working-class males often appear to display a delinquent value system. Willis concluded that the British education system was one that failed the working class by promoting middle-class values. Thus, in rebellion, working-class youths occasionally adopted delinquent attitudes towards education but nonetheless still adhered to the overall conventional values of mainstream society. Such views were supported by several other theorists. The Birmingham School of thought helped spearhead subcultural literature, and examined Mods, Rockers, Skinheads and Punks, among others (see Hall and Jefferson, 1975; Hebdige, 1979; Gilroy, 1987). Subcultures were ultimately considered as resistance through rituals (Cohen, 1972). Yet, Cohen notes that much of the subcultural values came by way of media sources, which regularly constructed group characteristics. This latter point would be explored by Cohen (1980) as he analysed the role that control agents played in subculture identity.

While researching Mods and Rockers, Stanley Cohen found that subculture identity was largely constructed via media reporting. Often sensationalised, reporting influenced public opinion and created moral panics. As such, typically diffused groups who adopted subcultural styles were regularly presented as dangerous and corrosive to traditional values. Moreover, such groups enter a self-fulfilling prophecy during this process by adhering to the media images being presented (see Becker, 1963). Yet, Hall et al (1978) would continue to refine this process and argue that this creation of folk devils was often done in the guise of reinforcing long-standing illusions that young people, and more specifically young ethnic populations, were to blame for a variety of social ills. These groups were consequently seen as being corrosive to the very moral fabric of British society. This allowed the political establishment to scapegoat what was already a marginalised population lacking a social voice. Ultimately, the point that Hall makes is that so-called problematic movements, cultures or groups are often as much a consequence of response as initial formation. Hall suggests that these populations may already exist and have done so for some time, yet they remain diffuse and largely benign; however, sensationalised media reporting heightens public opinion, which, in turn, often creates a knee-jerk reaction by way of political response. This, in turn, only serves to solidify subcultural or group identity. Many contemporary scholars who oppose the idea that the UK has become infiltrated with a growing US-style gang epidemic follow a similar line of argument to that which Hall presents. The gang phenomenon is largely seen to be the result of a new moral panic, influenced by complex processes aligned to increased globalisation.

Revisiting the British gang

While early British researchers failed to identify US-style gangs on UK soil, this resulted in the conclusion that gangs were particular to the US. UK scholars instead focused on subcultures to explain youth, and group, delinquency (Campbell and Muncer, 1989). This perception has gradually declined as increased globalisation has impacted upon the transnational movement of people, ideologies, politics, cultures and postmodern thinking. As part of this process, criminology has also risen as a discipline and steadily replaced sociology in criminal research. Alexander (2008) suggests that this movement away from the sociological investigation of youths and subcultures towards the American positivistic approach of criminology constructs gangs as a primary mechanism for criminality. As such, there is a growing perception that the suppression of the gang is ultimately the suppression of crime. Yet, recognising contextual differences between the US and the rest of Western society, the Eurogang Network helped catapult the discipline of criminology into a European context, using fixed and inclusive definitions to be applied across Europe when exploring youth delinquency and identifying gangs (see Klein, 1995; Klein et al, 2001; Weerman et al, 2009). This process of making research transferable helped cement not only criminology as a discipline to investigate delinquency, but also the gang's position as a centralised component in its analysis. In subsequent years, whether due to the identification of previously unlabelled groupings, being socially constructed or the extrapolation of US-style gangs, the reporting of violent street gangs in major European, and in particular British, cities has consequently increased. The gang now holds a prominent position in research, political debates and media reporting (see Hallsworth and Young, 2008).

Contemporary gang research in Britain is concerned with identifying whether, or not, British gangs are, indeed, adopting US gang styles and, in doing so, proliferating across the country and organising as a means for gang business, whereby organising priorities consequently mean that they retain evolving capabilities. The debate as to whether this is occurring or not has resulted in the dichotomisation of UK gang research. Yet, in summarising this debate in his book *The street casino*, Harding (2014) reviews the main scholarly pieces and helpfully locates these in their ideological context. Harding argues that contemporary UK gang scholars can be loosely located into three categories: governance-through-crime Left idealists; latter-day Left labelling theorists; and Left realists. The first, Left idealists, argue that the creation of gangs helps the political establishment to govern populations through crime. Consequently, the gang is largely a social construct, often aided by media reports (see Hallsworth and Young, 2006; Hallsworth and Brotherton, 2011). The second, latter-day Left labelling theorists, adhere to labelling theories. Yet, while they acknowledge the gang, they likewise argue that via consequential labelling and social reaction, groups that have existed previously have become acutely identified (Ralphs et al, 2009). However, this does not mean that they are proliferating or becoming any more organised; rather, the public simply has more awareness of their existence. Lastly, Left realists argue that we are witnessing the proliferation of gangs as they increasingly organise as a means for gang business. Traditional Left realist criminologists such as Jock Young, John Lea, Roger Matthews and Richard Kinsey argue that crime, in a general sense, is real and on the rise in the post-war era. The role of the criminologist is therefore to explain crime in order to effectively tackle crime. Lea and Young (1984) argue that although issues such as poverty and deprivation may share close links with many crime types, this does not mean that they are the causes of crime per se. Rather, causes may be much more deeply embedded in society. Only by addressing wider socio-economic, political and structural causes can crime be truly addressed. While my own perspective arguably adheres to this latter approach, of course, context, researcher subjective perceptions and agenda, as well as other factors, all play an important part in the interplay and situate where one scholar may conceptually sit next to another. Nonetheless, as I adhere to the Left realist perspective, this is the perspective that I will particularly emphasise in this review of gang literature.

Analysing gangs in Manchester following a rise in gang-related shootings, Bullock and Tilley (2003) identified several loose turf-based gangs who shared several characteristics with US gangs. First, turf was not totally unchangeable, as commonly assumed with Scottish gangs (see Patrick, 1973; Miller, 2015); rather, turf allowed business operations to be conducted and could thus be expanded accordingly. Second, members were often found to be young ethnic adults as opposed to solely delinquent teens. Lastly, the gang's sphere of criminal activity went beyond that of territorial violence and included several crime-for-profit ventures. Bennett and Holloway (2004) would likewise investigate gang activity in Manchester. They too found similarities between US and UK gangs relating primarily to socio-demographics and behavioural characteristics. However, they also concluded that ethnicity was not found to be an issue. Furthermore, when gang members were compared with non-gang members, the data revealed that gang members tended to be involved in both a disproportionate amount of crime and a substantially greater range of crime. Activity notably included drug supply and firearm crimes, over half of which were gang-related. Both studies helped mark a gradual shift in the way that gangs would come to be identified and defined in contemporary Britain.

As England's capital city, London is particularly exposed to the effects of globalisation. Thus, like Manchester, London has frequently been investigated as a site for criminological research and gang studies. John Pitts (2008, 2012) identifies the presence of not just organised street gangs, which share considerable characteristics with US gangs, but also US-style 'supergangs' operating within London's boroughs, although Aldridge (2011) notes that even in the US, such gangs are very much the exception as opposed to the norm. Pitts (2008) outlines a six-point typology that describes the drug-dealing gangs of Waltham Forest. Each level of the gang typology is linked through criminally harmonious transactions and a degree of subordination to the higher echelons of the gang. Essentially, each level is presented as a somewhat extended arm of the gang. By illustrating the gang in such a way, Pitts presents it as a cohesively functioning unit. Those characteristics often attributed to US gang models, that is, subordination, hierarchy, a defined division of labour and leadership, are found in the Waltham Forest supergang. Gang behaviour therefore covers a range of activities, from theft and violence, to racketeering and drug distribution (see Pitts, 2012).

Concurring with Pitts, Simon Harding (2014) applies Pierre Bourdieu's principles of social field analysis and habitus to urban street gangs and similarly argues that processes of globalisation have resulted in the increased criminality of contemporary gangs in London, which have been refined and organised as a means to engage in gang business. Through intense competition for sparse resources and survival within violent street worlds, young gang members are forced to play in 'the casino of life', whereby success and status is determined by accruing what Harding terms 'street capital' through gang participation. Likewise, James Densley (2012, 2013) argues that complex processes of economic and cultural globalisation have resulted in the organisation of street gangs as a means for gang business. Yet, Densley is aware that even within the discipline of criminology, there has been a polarisation among academics concerning gang structure and organisation. While an empirical body of work concerning English gangs has emerged in recent years, the literature is often framed in the language of cultural criminology, which emphasises the manufactured meaning around the term 'gang'. Adopting a more pragmatic approach to gang structural and organisational features, Harding (2014) argues that British scholars like Alexander (2008) and Hallsworth and Young (2008) are overly cautious when conceptualising the gang for fear that the label itself may imply that US gang models do exist in the UK, and that by emphasising alternative terminology, they create terms in themselves that appear no less ambiguous or unhelpful. Yet, accompanied with the Eurogang paradox, UK gang literature has become home to an assortment of confusing amalgamations of gang types that often conceal more than they reveal. Densley thus argues that the term 'gang' is no less perplexing than the existing alternatives. Furthermore, Densley suggests that these typologies have essentially resulted in a gang spectrum being created. One of the key points of disagreement among gang scholars is where the street gang ends and organised crime begins, particularly given that the association of criminals and criminal association are one and the same (see Morselli, 2009). If a term is too broad, it can lead to the criminalisation of minor offenders; yet, if it is too narrow, offenders remain unidentified.

Acknowledging Hallsworth and Young's (2008) three-point typology as perhaps the most influential gang definition in contemporary Britain, Densley argues that its distinctive features distinguishing gangs from organised crime are nonetheless too narrow. Hallsworth and Young's conceptualisation of organised crime as crime carried out by groups of adults for whom involvement is for personal gain simply does not go far enough. Drawing upon Varese's (2010) systematic content analysis of over 100 definitions, Densley demonstrates that much of Varese's work reveals organised crime to be more than just the attempts to unlawfully regulate/control the production and distribution of a commodity/service. Rather, much of Varese's work finds that those characteristics associated with drug-dealing gangs like those described by Levitt and Venkatesh (2000) actually also fit the criteria of OCGs, namely, in that they provide illegal goods and services while similarly making efforts to be sole suppliers within the sphere of operation. Thus, gangs may fit the criteria for both crime that is organised and organised crime. Exploring this possibility, Densley analysed gang structure and organisation in London and found that gangs often exist on a continuum in reference to both structure and organisation.

Densley argues that while not all gangs evolve, others do and will generally start out as recreational groups serving primarily social purposes. Membership is based upon friendship as individuals share history, interests, experiences and, not least, location. In turn, gang names at this stage are regularly derived from the neighbourhood. While gang activity is generally benign, it can sometimes be delinquent, particularly when alcohol and drugs are involved. Yet, delinquency can become intrinsic to group identity, especially given that criminal engagement can be both exciting and status rewarding. However, this can bring unwanted attention from other criminals and law-enforcement agents, to which gangs may respond by solidifying (see Klein, 1971). At this stage, gangs may alter their group name to more adequately represent their criminal components. As gangs evolve in response to external threats, they may likewise do so in response to financial commitments given that financial responsibilities typically ensue with maturity. Therefore, the pursuit of material goods supersedes a need for street credibility and, as a result, crime becomes the means not the end. Entry into the drugs business has had the most significant impact on gang evolution, first in the US and now the UK. While the gang's value is based on intangible assets in its early recreational and criminal stage, with the transition from the criminal to the enterprise stage, the gang can be used to gain tangible rewards. The internal organisation now becomes a main concern for members, who organise in response to business opportunities and incentives. Ultimately, the gang evolves from being relatively disorganised at the neighbourhood level, into what resembles a corporate entity in many ways. Structural models of OCGs provide a template for gangs to work from as they increase in organisation. After gangs organise, members quickly find themselves able to bulk-buy drugs and firearms, and thus move beyond those original lines of supply, progressing ever closer to the source itself.

Gang structure

Having outlined the conditions and settings in which gangs are thought to emerge, or not, I now look to discuss the gang from the approach of structure, looking at definitions, typologies and gang models. Ultimately, gang literature has been separated into cultural criminology and administrative criminology. This has resulted in the creation of ever-more gang models. Definitions are typically constructed in relation to research purpose. Thus, early gang research was not intended to be used as a tool for gang suppression. Thrasher's (1927) classic study on Chicago's gangs and Miller's (1982) contemporary perceptions encapsulate this current dilemma. For Thrasher (1927), a gang is:

> an interstitial group originally formed spontaneously, and then integrated through conflict. It is characterized by the following types of behaviour: meeting face to face, milling, movement through space as a unit, conflict, and planning. The result of this collective behaviour is the development of tradition, unreflective internal structure, esprit de corps, solidarity, morale, group awareness, and attachment to a local territory.

Emphasising the spontaneous nature of gang formation, Thrasher regards delinquency as a potential outcome rather than a given. As such, delinquency is to be examined independently; any construction of gang classification based upon delinquency alone would prove to be only a narrow concept. Yet, by the mid- to late 20th century, American scholarly research was to become part of the fight against gangs, which was, in turn, a key element in the intensified war on drugs. Thus, gang expert Walter B. Miller's (1982) scholarly definition suggests that a gang is 'a group of recurrently associating individuals with identifiable leadership and internal organisation, identifying with or claiming control over territory in the community, and engaging either individually or collectively in violent or other forms of illegal behaviour'.

Such definitions have been incorporated by a number of US law-enforcement agencies. As Pitts (2008) points out, even though gangs were once perceived as boisterous groups, the overarching discourse concerning gangs has turned progressively punitive as street-gang escalation has coincided with an upsurge in a globalised gang culture (see Densley, 2012) and increased accessibility to illegal drug markets (Alonso, 2004; Kenney, 2007; Gootenberg, 2011).

Contemporary definitions being incorporated by law-enforcement agencies when creating workable criteria largely overlook much of the scholarly caution that has been highlighted. Drawing upon Matza and Syke's (1961) early work, problems emerge when current definitions present loose peer groups and associates as solidified units involved in delinquent or criminal behaviour. Yet, as the scholars point out, the level of gang involvement that each individual retains alternates regularly as they drift in and out of association when expressing subterranean values. Likewise, Short (1968: 11) points out that 'among gang boys most delinquencies do not involve the total group'. Gang models are all too often simplistic in their outlook as core members and loose associates are labelled alike, with delinquency being a unified activity. Instead, Short (1968) suggests that perceiving gang involvement as existing on a continuum is more appropriate than applying an either/or status (see also Yablonsky, 1959). Such critiques are arguably given more attention in a contemporary European context where the gang phenomenon has not been so explicitly studied or criminalised. While European definitions are less inclined to directly apply US definitions, they have nonetheless undoubtedly been influenced by such conceptualisations. However, such influence is arguably becoming ever-more amplified and adoptable, as is evident in the contemporary tone of the literature, particularly in the UK, where many now see criminality as an integral feature of the gang (see Pitts, 2008; Densley, 2012).

Referring to this process and acknowledging recognisable differences between gangs, as well as growing gang complexities, Klein et al (2001: 428) expand Klein's (1971) gang definition and state that a gang is defined as:

> any denotable adolescent group of youngsters who (a) are generally perceived as a distinct aggregation by others in their neighbourhood, (b) recognize themselves as a denotable group – almost invariably with a group name – and (c) have been involved in a sufficient number of delinquent incidents to call forth a consistent negative response from neighbourhood residents and/or law enforcement agencies.

Klein et al (2001) also supplement this definition with a five-point typology:

1. The Traditional Gang is typically a large, enduring, territorial gang encompassing a significant age range with several internal cliques based on such characteristics.
2. The Neo-Traditional Gang refers to newer territorial gangs that are evolving towards becoming a traditional gang in time.
3. The Compressed Gang is relatively new, small, has no subgroupings and may not always be based on territoriality. Thus, it is unclear whether it will solidify into more traditional forms.
4. The Collective Gang is a kind of shapeless mass of adolescents and young adults that has not developed the distinguishing characteristics of other gangs. They are often medium to large in size and age range and may have existed for over a decade.
5. The Specialty Gang is crime-focused in a narrow way. Its principal purpose is more criminal than social. It is smaller in size and may even be territorial.

Yet, while similar characteristics like criminality, territoriality and structure are emphasised in the UK, many scholars – perhaps none more so than Simon Hallsworth – have been concerned that contemporary gang talkers increasingly define gang deviance up by overplaying the roles that delinquency and criminality play in gang activity, thus drawing it closer to characteristics primarily found in US gang models. Similarly, some definitions closer to home (like the Eurogang definition) may prove overly complex and not specifically relevant to the UK (see Hallsworth and Young, 2004, 2006; Hallsworth and Brotherton, 2011; Hallsworth, 2014).

Contending with both US and European gang concepts, Hallsworth and Young (2004, 2006) adopt the description 'urban collectives' in an attempt to avoid preconceived assumptions and designations. Providing three distinct urban collective typologies in an English context, the model operates on a pyramid structure, with OCGs situated at the pinnacle, gangs in the middle and peer groups at the base. The peer group is described as a 'relatively small, unorganised transient congregation of confederates who may coalesce in public space. Its members will be known to each other principally because they share the same space along with a common history and biography' (Hallsworth and Young, 2006: 64). Neither criminal intent nor delinquency is integral to identity and this is what primarily distinguishes it from the gang. If delinquency occurs, it is often in correlation to particular staging points (see Anderson, 1999).

The gang is described as a 'relatively durable, predominantly street-based group of young people who see themselves and are recognised by others as a discernible group for whom crime and violence are intrinsic to identity and practice' (Hallsworth and Young, 2006: 68). The minimal criteria require the group to have a name and be predisposed to engage in crime, which, in itself, promotes group solidarity and identity. The authors suggest that other attributes like structure, leadership, organisation, crime-for-profit activity and so on are supplementary features more akin to US models. Yet, US scholars like Hegadron (1994, 1998, 2008) and Huff (1990) point out that groups often begin as peers but external pressures help consolidate group identity and subsequently resulting behaviour. This transition from one group to the next is perhaps somewhat blurred – more so in the eyes of law enforcement – and is subject to interpretation. Furthermore, by adding a number of supplementary features, the gangs described by Hallsworth and Young (2006) are more closely aligned to OCGs than street-based youth gangs. Gangs may easily resemble the OCGs for whom the authors argue 'involvement in criminal behaviour is intrinsic to their identity and practice' (Hallsworth and Young, 2006: 74). The OCGs are comprised of men who do business, and the business is crime. Yet, gangs retaining considerable supplementary features may well prove equal to their adult counterparts in all aspects bar one – age. Densley (2012) describes how gangs retain the ability to organise as a means of business in a globalised consumer society. Thus, while Hallsworth and Young's (2006) three-point typology provides a firm foundation from which to work, it nonetheless requires additional detail while also recognising that young adolescence can very well engage in the same level of criminality and maturity as adults.

However, derived, in part, from the work of Klein et al (2001), Gordon (2000) and Hallsworth and Young (2004), Pitts (2008) does expand on the work of his peers and demonstrates the growing complexities concerning contemporary UK gang models as they increasingly organise for illegal propose. Arguing that London street gangs contain a variety of hierarchical levels, Pitts provides a six-point typology to incorporate subdivisions, specified roles and assigned responsibilities:

1. The named Articulated Super Gang is a local, originally familial, grouping with historical ties to organised crime. It can exert high levels of control over both residential and drug-dealing territories, and being a hierarchical 'institutionalised' enterprise with subgroupings, it has horizontal links to other gangs and vertical links into higher-echelon organised crime.
2. The Street Gang is a relatively durable, predominantly street-based group of adolescents who self-define (and are seen by others) as a discernible group, with subgroups defined by age. Crime and violence is integral to group identity. Territory can be residential or based on criminal opportunities.
3. The Compressed Street Gang is a new, small group with no subgroups. With a narrow age range, members see themselves (and are seen by others) as a discernible group. Crime and violence are integral to group identity within residential territories.
4. The Criminal Youth Group's purpose is more criminal than social. It narrowly focuses on specific offences. It is small and territory is either residential or based on opportunities for crime.
5. Wannabees have not developed structural characteristics like traditional gangs, despite claiming territory and displaying similar gang insignia, signs, symbols and names. They are loosely structured groups who engage in spontaneous social and criminal activity.
6. Middle Level International Criminal Business Organisations primarily consist of adults and are at the end of an international crime network. Often engaged in drug dealing (using local adolescents), prostitution and trafficking, they generally retain a low profile.

However, Pitts (2008) is criticised for all too readily accepting evidence of loose partnerships, crime syndicates, organisations, street gangs and middlemen as existing before consolidating them as one cohesive unit under the umbrella term 'gang' (see Aldridge et al, 2011; Hallsworth, 2014). Criminal networks often contain a variety of organisations or partnerships that work together at different points, yet they are nonetheless far from being a cohesive unit or single entity (see Decker and Van Winkle, 1996). Aldridge (2011) points out that even in the US, these 'supergangs', as described by Pitts, are very much the exception rather than the norm. However, what Pitts (2008) does achieve is to demonstrate that, ultimately, any broad definition of what constitutes a gang within an era of globalisation will inevitably fail to acknowledge appreciable differences regarding levels of involvement and complexity but will nonetheless still affect policymakers (see Roger, 2008). Equally, though, narrow definitions may prove specific but, at times, irrelevant within a given context as researchers choose between limited criteria.

Yet, drawing on the work of scholars like Short (1968), as well as contemporary scholars identifying the increased ability of gangs to organise and act cohesively as a means for business in a globalised climate, Densley (2012, 2013) puts forward an evolving gang model as opposed to fixed typologies as a way of explaining appreciable differences in gangs. Similarly, such a model allows gangs to be linked to both street-level crime and organised criminal activity. Pointing to recreational, crime and enterprise as sequential stages of development, Densley (2012) argues that gangs are able to move along the continuum as their organisational aspects evolve. Originating from localised adolescent peer groups partaking in common features affiliated with street life, gangs respond to external threats and financial commitments by using acquired resources for the successful regulation of unlawful commodities or services, thus becoming more organised. However, whether such group behaviour is organised crime or simply crime that is organised is ambivalent (Schelling, 1971). While Densley (2013) favours the latter when considering the majority of UK-based street gangs, he acknowledges the potential for gang evolution towards becoming an OCG. In many ways, this is similar to the points made by Hallsworth and Young (2006) via a typology model. Furthermore, Densley (2012, 2013) is one of the few authors who provide a detailed description of those sequential steps that gang members undergo at the individual level, as opposed to the group level, while transcending towards involvement in organised crime. Where Densley's model succeeds over the likes of Hallsworth and Young's (2004, 2006) typology is that it ultimately incorporates globalised complexities that allow contemporary gangs to organise in response to not only immediate external threats, but also structurally globalised ones.

Gang activity and (dis)organised crime

Having first considered the gang from the setting in which it is most to likely emerge, or has disproportionately been found, and then subsequently analysed the structure in which these manifest, I now consider gangs from the perspective of activity. This is because one of the key aspects by which gangs are thought to differ from lesser peer groups and more organised outfits is whether criminal behaviour is organised or not (Densley, 2013; Harding, 2014; Von Lampe, 2016). Essentially, what this means is that a brief review of organised crime is needed.

What is organised crime?

So, what exactly is organised crime? In the contemporary era, it is stereotypically, and often inaccurately, used to describe particular criminal activities carried out by particular criminal groupings. However, as we have seen in the review of gangs so far, there has been a lack of consistency when academics, practitioners, the media and, indeed, even the general public apply the term. Von Lampe (2016) argues that even when the term is being applied by many to describe the same phenomena, what exactly makes such phenomena organised may be seen to differ. Is it the crime itself, or those who are involved, or even the power that is being exercised? Arguably, though, much of what is believed to make a criminal phenomenon organised is typically attributed to the fact that it provides the provision of illegal goods and services. This is because numerous goods and services are prohibited in one way or another, whether due to products/services being outlawed, strictly regulated or highly priced. This essentially means that they become unavailable to the masses (Croall, 2011).

Of course, people often look to capitalise upon such circumstances by providing consumers with the products/services that they desire. It is in this niche that organised crime is generally perceived as operating. Yet, does this mean that all who provide illegal goods and services should be considered as involved in organised crime, regardless of what these goods/services may be, by whom they are distributed or the degree to which this is done? Similarly, by only focusing on market-based crime, there is a tendency to neglect and exclude predatory crimes like fraud, robbery and bribery. The discussion of organised crime is often used in a multidimensional manner, whereby it is used to describe not only a particular activity, but also those structures/networks in which, and by which, it is carried out, either as a precondition or consequential result itself. Again, this is often also dependent upon the wider setting in which such phenomena take place.

We must also consider that organised crime is by no means confined to groups; however, it is widely recognised that criminal cooperation means that crime is much easier to carry out when situated on a continual basis. This is because group activity, involving two or more, means that resources, skill sets and other forms of capital can be pulled together for the commission of crime, particularly as ongoing crime, like market-based crime, requires the need for numerous tasks to be interlocked with one another. An example may be the global supply of drugs, which are produced, transported and then distributed, with money and other goods coming back along the same supply lines to various degrees. Another example in relation to predatory crimes is the sale of a stolen motor vehicle, which requires the car to be stolen, the manipulation of the vehicle to take place and the resale of the car to be made possible. Therefore, when discussing organised crime, we often generally speak of both the commission of crime and those carrying out the crime simultaneously. More often than not, law enforcement attributes definitions of crime to groups (to varying degrees), as typically used in organised crime-mapping techniques.

Origins of organised crime

How we apply the term 'organised crime' in the contemporary era is largely subjective and used quite differently from its original application. Thus, it is helpful to consider how the term, as with 'gangs', originated. While the term 'organised crime' pre-dates the 20th century, the way in which it is applied in the contemporary arena is essentially a US invention, whereby the words 'organised' and 'crime' were brought closer in a consistent manner and used to describe particular crimes carried out by particular groups (Bell, 1953; Hobbs and Antonopoulos, 2013; Von Lampe, 2016). Since then, from around the 1970s and onwards, it has been steadily extrapolated into the European arena, and then on the global scale from around the 1990s in the run-up to the UN Convention against Transnational Organised Crime, also known as the Palermo Convention, in 2000 (see also von Lampe, 2016).

The two words 'organised' and 'crime' had occasionally been placed together as early as the 19th century, yet with no real consistency or meaning, and were commonly used to describe crimes that had been carried out in the context of war. Yet, both were deliberately brought together in the US in 1919 when the Chicago Crime Commission was created, whereby esteemed professionals sought to protect their assets from criminals engaged in predatory-based crimes. However, the term was used in reference to criminals who engaged in crime as a business (Chamberlin, 1920, 1921) as opposed to describing any link between criminal organisations, networks or ethnicities. Such usage of the term did not appear until around the 1950s,[1] when it was used to refer to the Italian Mafia. Throughout the Prohibition years of 1920–33, the term would be applied more specifically to 'gangsters', often operating in 'gangs' (Lashly, 1930).

During the 1950s, the resurgence image of the Italian Mafia would see organised crime and ethnicity brought closer together. The televised hearings of the US Senate chaired by Estes Kefauver and guided by information from the Federal Bureau of Narcotics (FBN) would focus attention on a group of underworld figures from Chicago and New York who were suspected of controlling illegal gambling operations throughout various parts of the US. The committee concluded that a number of powerful criminal groups were tied together by links to a criminal organisation known as the Mafia. Von Lampe (2016) notes that such findings marked a significant turn in the conceptualisation of organised crime, whereby it was no longer a localised problem and an ethnic dimension was added to it. For the first time, involvement by law enforcement was also seen, in the form of the FBN taking an active role in combating the phenomenon. Such conceptualisations of organised crime were reinforced by two key events: the Kefauver hearing's discovery of a national meeting of Italian American criminals in New York; and the 1963 Mafia testimonies by 'supergrass' Joe Valachi, presenting the Cosa Nostra as hierarchical, nationwide and having clear divisions of labour and rules of conduct. In 1967, the Presidential Commission on Crime would consequently declare the Mafia to be the embodiment of organised crime. Following such events, Mafia conceptualisations and stereotypes have since been influenced by numerous reports, novels and films (Levi, 1998; Paoli, 2003, 2004).

Yet, while it is acknowledged that other types of criminal organisations engaged in various criminal activities have long existed in the US prior to hysteria surrounding the Mafia, Mafia models of organised crime were simply placed over other 'non-traditional' organised crime (Von Lampe, 2016). As such, Asian, Latino and Russian groups have all been defined within the same paradigm as the Italian Mafia. In addition, since the late 20th century, other countries, in particular Western countries, have looked to US think tanks in an effort to tackle their own social ills. While organised crime terminology has been thoroughly adopted, US paradigms of organised crime were nonetheless found to fail in giving an accurate account of the range and varying degree of differences found in the given European context. As such, the initial response to organised crime as being orchestrated by organised and politically entrenched criminal outfits was to either reject or, more commonly, adapt it. Thus, European models tend to describe organised crime as occurring in primarily criminal networks in which various criminal groups operate who can transcend local environments and enter transnational ones. This perception of criminal groups working in transnational criminal networks is one that has been favoured, and significantly developed, by law enforcement. While the narrow perception of Mafia organisations is one that is generally adopted by the public and media, law enforcement continues to retain this broader perception of organised crime, which encompasses all profit-motivated criminal activity that is carried out by more than two/three individuals working together in a coordinated manner. However, some scholars have been critical of the perceived increase in organised crime and have pointed out that by increasingly defining certain behaviours as belonging to the domain of organised crime, law enforcement are able to ask their respective governments for greater levels of funding in order to tackle such problems: often via the creation of specialised units (Symeonidou-Kastanidou, 2007).

Organised crime research

Von Lampe (2016) argues that, ultimately, the study of organised crime has been approached from three perspectives. How organised crime is viewed usually depends on whether it is analysed by studying: the crime; the criminals; or the power that is exercised. To understand organised crime, we need to look at how criminal *activity* affects, and is affected by, criminal *structures* and the *illegal governance* that takes place.

Organised crime by activity

To understand organised crime from the aspect of activity is to analysis what type of crime is taking place? How is the crime being carried out? What level of sophistication, planning and potential harm is involved? Criminal activities can be placed on a continuum, with spontaneous, impulsive and one-off behaviour at one end and planned, coordinated and continuous behaviour at the other. Von Lampe (2016: 31) argues that 'where exactly organised crime should be positioned on this continuum is not as important as understanding how under conditions of illegality, in an essentially hostile environment, fairly sophisticated, continuous activities are possible'. Regarding activity, there are three main types that help us get a better understanding of organised crime from the approach of activity: predatory crimes; market-based crimes; and governance crimes.

Naylor (2009) argues that it is helpful to distinguish between predatory-based crimes and market-based crimes in that while both may be driven for profit, how they are carried out and who the intended victims are, as well as how the victims may view the crimes, may nonetheless differ remarkably. As briefly mentioned, the term 'organised crime' has its roots in predatory crimes, whereby gangs of criminals would rob merchants along trade routes in what was once British India. While predatory crimes can, and do, occur over a given duration in some cases, or may even have preferred and replicated techniques for carrying out such crimes, they can nonetheless be thought of as essentially crimes that are primarily one-off events in that they do not always require a number of working parts acting together for criminals to yield a profit. Predatory crimes can essentially be thought of as involving the distribution of existing wealth from one party to another resulting from bilateral transfers between the victim and perpetrator, creating identifiable victims.

Market-based crimes, on the other hand, are viewed as crimes that are driven by supply and demand. While there is a staunch argument that demand may well be significantly influenced by production itself, to keep it simple it nonetheless helps to view demand as when certain consumers want something but the product/service is difficult to obtain. This means that the supply of the product is driven by a need to fulfil the demand. To this end, demand is seen as being met by criminals who exploit market restrictions on products/services. Traditional images may well conjure up thoughts of Al Capone distributing alcohol to the American public during the Prohibition era, or more contemporary drug trafficking by Columbian cartels to a willing American public (see Roldán, 1999). This has seen the populist argument emerge which suggests that the way to address market-based organised crime is to simply legalise, to various degrees, the commodity or service in demand; yet, this is to oversimplify the matter. However, it is important to note that market-based crimes are not always directed at large sections of the population, but may also cater for smaller, and even hidden, segments of the population, for example, as regards child pornography, sex workers or slavery.

It is helpful to think of market-based crimes as operating much like a business, whereby willing consumers are being supplied with desired goods and services by those who have access to them. Market-based crimes typically operate much like a supply chain, including production, exchange and distribution. However, this is not to say that the supply chain is overseen by any one person or group; rather, the mode of exchange, currency, motivation and the relationship between those along the supply chain may differ considerably, and in form, from one section to the next. Furthermore, with market-based crimes, it can, at times, be very difficult to identify who the direct and indirect victims are, as well as who is involved in the crime itself and who is not, even regarding suppliers. Market-based offences can be further subdivided into three subsets: those encouraged by regulatory restrictions; those driven by taxation; and those that result from prohibition (Canadian Justice, 2018).

Von Lampe (2016) argues that another way to think of organised crime is in terms of 'illegal governance'. Crimes of this nature do not necessarily mean that perpetrators engage in market-based or predatory crimes; rather, by retaining some degree of power, via various means, over others operating within illegal markets, or even where legal governance is weak, they are able to 'tax' others and control criminal behaviour in a given location. The Mafia is a good example of a quasi-governmental structure. Taking a simplistic and somewhat stereotyped image here, it can be argued that the control that the organisation has over a given sphere (tangible or non-tangible) allows the Mafia to exercise power over other criminal, and on occasion legitimate, individuals. They can dictate which acts are allowed and which are not, they can also tax other criminals, whereby a percentage of profit is paid as tribute to those in power. This means that although the organisation may not necessarily be carrying out crimes per se, it nonetheless controls the actions of those who do, as well as outlining which activities are acceptable and which are not. The organisation may even act as a third party in which disputes, where recourse to law is not possible, can be settled. Yet, while the Mafia is a good example (though stereotyped in this example), illegal governance can also be carried out by legitimate institutions, such as a corrupt government.

Gangs and organised crime

Ultimately, when considering the role of the gang regarding activity, we see that, over time, there has been a tendency to view gangs as retaining not only delinquent properties, but also criminal ones. This is because the context in which the gang was first studied has changed. The gang and those who view the gang have both responded to complex changes that have occurred because of increased globalisation. With greater access to illegal markets, greater diversity in the ways in which crimes can be committed and greater exposure to alternative gang models to replicate and build upon, gangs have adapted their structure and activity to suit the environment in which they find themselves (McLean, 2017, 2018a, 2018b, 2018c). In addition, greater complexity has also meant that where gang structure ends and OCG structure begins, and whether they are engaging in organised crime or not, has become increasingly difficult to determine. Yet, many gangs are now engaging in behaviour that is technically deemed to be organised crime (Miller, 2000; Densley, 2013; McLean et al, 2017). This is particularly true when gangs are involved in the provision of illegal goods and services at various points of drug supply chains. The expansion of the global drugs trade has meant that drug supply chains are now extending further than ever before and penetrating every level of society (Pearson and Hobbs, 2001). This has brought many youth gangs into supply networks where, in previous decades, they were not needed or wanted, nor able to access themselves.

Therefore, I argue that when discussing whether a gang, which is an ambiguous and highly subjective term, is engaging in organised crime or not, it is ludicrous to also draw upon the term 'organised crime' as a method of distinction alone, considering that it is also a highly ambiguous and subjective term. So, to call one gang a group as opposed to a gang because they are involved in organised crime is no longer applicable given that those that we traditionally called 'gangs' are also now involved in similar processes. The point of this section is not to give refined organised crime definitions, or otherwise, but merely to point out the flaws that exist in using set markers such as context, structure or activity independently as a way of distinguishing a peer group from a gang and a gang from an OCG, and in doing so to further justify my argument for adopting the term 'gang' as an umbrella term within which everything else can be located. Yet, given that an increasing variety of gang types are becoming involved in these organised criminal supply chains, there must be some degree of workable distinction as current definitions bring many into the fold of organised crime. Therefore, I argue that existing 'official' organised crime criteria used by the NCA and Police Scotland should be termed *organised efforts of crime*, while organised crime has the additional feature of illegal governance, similar to Von Lampe's (2016) suggestion. This additional feature makes a distinction between those gangs in the higher echelons and those working within the markets that OCGs attempt to control and orchestrate.

Chapter summary

This chapter has explored the gang from three different aspects in order to bring the reader up to speed with the gang literature. This has been done by chronologically tracking the development of the gang literature and how gangs were originally thought to be a product of their environment. The chapter explored this in detail and analysed how the rise of the multidimensional factors of globalisation, overnight deindustrialisation and greater access to drug markets have all contributed to the extrapolation of gangs from their origins in the US, into the European arena, and evidently UK soil. The chapter then moved on to exploring the structure of the gang, or at least how academics have conceptually viewed them. This section traces how the definitions, typologies and models have tended to reflect wider gang discourses. However, pinpointing a universal gang structure is an impossible task on its own given the sheer scope for variety. This variety is often impacted upon by the relationship that structure shares with activity, as both continue to influence one another. Consequently, activity, in conjunction with structure, is often used as a method for distinguishing between gang variations such as peer groups and OCGs. Yet, in order to help uncover the true complexities involved, activity was examined not so much by exploring the interplay between structure and activity, as this will take place in Part III of the book, but rather by drawing attention to the contradictory and highly ambiguous nature of what exactly constitutes organised crime. This is because organised crime is used as a key characteristic for differentiating between gang and non-gang typologies; however, as seen, what organised crime is to some it may not be to others.

Note
[1]   Media and public attention had been raised with regard to two notable incidents that occurred in the decades prior (see Lombardo, 2010).

3

Scottish Gang Literature

Chapter 2 outlined gang research in three main ways. These were regarding context, structure and literature. Yet, while this discussion was placed in the wider US, European and, finally, UK context, Scottish gang literature was excluded. This is because I did not want to present the complex picture of what has been happening in Scottish gang literature without first setting the background in which it can be understood. This is particularly important given that this book is not just for the established academic. Yet, this chapter is written in a manner that hopes to fuel a renewed rejuvenation of Scottish gang research. This chapter can essentially be broken down into two parts. The first part of the chapter will look at Scottish gang literature and will cover, in an intertwined manner, the context in which gangs are studied, the structure with which they are generally attributed and the activities in which they are thought to engage. The second half of the chapter will then look at some of the reasons that have contributed to the stagnation of Scottish gang literature and how gangs are believed to be in Scotland. This will be explained by exploring several contributory factors, though these are by no means all of the reasons why, but are rather a specifically selected few. A summary will then be given to conclude the chapter.

Gangs in Scotland

Scottish gang literature

Left idealists argue that governance-through-crime approaches are the primary factor for why the UK landscape is now seen to be dominated by gangs. They argue that increased levels of global immigration are the primary driving force behind the spike in UK gang research. Interestingly, whether this is true or not, and as with English gang literature, immigration played an important role in the emergence of gang formation in late 19th-century Scotland. While gangs have been found in almost every major city in Scotland, it is the country's largest city, Glasgow, and the immediately surrounding urban environment, that has become known as a hotbed of gang activity (Deuchar et al, 2018). Therefore, to understand gangs in Scotland, one needs to understand gangs in the Glasgow conurbation (Holligan and Deuchar, 2015; Holligan et al, 2016; McLean, 2017, 2018a, 2018b). Therefore, much of the debate in this chapter will revolve around gang research within the city. Of course, this is also because the Glasgow conurbation is the location where my own research was carried out, and I firmly believe context to always hold a degree of relevance to the research taking place or phenomenon being studied.

As mentioned, immigration played a key role in the city's original gang formation. In particular, the rise of the razor gangs during the 1920s/30s coincided with large-scale Irish immigration into the region. While immigration into Glasgow had already been underway for several decades beforehand, a sharp downturn in economic output resulted in widespread recession and high unemployment rates, for which the Irish were duly scapegoated. In Glasgow, migrant communities typically bordered indigenous communities; thus, growing tensions would regular spill over into violent confrontation. As migrant populations were almost physically indistinguishable from indigenous ones, religious practice would be used as a tool for identifying the 'other' (see Bauman, 1989) that threatened the Glasgow way of life (Davies, 2007, 2013). Such confrontations would gradually see youths form gangs, which adopted 'scheme' names as a way of signifying territorial jurisdiction and religious practice, for example, 'The Bridgeton Billy Boys' were from the Bridgeton district and Protestant in religious genealogy. Many razor gangs also had junior outfits that would likewise engage in territorial violence and come to play a key part in the rise of YSGs (Davies, 1998; McLean, 2018b).

This practice of knife use would gradually give rise to what became an embedded knife culture, as evident in repeated calls for knife armistices throughout the post-war period, perhaps most notably celebrity Frankie Vaughan's 1960s' appeal to gang members on the notorious Easterhouse estate (see Bartie, 2010). Knife culture would eventual culminate in the city being branded Europe's Knife Capital during the early 2000s (Holligan et al, 2016). However, it is important to note that razor gangs were not just fighting outfits, but would also engage in other types of crime aimed at securing financial rewards, including armed robbery, racketeering and extortion (Davies, 1998). Although rooted in territorial violence, as an expression of sectarian division, the gang was also used to reward members financially. Thus, gangs organised as a means for carrying out gang business (Sillitoe, 1956). Gang members were also typically older, a feature that Davies (1998) attributes to the economic recession. While older members and junior members alike would regularly get involved in gang violence, it was primarily older members that engaged in criminal activities aimed at financial gain. However, Sir Percy Sillitoe (1956) gives one of the few accounts of the inner workings of the razor gangs. In doing so, Sillitoe identifies the gang as comprising two units: those who are 'core members' and those who are on the 'periphery' of the gang. While core members were often hardened criminals who specialised in a range of criminal activities in addition to territorial street fights, those on the periphery could be considered loose associates who attached themselves to the gang primarily for fighting, as well as sociable, purposes. Those on the periphery rarely got involved in organised crime (see Davies, 1998).

As outlined, Glasgow has displayed a long and synonymous history with gangs; yet, while one might have expected the city to perhaps lead the way in Britain's more contemporary revisiting of the gang, this has not been the case. Although the city – like its English counterpart, London – has received considerable attention from gang talkers in the media and law enforcement, unlike London, this has not translated itself into a new wave of academic research. Even the analysis of early gang formation in the city has primarily been confined to the later writings of a few, including Bartie (2010, 2014), Davies (2007, 2008, 2013), Sillitoe (1956) and Humphries (1981). Even though 'gang' exploits would dominate the media in post-war Glasgow, more specifically, focused on the housing estate of Easterhouse, Bartie (2010, 2014) acknowledges that such discussion was primarily located within media and political spheres. Even here, the term 'gang' was being applied to what were essentially youth groups socialising in public urban areas, as opposed to criminally intent gangs. Nonetheless, though, prior to the 21st century, contemporary writings on gangs in Glasgow, or Scotland, were few and far between. The only real piece of academic literature was James Patrick's (1973) ethnographic study, *A Glasgow gang observed*, in which Patrick details his experiences of 'hanging out' with a Maryhill-based YSG. The work of Patrick has remained influential over more contemporary writings.

Since then, gang literature would remain silent until a handful of academics took it upon themselves to revisit the contemporary gang in a Glasgow context. Since the early 2000s, there have been several key pieces of research concerning gangs in Scotland, and more specifically Glasgow. Yet, this revisiting of the contemporary Glasgow gang has taken its own unique form, different from that which has taken place in the English context. This has led to the conclusion that gangs in Glasgow, and Scotland more broadly, are inherently different – always have been and perhaps always will be – from those found in major English cities and further afield. Key studies by Deuchar (2009, 2013), Fraser (2013, 2015), Holligan (2013), Lawson (2013), Miller (2015) and the Violence Reduction Unit (VRU, 2011) into Glasgow gangs, as well as Bannister et al (2010), Bradshaw (2005), McAra and McVie (2007, 2010), Smith (2006) and those other scholars involved in the Edinburgh Study of Youth Transitions and Crime into Edinburgh gangs, all suggest that they are recreational youth groups involved in territorial violence with no structure, no organisation and no intent to engage in criminal activities for the purpose of gains.[1]

Concerning the investigating of gang organisation in Scotland, Squires et al (2008) sum up the overall argument well as to how Scottish gangs are perceived. They suggest that the weapon of choice in Glasgow is the knife, as opposed to the gun, and violence is inherently tied up with issues related to territoriality among youth groupings, as opposed to being directly related to drug distribution and drug supply by late adolescents and young men in gangs (see also Bullock and Tilley, 2003; Pitts, 2008; Deuchar, 2009; Densley, 2012, 2013; Miller, 2015). Furthermore, a popular, and typically indirect, way in which knowledge of Scottish gangs has been built up is that when exploring other areas of scholarly interest, YSGs have often been used as a vehicle. This is particularly true regarding the likes of masculinity studies. Thus, such contributions have meant that our perception of Scottish gangs has been somewhat distorted and stifled. Therefore, as a consequence, any direct comparison with gangs in the North American, European or even English context has become increasingly difficult given that assumed differences in age, structure, activity, intent and purpose are inherent.

I have made considerable effort to look beyond such gang formation in an effort to shed light on other typologies (so often described elsewhere), as well as to re-engage Scottish gang literature back into the wider UK discourse, thus helping comparable analysis between gangs in the Scottish and English contexts to take place and, in the process, reveal those developments that occur in, and the interrelationships between, YSG and OCG formation. Likewise, such insights are consistent with data findings and broader discussions outside academia, such as in (auto)biographical accounts by (ex-)gang members and 'gangsters', practitioner services, the National Crime Agency (NCA), and public discussions typically involving concern about drug-dealing gangs in the community (see Scottish Government, 2013). Following fieldwork carried out in the Glasgow conurbation between 2012 and 2016, and continued ongoing data analysis thereafter, it was found that contrary to existing contemporary gang research in the Scottish context, gangs, in fact, retained evolving properties and, in many ways, identifiable features with those criminal gangs south of the border (see Bullock and Tilley, 2003; Pitts, 2008; Densley, 2012, 2013; Harding, 2014). Gangs in the Glasgow conurbation exist on a continuum, whereby some progress from YSG formation towards other gang typologies that engage in organised efforts of crime and organised crime. This was particularly found to be true with regard to involvement in drug supply networks, firearm crimes, money laundering, fraud, loan-sharking and even carrying out 'hits'.[2]

Seeking to negotiate the structure–activity nexus when situating gang/group positions on the continuum, in defining gangs, I first did so by looking at YSGs and their behavioural attributes and activities from which structural properties may, or may not, emerge thereafter. However, regarding evolvement, both activity and structure are largely inseparable and influence one another, for example, while all diffuse and disorganised gangs retain evolving capabilities, it is often only those that seek to organise as a means for 'business' that evolve. Typically, organisation occurs when individual group members seek to respond to external threats, motives, pressures of the adult world and financial commitments, and, in doing so, band together with likeminded, and trusted, individuals with whom they share history, experience and, in many cases, some degree of kinship, even if through reordered family structures (McLean, 2017). Like Densley (2012), I argue that persistent high-end offenders involved in the hard drug economy seldom arise from nowhere (see Windle, 2013; Windle and Briggs, 2015); rather, they harness and refine their criminality over sustained durations, often in groups or with co-offenders (see Decker and Kempf-Leonard, 1991; Decker and Chapman, 2008).

Findings from the research indicated that gang organisation exists on an evolving continuum, whereby organised groups of criminal adults (OCGs) occupy one end and disorganised delinquent youth gangs (YSGs) occupy the other end. This continuum is presented as having three main identifiable stages of development. While it was typical for gangs to progress from the bottom of the scale, it was not always necessary for a gang to have to do so as some managed to manifest and come into being further up the evolutionary ladder. Likewise, while this continuum represented the majority of gangs in the given context, and, indeed, all from the research, I recognise that other gang types also exist in the given context that do not adhere to this continuum, particularly given the broad definition I use to apply the term 'gang' itself, for example, biker gangs. The study of these alternatives typologies, which are the exception as opposed to the rule, is beyond the scope of this book.

As seen earlier, the evolving gang model in Scotland, which I present, is split into three generic stages: recreational; criminal; and enterprise.

Figure 3: McLean's evolving gang model

RECREATIONAL *Occupied by YSG;* *Age range*: 12–16 *Relationships*: social *Terminology*: self-labelling *Membership*: open, residentially assigned *Group activities*: recreational, occasionally delinquent and typically revolve around territoriality	**CRIMINAL** *Occupied by YCG;* *Age range*: 17–25 *Relationships*: social *Terminology*: non-labelling *Membership*: closed, assigned via friendships *Group activities*: primarily delinquent and criminal. Wide ranging	**ENTERPRISE** *Occupied by OCG;* *Age range*: adulthood *Relationships*: economic *Terminology*: non-labelling *Membership*: closed, assigned via business arrangements *Group activities*: criminal and typically specific

Within each stage, gangs can be quite different but they will typically display most, if not all, of the listed criteria. Thus, gangs that typically occupy the recreational stage are YSGs. YSGs are typical of the listed criteria in that they are generally youth groups, with open membership based on street socialisation and postcode residency, and when delinquency occurs, it primarily revolves around territoriality. However, these are by no means set in stone as some YSGs do have older and younger members, some are more coherent than others, and some are engaged in much greater levels of violence. For example, while the YSG in the affluent area of Bearsden shares these characteristics with the YSGs in the 'rough' Govan area of Glasgow, they are very different in the level of harm they pose, aggression and cohesion. While it was suggested during interviews that the Bearsden gang had carried out very little knife crime, two of the YSGs in the Govan district were reported to have had several members who had carried out between them several murders on rival gang and non-gang members.

YSGs are essentially recreational youth groups engaged in territorial violence. YSGs can be split into two sub-units: the 'outer layer' and the 'core'. The outer layer consists of local youth who affiliate with the core body but only minimally engage in offending. They are the least 'embedded' (Sweeten et al, 2013), and thus typically disengage from the group once they reach adulthood. The core body, by contrast, is the gang 'mainstay'. Although they constitute a minority, core members are the most embedded in the gang and become the most prolific offenders (see also VRU, 2011). They view crime as intrinsic to their own identity and are thus deemed 'life-course persistent' offenders (for example, Moffitt, 1993; Farrington et al, 2006). Core individuals (working with other core members) were typically the most likely to contribute to gang organisation. The process entailed criminal identities transcending the individual to become part of overall group identity. In other words, the core body underwent refinement to become a more coherent unit. Criminality became part of group intent, behaviour and activity, at which point the YSG changes into a YCG. However, as YCGs exist on an evolving continuum, differences remained even within gangs under the same stage of development. The term YCG can thus only be applied to those who engage in organised efforts of crime, and in regard to drug distribution (which all engaged in), had managed to effectively move beyond retail-level supply to bulk-buying and even high-end wholesaling practices. It is important to note that while YSGs tended to label themselves as a gang, for example, 'Pollok Young Team' or 'Young Linty Goucho', YCGs no longer adhere to issues of territoriality and thus cease using related terminology.

Police Scotland uses the term SOCG as equivalent to OCG in the English/Welsh context. This term describes those adult criminals engaged in organised crime and large-scale wholesaling drug distribution practices, or even importation, who generally operate in the upper echelons of the supply chain. OCG membership is based on economic properties first and social properties second, although, in many cases, OCG members actually socialised very little with one another outside 'working' relationships. While it was possible for a YCG to become an OCG in its own right, this was rarely the case. Rather, particularly successful YCG members ceased associating with other YCG members deemed as 'risky' or a 'liability' and instead formed 'business alliances' with colleagues at the top of the supply chain, often by way of being recognised in the underworld and thus brought into the fold (see Katz, 1988). Due to the level at which they operate, there is a real need for OCGs to launder money and they thus typically operate in the gaps between the illegal and legal markets, consequently ceasing to handle illegal commodities (like drugs) directly and instead handling money (see also Murray, 2016). As OCGs typically occupy the higher echelons of their respective markets, they retain features akin to illegal forms of governance within their sphere of influence. Thus, OCGs engage in what can be deemed organised crime given that all official criteria for organised crime are met in addition to the added feature of illegal governance.

Not all gangs will evolve. In relation to YSGs, very few gangs do evolve. Yet, there are a number of YCGs simply because in the Glasgow conurbation, due to issues of territoriality, there are actually many YSGs.

Furthermore, as these YSGs are typically associated with age, with only a few years between the upcoming YSG and the outgoing YSG in a given location, a number of YCGs may be turned out. Thus, it is not that every YSG becomes a YCG, but rather that there are a number of YCGs simply due to there being a disproportionately high number of YSGs in the given context. As for YCGs, they may arise from a YSG; however, in many cases, they actually come about with the merging of two or more YSG core members (often from different schemes but within the same housing estate) as they begin to move beyond territoriality with age and maturity (these are also reasons for the lack of self-labelling). While YCGs may become OCGs in their own right, more often than not, select members will be absorbed by existing OCGs.

Why has gang organisation gone unnoticed?

Having drawn attention to the fact that Scottish gang literature has effectively failed to engage in the wider revisiting of the British gang, and having outlined some of the key pieces of literature to justify my argument that there is a need to fill this gap, I will discuss why gang organisation had remained hidden from contemporary Scottish gang literature. This will help remove those barriers that stifle academic research into gang organisation and help address the overly fixative gaze placed upon recreation-based street gangs who occasionally engage in territorial violence. These factors are by no means the only ones that have contributed to the fixative academic gaze, but they are some of the most influential ones.

The conventional wisdom of gang research

Levitt and Dubner (2006) point out that conventional wisdom draws our attention towards that which is most apparent and readily fits our own subjective schemas. The scholars note that conventional wisdom all too often points us in the wrong direction as researchers, providing several insightful examples. Just as this process plays itself out every day, these same procedures have played themselves out in relation to contemporary Scottish gang research. Even with a considerable personal knowledge of gang activity at all levels, I likewise initially failed to recognise the error of conventional wisdom until making a complete re-evaluation of the gathered data in order to make theory accurately reflect reality. Let us explore this issue by drawing upon some of the key pieces of contemporary Scotland gang research. Studies by Bradshaw (2005) and McAra and McVie (2010) adopt a self-referral questionnaire used to measure membership and levels of delinquency. Deuchar (2009, 2013), Fraser (2013, 2015) and Holligan and Deuchar (2010) use a more ethnographic approach and subsequently interview youths who self-identify as gang members. More recently, Miller (2015), adopting a mixed methodology, also used self-referral questionnaires to identify members. Lastly, the VRU (2011) applies a somewhat early intervention approach to identifying potential persistent offenders and highlights YSGs as the main body from which persistent offenders arise. However, interestingly, while acknowledging YSGs as being central components in creating persistent offenders, it fails to build upon such findings by establishing links between YSGs and serious organised crime. Regardless, the recurring theme here is that all these studies first need to identify gang members in order to study gang behaviour. In doing so, gang members are often identified through a system of self-labelling and, to a lesser degree, labelling by 'official' sources. Let us now look at how gang members are sought out.

It is in this process of labelling that contemporary Glasgow gangs are misrecognised, resulting in an overly fixative gaze being placed upon essentially early adolescents who display 'protest' masculinity (see Holligan, 2013) via territoriality in particularly deprived communities. These groups often share location, proximity and history, and as a by-product, they take on what Miller (2015) suggests is their local scheme name to identify themselves to others, or can likewise have this label projected upon them. Ultimately, what is being studied is essentially street socialisation among youths in these schemes, as opposed to actual gang organisation. Such groups more readily identify with Hallsworth and Young's (2006) description of young peer groups in the English context, which perhaps, at times, transcend the boundary towards being a gang, but only really by way of a few core members – a process that I acknowledge (see McLean, 2017, 2018b). Similarly, at this stage, the YSG matches that description of reactional youth groups identified by Densley (2012) in London. At this stage, the gang is more a group of friends who, at times, display 'gang-like' features and retain potential – as opposed to given – evolving capabilities. YSGs, when considered as a whole, cannot be compared with those labelled as 'gangs' in either the English or North American context simply because what is being label as a gang in Scotland is being labelled as a youth/peer group, for example, in another context. McLean (2017) argues that the group to which the term 'gang' is typically applied in Scotland is, in fact, the equivalent of early pre-gang formations elsewhere, essentially what many consider 'pre-gangs (Hallsworth and Young, 2006; Densley, 2012; Harding, 2014).

In addition, when identifying gangs, researchers need to label the gang and thus target gang members. When defining who a gang member is, where to find gang members and what criteria must be met, researchers typically draw upon existing literature from prominent scholars in the field. In the case of gangs, this often includes: (1) North American literature, which itself draws upon early Chicago School theorists, leading researchers to go to those deprived, often socially disorganised, communities where there has been high migrant settlement, a lack of social control and a visible street-corner society as a consequence (Thrasher, 1927; Whyte, 1942); and (2) European definitions of what criteria are needed before the term 'gang' may be applied in the European or UK context (Klein et al, 2001). Looking at the Eurogang definition, Klein et al (2001: 428) state the gang to be:

> any denotable adolescent group of youngsters who (a) are generally perceived as a distinct aggregation by others in their neighbourhood, (b) recognize themselves as a denotable group – almost invariably with a group name – and (c) have been involved in a sufficient number of delinquent incidents to call forth a consistent negative response from neighbourhood residents and/or law enforcement agencies.

Yet, closer analysis reveals that the traits of youth, visibility and self-labelling are all equally emphasised as key components of gang criteria. Therefore, within a Scottish context, when researchers seek the gang, typically adhering to such definitions and located in those socio-economic environments as outlined by early Chicago School scholars, they find it in the YSG. This is because YSGs are often located in deprived communities, youthful and also highly visible in that they socialise in public urban space and are easily identifiable through dress styles. Yet, most importantly, YSGs also retain self-labelling properties. Drawing upon the work of early scholars and the Eurogang network as a foundation to work from, researchers typically begin to seek out visible youths in deprived communities (often with strong ties to immigrant populations), who likewise self-label as a gang.

When placed in the Scottish context, this typically leads researchers to Glasgow, and more specifically the city's East End, due to its history of Irish settlement, deprivation, violence and visible anti-social behaviour (Deuchar, 2009; Davies, 2013). Drawing upon conventional wisdom, researchers look for that which is most apparent (Becker, 1963). Throughout gang research, this has led to the targeting of rowdy teenagers who gather in groups in deprived communities. Thus, displaying gang-like features, being younger and perhaps having already been labelled by local law enforcement, youth workers or elderly residents as a gang, the researcher becomes more inclined to approach such youth groups. This is also due to feasibility as the targeting of such groups carries significantly less fear of reprisals, danger or just being disregarded than, say, approaching those who are known by locals to be adult drug dealers in their own homes who are known to carry out criminal activities. It would seem that to approach such individuals and ask if they are dealers, gang members or involved in gang-like structures or organised crime may be unreasonable and carries much risk, as well as considerable ethical consequences. Thus, it is much easier to approach visible youths in the street or, more often, in local youth community centres, where most core gang members do not 'hang out'.

Importantly, though, in a Glasgow conurbation context, when approached, such youths are likely to respond with positive feedback for the researcher by self-identifying as 'gangs', having gang membership or at least being gang associates who perhaps drift in and out of gang affiliation (McAra and McVie, 2010). This happens for many reasons, some of which we will explore as we continue. Yet, because of this process, the researcher has now ultimately identified the gang they sought, and thus the study of the gang, or the group that labels themselves as a gang, may begin. It is argued here that this process has led to an overly fixative gaze being placed upon the study of what are essentially youth groups. Furthermore, although these groupings may retain the potential to evolve into those gangs described by, or more readily sought out among, scholars in the English or even North American context, such potential is never explored in Scotland for several reasons, most notably, because the YSG is often studied as a whole, and as members age, mature and become involved in more serious crime, they tend to no longer self-label in the manner that they once did, if at all.

Labelling and scheme identity

Given the importance of self-labelling in this process, I will now explore how and why youths in this context label themselves as a gang per se. First, Glasgow gang identity is bound up with what Miller (2015) argues is scheme identity, much like Vigil's (1988a) study of Latino gangs in the US barrios. These schemes are found to have regenerating properties primarily through intergenerational gang membership and, more importantly, gang narratives, whereby gang stories are initially told by older generations to younger generations in the scheme. Youths looking to resemble older-generation gang narratives begin to socially construct their own version of these narratives, which gives the narratives life. Scheme identity thus becomes part of street socialisation. This street socialisation sees large numbers of youths in these areas having their own identity bound up with that of the scheme's history. In this process, youths may also label themselves or be labelled by others with old and pre-existing gang names that reflect that of the scheme. This process is evident in a number of books written by, or about, infamous Glasgow gangsters like Jimmy Boyle (1977) or Paul Ferris (Ferris and McKay, 2001, 2010; Ferris, 2005). The former sought to replicate the behaviour of local 'hard men' who, like himself, built a fearsome reputation initially via peer group engagement in territorial violence. As mentioned, Vigil (1988a) points to a similar process occurring within the barrios of North America, where youth identity is inherently tied to the barrios' history and, in the process, gang activity itself develops in relation to age. Thus, the gang refines and matures over time, having begun in street socialisation and peer group delinquency.

These processes also exist in Glasgow and are evident in the particularly young age from which gang membership regularly begins (12–16 years) (Bradshaw, 2005; Deuchar, 2009; VRU, 2011). Yet, it is argued here that visible youths in deprived communities are, through regenerative properties, essentially making immature efforts to replicate those intergenerational gang narratives that they are being presented with. Thus, youths are labelled as belonging to a scheme via street socialisation and, in turn, self-label as gang members as a consequence. When combined with delinquency, these youth groups, which are very visible, may display gang-like features while, in the process, also forming the basis or early foundations from which criminal gangs may emerge (Densley, 2012). Yet, due to youthful age and immature efforts to replicate gang narratives, only certain traits of those older, or former, gang types may be displayed in YSGs, such as delinquency and anti-social behaviour, as opposed to outright criminality.

Applying the term 'gang' to YSGs, along with some of the features they present, sees YSGs essentially labelled as a gang per se. Yet, YSGs nonetheless remain largely incomparable with those more organised, or criminally intent, street gangs engaged in criminal behaviour in the English context. This is because the revisiting of gangs in an English context has focused more upon the next sequential step in gang evolution, where the YSG or peer group begins to organise and carry out criminal business. This is evident in the works of Bullock and Tilley (2003), Densley (2012) and Pitts (2008), to mention a few prominent scholars, as well as in the political establishment, such as with the Centre for Social Justice (2008). All approaches view the gangs as organising as a means for business. Thus, these gangs in the English context are more fitting with those found in North American gang literature. Yet, such gangs are not found in Scotland, not because they do not exist, but rather because research has failed to seek them out, failed to identify them altogether or simply overlooked their existence. However, this is not the fault of the researchers, but rather the consequence of conventional wisdom, as discussed earlier, as well as several other factors that we shall now move on to. One of these factors is the juxtaposed position of Glasgow's own historical gangs and the incompatible features required for a revisiting of gangs in wider UK discourse. When the contemporary revisiting of the gang began, those features emphasised, such as gang labelling, intrinsic criminality, organised crime and increased violence, could not be neatly packaged into a Glasgow context in the YSG.

Self-labelling, or a lack of it?

That YCGs do not label themselves as a territorial gang – but nonetheless are somewhat organised, semi-structured and involved in criminal activity for financial gain (namely, drug supply) – is one of the crucial factors in determining why YCGs have remained hidden from the conventional wisdom of other contemporary researchers who seek the gang in Scotland. By no longer adhering to territorial or scheme labels, YCGs take on a very different form of labelling from that which is expected of preconceived gang labelling in a Glasgow context. While YSGs take on the scheme name, traditional British groups involved in organised crime often take on the family's name because organised crime was historically situated within kinship and ethnic networks, for example, the Kray twins,[3] the Thompson family, the Noone family and so on. Even now, those involved in high-level organised crime in Scotland are referred to by kinship names, that is, the Daniel clan or the Lyons family. However, Densley (2012) suggests that with increased globalisation, contemporary gangs involved in organised crime in the English context are now more inclined to take on names that more accurately reflect gang activities. The move away from naming gangs in reference to specific family ties has diminished as, in a globalised setting, family ties are no longer a relevant requirement for entry into, or continued access to, organised crime, particularly where drug dealing is involved. Likewise, as Bauman (2005) points out, liquid life has meant that traditional lines of kinships are regularly replaced with ones based on friendship or even habit. Thus, situated between YSGs and OCGs, the YCG generally lacks a definitive label as it is no longer based on territorial or a kinship group involved in organised crime.

Consequently, YCGs do not self-label and are not labelled by others in this traditional way; instead, when outsiders make reference to the YCG, they often do so by referring to the gang member they know, or have heard of, personally. For example, if a certain YCG has three members called Boab, Del and Lenny, Mr X may call the group 'Lenny and his boys' if he is most acquainted with Lenny, but Mr P may call the same YCG 'Boab and his mates' if he is most acquainted with Boab. In a similar vein, Mr Z may refer to the YCG as 'Boab's crew'. In addition, YCGs are often an amalgamation of once rival YSGs; thus, scheme-specific labels become obsolete. Therefore, specific gang terminology or labelling is not being applied to the YCG. Also, as YCGs are not strictly seen to be involved in OC (for various reasons, namely, related to age and group purpose), they are also not labelled as such by law enforcement – although, at times, individual members, but not the gang as a whole, may be occasionally targeted as being involved in crime syndicates or networks.

For gang researchers, self-identifying as gang members is often one of the most crucial factors in identifying or defining gangs (Klein et al, 2001). Therefore, when labels are removed and offenders no longer self-label as gang members (in terms of the expected YSG label), this can prove problematic in terms of identifying the gang. This is particularly the case for gangs in a Glasgow context, where there has been a long history of gang identity typically being intertwined with scheme identity, whereby people inherit, and import, the scheme's history into their own identity and thus identify with the scheme when partaking in YSG activity revolving around territorial violence. These processes have helped cement the historical assumption that Glasgow gangs always self-label in accordance with their schemes. This image is also regularly portrayed by: (1) the schemes' population due to intergenerational narratives; (2) the media and social media, particularly when presenting stereotypes; and (3) the political establishment. In addition, McLean (2017) found that YCG members also considered the use of scheme names as immature and detrimental to being taken seriously in the adult criminal world, and thus will often make efforts to distance themselves from such labels.

The ability to accept or reject labels can be powerful. Many multinational companies, as well as agents of law enforcement, have been accused of acting like a gang. Yet, having the political voice and power to reject gang labels means that these labels do not typically stick. Yet, it is important to remember that YSG members often want to be seen and labelled as a gang. While the term 'gang' may be viewed as a negative connotation by those mentioned earlier, for YSG members living in deprived communities, the gang label can often be seen as a source of empowerment, status and reputation. This adds to YSG willingness to be viewed as a gang per se. The researcher essentially proves this platform for these youngsters. For Becker (1963), linguistics retains the power to attach labels, which, in turn, can lead to the formation of preconceived ideas whenever such labels are being reapplied. In this context, the gang label is often applied to that which we already believe to be true or assumed, often to the detriment to alternatives, changes or modifications (see Berger and Luckman, 1966; Stryker, 1967; Levitt and Dubner, 2006). Therefore, in Scotland, where the public, media and political gaze continues to intensify on youths, with their prominent subcultural display and self-defining gang membership, YSGs' willingness to be labelled as a gang,[4] and YCGs' efforts to avoid labelling, play an important part in shaping the researchers' sample group and research methodology.

Glasgow's assumed gang history

Another factor leading to an overly fixative gaze being placed upon the YSG is that of Glasgow's assumed gang history. Given that much of Glasgow's gang history is situated not in empirical data, but rather in (intergenerational) narratives, media sources and local stories, it has proved hard to distinguish fact from fiction (Davies, 2013). However, as Sandberg (2010), and later Presser and Sandberg (2015), note, what is important is not whether these stories are real or not, in the strictest sense, but rather that they carry the power of meaning. This can subsequently result in action. Therefore, what begins as a story can have real-life consequences upon which actors can act. Similarly, through the narrative process, certain traits and aspects of the gang become emphasised. As these traits become emphasised, other traits that also exist in the narrative become diminished.

Over time, Glasgow's long history with gangs has accumulated certain indispensable traits that are now assumed to be inherent to gang formation. This has impacted considerably upon contemporary gang studies. First, if we look at the narratives revolving around the scheme, this has created the perception that Glasgow gangs are territorially fixed (Kintrea et al, 2008). Second, this process of territoriality is interwoven with sectarianism as communities were religiously divided following Irish migration into the city (see Davies, 2008, 2013; Bartie, 2010). Third, gangs are violent and often adhere to knife culture, as opposed to using or carrying firearms (VRU, 2011). Lastly, Glasgow gangs are fighting outfits and have no links to drug supply or distribution (Deuchar, 2009, 2013; VRU, 2011). These points, in particular, continue to emerge within the Glasgow gang discourse. When combined, the assumed traits run contrary to those traits sought within the wider revisiting of the UK gang, with gangs in the English/Welsh context seen as: not territorially fixed in the sense that

Glasgow gangs are bound to schemes; the consequence of globalisation and immigration; carrying firearms; and seeking to control local drug markets (see Pitts, 2008). Yet, being territorially fixed, religiously divided and too violent to compromise, Glasgow gangs are perceived as incapable of engaging in organised efforts of crime (OEC), and along with being younger in age, they are thus assumed to be uniquely different. Yet, these differences arise through the historical narratives that the Glasgow gangs are situated in.

Thus, while complex processes apropos of globalisation are contributing to a review of the extent of UK gang organisation as a means for gang business, Glasgow is overlooked due to historical assumptions. Yet, while these assumptions may be readily accepted and subsequently projected by the political establishment and mass media without question, this is not so in academia. The reason academics have misrecognised the true gang is not that they have not been trying to find the gang, but rather that the gang has found them by fitting with conventional wisdom, self-labelling practices and subjective assumptions as to what constitutes being a gang in Glasgow. The self-labelling of YSGs who adhere to many of the historical assumptions – in that they are territorial and may carry weaponry, particularly knives – leads the researcher to identify the gang in them. Yet, it is not that the academic has not found the gang, but rather that the academic has only identified the highly visible, recreational gang in its early stages of gang evolution prior to organisation and intrinsic criminality. The YSG is only a branch in gang evolution, as opposed to the trunk. If we explore this argument that such traits are assumed, then we need only look at the evidence itself, often hidden within the text of the literature.

Let us begin by dismantling this perception that Glasgow gangs are not involved in, nor have ever been involved in, organised efforts of crime or organised crime. Contrary to contemporary perceptions of YSGs in Scotland, a detailed analysis by Davies (1998, 2013) and, to a lesser extent, Humphries (1981) explored the possibility of early 20th-century Glasgow gangs being able to organise as a means for gang business. They found that while gangs retained a territorial fighting capacity, they nevertheless also engaged in organised crime or made efforts to do so. Such accounts are supported by police reports, such as Sillitoe (1956). Before the rise of globalisation and consequently access to the illegal drugs market, Glasgow gangs would carry out a range of criminal activities for financial gain. These early razor gangs were, in fact, organised. Members often paid dues (a membership fee) and wore military-styled outfits, as in the case of the Billy Boys (see Davies, 2013). Razor gangs likewise engaged in a range of activities that would be labelled organised crime in the contemporary context, and Sillitoe's (1956) account recalls that many a gang member was arrested for being unable to explain large sums of money on them when stopped and searched by police. In part, Davies (2008, 2013) attributes such gang organisation at the time as a consequence of the economic downturn during this period. This resulted in gang members retaining gang membership for greater durations, and it was not uncommon to have members in their 20s and 30s. Thus, those mature developmental properties that both Hagedorn (1988) and Decker and Van Winkle (1996) stress as being essential criteria for the successful engagement in organised crime were present.

Further to this, gangs were also found to generally consist of a core membership of primarily elder members who had built solid reputations as hard men through fighting, and professional criminal personas by acquiring unique skill sets. The core typically consisted of persistent offenders for whom criminality was integral to their identity, and the gang centred on them (see Farrington et al, 2006). In addition, they regularly had both family ties to criminal networks (see Eitle et al, 2004; Sharp et al, 2006) and family members who had affiliations with gang memberships (see Patrick, 1973; Spergel, 1995; Hallsworth and Young, 2004; CIRV, 2008, 2009; Pitts, 2008). Their fearsome reputation – initially gained through territorial violence – afforded them with criminal opportunities and community social status not available to others. This reputation is somewhat similar to Anderson's (1999) code of the street, whereby individuals adhering to an unofficial street code come to value and hold in esteem musculature, criminal ventures and violence. Being able to demonstrate such traits gives individuals a high degree of social status, as well as acceptance into criminal underworlds (Katz, 1988). As a result, core members would regularly exploit their status, along with those readily accessible means or resources, to partake in organised crime (Sutherland, 1939). Such accounts are supported by Percy Sillitoe (1956), Jimmy Boyle (1977) and Jeffrey's (2003) *Glasgow's godfather*, detailing his account of gangster Walter Norval.

Yet, these gangs involved in organised crime and organised efforts of crime, in some cases, were still centred on issues of territorialism. This was particularly true of younger members who had yet to establish fearsome reputations through fighting and fully acquire the much-desired criminal skill sets. However, territorial violence during this period was quite different from that which we see now; often, this insight is lost in contemporary research. High rates of Catholic Irish migrants flocked to industrialising Glasgow and settled in communities that were juxtaposed alongside indigenous Protestant communities. Territorial violence did not simply retain territorial properties, but was rather embedded in immigrant hatred. This hatred expressed itself through religious practice.[5] Territorial gang violence was merely one of a number of areas where religious division was expressed; another most notable sphere was in sports, with the rivalry between the Glasgow Rangers and Glasgow Celtic football clubs. Gang members not only expressed religious hatred in territorialism, but also found that these highly visible confrontations helped express protest masculinities and build social status and reputation. Yet, following tougher and more resilient policing strategies (Sillitoe, 1956), corresponding economic growth, and the post-war situation in which Catholic and Protestant Scotsmen had previously fought side by side against, primarily, Hitler's Nazi Germany, Glasgow's infamous razor gangs would diminish considerably, most notably, among older members (see Humphries, 1981; Davies, 2008, 2013; VRU, 2011).

The lasting legacy of the historical razor gangs lies in the narratives told to younger generations, who would form the YSGs we see today.[6] During the storytelling process, either through older generations, media or fictional books like *No mean city* (Kinsley and McArthur, 1957), certain traits of these older gangs became significantly emphasised. The traits of territoriality, violence and knife carrying are often those traits that are brought to the forefront. Thus, in an effort to replicate the older gangs, and older family members (who were themselves former gang members), that contemporary youths so readily admired and held in awe (Boyle, 1977; McGrath and Boyle, 2011), they came to copy and emphasise particular traits. In this process, such traits are themselves often magnified. This magnification of certain traits is also a consequence of other traditional traits in the older gangs becoming diminished. For example, while YSGs now emphasise the traits of territoriality, violence and knife culture, as a consequence of improved economic conditions, increased social integration, population assimilation, rehousing policies, the amalgamation of the schooling system and a rise in secularism and interfaith marriages, the traits of sectarianism have become considerable diminished, so much so that religion is no longer considered a relevant factor in gang membership in Scotland (Deuchar and Holligan, 2010).[7]

In addition, the trait of being involved in organised crime has also become extinct as a practice among contemporary YSGs. This has occurred for several reasons. First, improvements in security, increased globalisation, money being moved electronically, the rise of the digital age, the local now becoming the 'glocal' and increased technology in surveillance, among other factors, have all contributed to changes in how organised crime now presents itself. As razor gangs controlled local turf, among the youth and adult population, they consequently also controlled the means to commit and monopolise a wide range of criminal activity at the local realm. Yet, this is not possible for YSGs, who now live in a globalised world where local businesses are elevated to the global sphere. Second, given that YSGs are the prerequisite of YCGs, and thus actually just youths undergoing street socialisation, they are therefore developmentally too immature, both psychologically and physically, to challenge the authority of adults, whether other criminals or the police. Likewise, being young also means that they do not have access to those resources needed to carry out organised crime successfully and over a sustained period, such as housing, automobiles, phone contracts and so forth (see Hagedorn, 2008; Densley, 2012). Thus, for the reasons outlined earlier, YSGs overlook sectarianism and involvement in organised crime, and instead overcompensate by emphasising territoriality, violence and knife culture. This means that researchers often assume gang organisation as being an impossibility regarding YSGs.

Globalisation, immigration and research

Historically, the gangs described by Bartie (2010, 2014), Davies (1998, 2008, 2013) and Humphries (1981) were territorial gangs who had the power to control the street and local population through numbers, fear, intimidation and violence (see Anderson, 1999; Jeffery, 2003; Pitts, 2008). Territorial violence expressed religious hatred but also aided gang reputation in the process. Within close-knit communities – and with a lack of sufficient means of travel – any form of potential crime was predominantly situated within the residential locality (see Thompson, 1995; Ferris and McKay, 2001; Jeffery, 2003). For example, post offices, banks and local businesses were all easy targets for robbery and extortion (see Windle, 2013). The gang was used to exploit these local sources of finance. Yet, as briefly mentioned earlier, improved security, better transport, technological advances and, arguably more importantly, the opening of globalised markets and networks (see Beck, 1992, 2007) – illicit or otherwise – saw profitable criminal pursuits change considerably from heist-based activities to market-based activities. Increased access to the drugs market proved significant in altering gang behaviour. Hobbs and Antonopoulos (2013), Pitts (2008) and Densley (2012) are just some of the prominent scholars who suggest that increased drug supply is often tied, even if only theoretically in some cases, to migrant networks. Therefore, contemporary gang organisation is typically affiliated with migrant communities given that migrant networks are assumed as paving the route for the movement of not only people, but also drugs from their source of origin.

Increased globalisation has also directly impacted upon how gangs have come to operate in crime. For example, with the move towards drug-based operations, gangs have been forced to refine themselves into smaller units. Therefore, having a large visible entourage, for fighting purposes, was no longer needed. Core gang members could move away from street fights and instead focus on refining their criminal skills and knowhow in the drugs market. Effectively, criminal gangs had to become smaller, more efficient, less conspicuous and more businesslike. Zhang and Chin (2003) identify a similar process at work in other countries, like China, where large 'Triad' organisations only prove cumbersome in a globalised world where emphasis is placed on speed, movement, the specialisation of skills and particularly close-knit networks. Alonso (2004) also outlines how US gangs responded to this new market and demonstrates how gangs would move away from being primarily fighting-based outfits to business-based ones. Essentially, gangs evolved in response to changes in the socio-economic environment that they found themselves in.

Therefore, my work similarly details how YCGs are essentially a remnant of core members from YSGs who have evolved into being a proper criminal gang, where the emphasis moves away from fixed territoriality and fighting purposes, towards being centred upon economic activities in what Bauman terms 'liquid society'. The YCG is the gang located in the criminal stage of this model. This is the gang that is essentially being sought and studied in the English and North American context, whereas in Scotland, the emphasis has remained upon the highly visible, territorial-based and violent young peer groupings, labelled the YSG in the Scottish context. To succeed in the drugs market, where partnerships operate much like a business, being territorially fixed, highly visible and engaged in random and, at times, public violence would only prove detrimental to those involved. Thus, while YSGs are not involved in drug supply (beyond social supply and occasionally low-level retail dealing), YCGs are. Going from a YSG to a YCG means that several changes must occur within the gang structure. As these changes to formation, age, structure, intent and so on are profound, the gang must be reclassified into two separate gang typologies (McLean, 2017).

As stressed so far, the revisiting of the British gang has not been effectively applied to the Scottish context, and in particular the Glasgow conurbation, largely due to those criteria used by gang researchers when seeking to identify 'the gang', such as self-labelling, assumed gang traits, and local narratives of gang stories. Yet, given that the revisiting of the gang typically calls upon North American literature to spearhead the investigation into gang organisation, criminality and proliferation, it has consequently brought along several pre-existing designations inherent in the North American literature. In the North American context, gangs are essentially seen to be ethnic in their make-up and most active in those estates that have a high influx of migrants. Gangs are overwhelmingly seen to be the product of immigration, and even more so where migrants tend to be visibly different from the indigenous population, that is, through skin colour, dress styles and, to an extent, language. Being immediately recognisable makes it easy to begin the process of creating the 'Monstrous Other' (Katz and Jackson-Jacobs, 1997). Similarly, differences in cultural practices make it appear as though their value system is inherently countercultural to that of the indigenous, mainstream, system (Miller, 1958). Furthermore, when migrants originate from regions associated with Class A drugs like cocaine and heroin, then affiliations are assumed between incoming migrants and incoming drugs (Gootenberg, 2011). While modern-day Glasgow and Edinburgh, like the rest of mainland Britain, have been subject to the processes of globalisation, and consequently immigration, both cities have not seen the same level of intense post-war or recent migration as those major English cities of London, Birmingham and Manchester.[8] Yet, other than studies by Deuchar (2009, 2011), this process is left largely unexplored in Scotland. Arguably, this process has contributed somewhat to the way in which the gang discourse has been applied to the Scottish context. The gang revisiting in an English context has focused upon the processes of globalisation, immigration and the rapid proliferation of cultures, as opposed to actual gangs in many respects; yet, in Scotland, this process has occurred on a smaller scale and has thus not warranted the same attention as perhaps that in London. Ultimately, these combined processes have resulted in the revisiting of the UK gang being largely overlooked in the Scottish context.

Reluctance and difficulties in applying organised crime terminology

In Scotland, gang activity and organised crime are viewed as innately distinct phenomena. While the identification of YCGs has gone by largely unnoticed, YCG formation has undoubtedly been aided by processes of globalisation (see McLean et al, 2018b); thus, they are not necessarily a completely new phenomenon. Coinciding with the distinction between gangs and organised crime following the demise of the razor gangs, behaviour that at one time may have been attributed to YSGs is now wholeheartedly incorporated into the void of organised crime. This has seen the misrecognition of gang typologies, or even individuals involved in organised crime. As gang organisation continues to increase as a method for distributing commodities such as illegal drugs (Bjerregaard,

2010), it has become ever-more difficult to verify where the gang ends and organised crime begins (Varese, 2001). Indeed, this is indicative of wider gang research and not just problematic in Scotland. Along with the difficulty of defining gangs, there is equal difficulty in interpreting what behaviour exactly constitutes organised crime (Symeonidou-Kastanidou, 2007; Savona and Vettori, 2009; Sproat, 2012; Hobbs and Antonopoulos, 2013; Lusthaus, 2013; Hutchings, 2014). Thus, the contemporary view is that YSG behaviour is not organised crime, yet nor is organised crime carried out by YSGs.

Adamoli et al (1998) outline the extent of difficulty faced whenever attempts are made to discuss organised crime as a unified topic. While identifying organised crime as characteristically transnational, national definitions are themselves subject to national preference. With national priorities and social issues driving government responses, the consequential result has often been to cherry-pick from a mixed range of defining criteria, which can result in criminalising tendencies (see Varese, 2010; David, 2012; Carrapico et al, 2014). Varese (2001, 2011) points out that such methods can have a profound impact on the way in which governments interpret and perceive their own gangs, that is, whether gangs are recreational groupings or an evolving species within a broader genus of organised crime. Whereas in England and Wales, considerable links are acknowledged between both, in Scotland, this is not the case. Instead, there remains a strict division between YSGs and organised crime. This division is not only due to historical assumptions concerning Glasgow's gang history, but also because Scotland's judicial branch adopts a 'welfarist' perspective to crimes committed by young people (see Deuchar and Sapouna, 2016). Given the way in which both gangs and organised crime are approached within Scotland and England/Wales, this has resulted in appreciable differences between the gangs of the English (and Welsh) context when compared to the gangs of the Scottish context. Yet, in recognising difficulties arising around national approaches to organised crime, the United Nations Convention against Transnational Organized Crime was created to form a unified base from which the international community can work. This convention was further supplemented by three protocols specifically targeting key detrimental areas of organised crime manifestations, namely, human trafficking, migrant smuggling and the trafficking of firearms (UNODC, 2004). Yet again, at international and national levels, a search for common denominators is further complicated by differences concerning national criminal laws (Sheptycki et al, 2011).

Traditionally, any investigation of organised crime tended to focus on criminal activities at transnational, international and, to a slightly lesser extent, national levels rather than the regional or local levels (Schiray, 2001;

Hignett, 2004; Lavezzi, 2008, 2014; Rowe et al, 2013; Albanese, 2014). However, globalisation has undoubtedly extended international markets and enabled them to penetrate even the most localised environments (Hobbs and Dunningham, 1998). Therefore, alongside the Scottish Government's (2009a, 2009b, 2013, 2015) reports, Stelfox (1998) stresses a real need for the low-level localised investigation of organised crime as events are no longer abstract from larger overarching processes. Sheptycki et al (2011) point out that criminal practices are usually associated with local opportunities and the deregulation of national laws. Much of the crime occurring within national borders primarily affects those citizens within that country (see Pearson and Hobbs, 2001). Yet, in localising organised crime terminology and concepts, we become dangerously close to engaging in the criminalisation of minor offenders. To help address these points, the EU has put forward several criteria to help reach consensus as to what organised crime is. At least four mandatory propositions must be met before the term 'organised crime' can be duly applied:

1. Collaboration of three or more people
2. Engaged in crime for a significant or indefinite period of time
3. Suspected or convicted of committing serious criminal offences
4. With the objective of pursuing profit and/or power. (Cited in Adamoli et al, 1998: 9)

While British law enforcement consensually agrees to the four propositions, little has been done to develop or apply any additional criteria that would help provide a clearer and more specific understanding of organised crime definitions. In addition, EU member states also tend to dismiss the adoption of generic terms like 'Transnational Organised Crime' (TOC), and instead prefer the terminology of 'serious crime' to refer to crime that despite being serious, is nonetheless largely disorganised and often related to specific localised opportunities (Sheptycki et al, 2011). The NCA (2013: 14) highlight this problem and state that 'There is no legal definition of organised crime in England and Wales. For the purposes of this strategy, organised crime is serious crime planned, coordinated and conducted by people working together on a continuing basis. Their motivation is often, but not always, financial gain'.

However, broad unspecified definitions can ultimately have a net-widening effect, drawing in activities previously non-affiliated with organised criminality. Likewise, difficulties concerning the diversity of activities typically go hand in hand with those difficulties in identifying precise group structures (Bakowski, 2013). However, in England and Wales, the NCA (2013) highlights a need to address how organised crime is defined within a contemporary globalised climate due to the changing nature and increased diversity of criminal activities. Furthermore, unlike the Scottish Government's (2015) report, the NCA (2013) report clearly situates the position of urban street gangs within the sphere of organised crime, acknowledging a growing relationship between the gang and organised crime in a modern globalised market and society:

> The differences are primarily about the level of criminality, organisation, planning and control. But there are connections between gangs and organised crime: urban gang members may engage in street drug dealing on behalf of organised criminals and some gangs aspire to, and may become organised crime groups in their own right. Areas of high gang activity in the UK tend to be areas where organised criminals are most active. (NCA, 2013: 9)

However, while this is acknowledged by the NCA, this is not the case in Scotland, despite Glasgow having a historic and prevalent gang culture, as well as retaining a disproportionate level of the country's organised crime (see Scottish Government, 2009a, 2015; VRU, 2011). Furthermore, while the NCA report recognises the potential of gangs to evolve into OCGs, in Scotland, the Scottish Government's (2015: 6) report states that organised crime 'a) involves more than one person, b) is organised, meaning that it involves control, planning and use of specialist resources, c) causes, or has the potential to cause, significant harm, and d) involves benefit to the individuals concerned, particularly financial gain'. However, unlike the NCA report, the Scottish Government's (2015) report does not identify YSGs as having any links to organised crime or any capacity to evolve into an SOCG (in any degree). Rather, YSGs and organised crime remain firmly distinct. While the Scottish Government's criteria for classification as an SOCG allow a greater degree of latitude than the NCA criteria for OCGs, in Scotland, YSGs remain independent and distinct from involvement in organised crime. This can be seen in the recent Community Initiative to Reduce Violence (CIRV, 2009) report, which was specifically targeted at core YSG members and aimed to reduce violence in the city:

> Street gangs in Glasgow are very distinct and separate from those organised crime groups which exist for criminal enterprise purposes. Glasgow's street gangs have no identified

> hierarchy.... The age profile is also considerably lower than in the United States: in Cincinnati the average age of a CIRV client is 32; in Glasgow it is 16. (CIRV, 2009: 7)

While no official unified definition exists in Scotland or Glasgow as to what constitutes a gang, the definition produced by the VRU adopts this workable concept by drawing upon elements developed by the Centre for Social Justice (2009) for identifying gangs, which considers a gang to be a group of three or more people who associate together, or act as an organised body, for criminal or illegal purposes. Yet, the VRU (2011) simultaneously overlooks gang capabilities to engage in organised crime or organised efforts of crime by stating that YSGs are 'distinct from organised crime' (CIRV, 2008: 7). This cherry-picking procedure is flawed in its approach as some gang aspects are adopted while others are neglected, based largely upon pre-existing assumptions. Arguably, Hallsworth and Young's (2004) peer group definition perhaps resonates most accurately with Glasgow's YSGs, which may engage in delinquent behaviour but are nonetheless most definitely recreational outfits. Delinquency is seen to be an end in itself rather than a means to an end.

Marshall et al (2005) argue that, all too often, gangs and organised crime are viewed through distinct and separate lenses of inquiry, which neglects the considerable overlaps existing between both. Situated within a 'welfarist paradigm' (Deuchar and Sapouna, 2016), Scotland's judicial branch has made considerable efforts to avoid the criminalisation of young offenders. Yet, failing to acknowledge gang evolution – as it organises as a means for business – means that, on the one hand, YSG members may not be criminalised as belonging to organised crime networks, but, on the other hand, those who retain the middle ground are subsequently absorbed into the black box of organised crime, even when behaviour may resemble crime that is more organised or organised efforts of crime as opposed to outright organised criminal practices. This net widening, and subsequent labelling, only further embeds criminality into the individual's identity (see Klein, 1971). As of right now, the Scottish gang model is found to be lacking and is in need of being replaced by a gang evolution model.

Therefore, I argue, it is for such reasons that all behaviour that gangs are involved in that meets the mandatory four propositions put forward for organised crime must be considered as organised efforts of crime, with organised crime retaining the additional feature of illegal governance put forward by Von Lampe (2016). This creates a distinction between those OCGs at the higher echelons of criminal markets and those increasing number of, and variation of, gangs that are now plugged into extensive criminal supply chains/networks.

Chapter summary

This chapter has sought to provide a brief review of gang literature in the Scottish context. This was followed up with what could be described as a brief summary of my own research, in which gang typologies situated on an evolving continuum were presented. Thereafter, the chapter proceeded to look at some of those reasons that contemporary Scottish gang literature has essentially stagnated and become overly fixated upon the gang in the recreational stage of development, to the detriment of discovering other existing typologies. A full review of these reasons is beyond the scope of this book, but those key reasons were nonetheless presented. This concludes not only this chapter, but also Part II of the book. The following three chapters in Part III of the book bring to the fore the voices of the participants and discuss, first, gang structure, labelling and membership, before proceeding to look more specifically at the various types of activities in which the identified typologies engage.

Notes

[1] Scottish gang scholars can likewise be separated into Harding's identified categories of Left idealists, Left labelling theorists and Left realists. However, unlike the English/Welsh context in the general sense, Scotland, and Glasgow in particular, has a long and deeply embedded gang history. Thus, most scholars do not debate the existence of gangs per se completely. Even Left idealists somewhat blur Harding's middle category of Left labelling theorists. Atkinson, Bartie and Fraser, in particular, could arguably be categorised as Left idealists. While Bradshaw, McAra, McVie, Miller and Smith could be identified as Left labelling theorists. Deuchar, Holligan and McLean could be considered Left realists. Yet, it should be noted that this is subjective and some authors have moved to and from different categories with different pieces of research.

[2] Although in the wider British context, the term 'hit' refers to the murdering of a targeted individual in exchange for primarily financial rewards, in relation to the current study, the term was applied more broadly and referred to anything from murder, attempted murder, serious disfigurement, abduction and torture, or even a particularly violent assault on a targeted individual in exchange for primarily financial rewards, although drugs were also a common currency here.

[3] On the Kray twins, see Pearson (1995).

[4] YSG willingness to be seen as a gang is also evident in social media, where the gang label can transcend the verbal realm and move into the digital. YSGs regularly access social media sites such as Bebo, Facebook and Mywebspace.com to present local YSG insignia. This process only further embeds the gang label.

[5] Religious practice was an important way in which the indigenous Protestant population could identify the Catholic Irish population. This was even expressed at the informal and formal level in the creation of separate schools and professional football clubs, for example, Celtic and Rangers.

[6] YSGs are also a practice reminiscent of the junior divisions that many razor gangs had established.

7   Only in regenerative scheme names such as Royston Shamrock or Brighton Billy Boys are the historical roots of sectarianism still evident. Yet, YSGs simply retain these names because they are traditional as opposed to actually reflecting the religious practices or beliefs of those members within.

8   However, it is important to note that since 2000, there has been a gradual rise in the number of immigrants moving into Glasgow and Edinburgh. Yet, a large number have also been from Eastern Europe; thus, being similar in appearance and skin colour, and not originating from countries commonly affiliated with the growth of cocaine or heroin production, much of this has been overlooked by gang researchers in Scotland.

PART III

4

Rediscovering Scottish Gangs: Towards a Typology

This chapter explores gang evolution and presents findings from original, and follow-up, data via participant voices. To achieve the chapter's purpose, I explore gang organisation by situating it on a shifting continuum, whereby gangs progress from one stage to the next. Yet, not all gangs will progress – in fact, few do – most tend to fade away over time as youths move through adolescence and into adulthood. When gangs do progress, it is often with the amalgamation of two or more gangs from a prior, less-developed, stage of evolution coming together and organising around gang business. This has significant consequences for how gangs self-label, which is a key factor in the misrecognition of gang evolution. While, in reality, gang progression is continuous, specific key stages of development that gangs tend to move through can nonetheless be identified. Differences may be slight between gangs within their respective stages but, overall, most of the common criteria outlined here can be found in all gangs at their respective stages, which are termed 'Young Street Gangs' (YSGs), 'Young Criminal Gangs' (YCGs) and 'Organised Crime Gangs' (OCGs) in McLean's evolving gang model (see also McLean, 2018a, 2018b).

While Chapters 5 and 6 explore the range of activity that gangs engage in at their respective stages and gang organisation in conjunction with involvement in drug networks, respectively, this chapter will set the basis from which such discussions can emerge. Specifically, this chapter explores how gang organisation occurs, and does so by looking significantly at structure and exploring how individual motives, ambition and activity give rise to group or gang motives, ambition and activity. Much like wider scholarly research, findings suggest that criminals often seek out the company of other criminals. Thus, individual preferences result in emerging group practice. After all, although driven by individual needs and desire, humans are social beings. Therefore, looking at gang typologies, we see how certain internal/external factors combine to create increased gang organisation. Much of the discussion on structure here is intertwined with the resulting labelling properties by which the members or others perceive the gang. While the chapter holds significance for a broad audience, certain sections are aimed more at the academic community in an effort to achieve the secondary purpose of the book: re-engaging Scottish gang literature back into the wider UK gang revisiting.

The chapter is divided into four main sections. The first section is a brief recap highlighting and summarising the evolving gang model that I put forward in Chapter 3. The second section, on YSGs, then proceeds to explore what YSGs are exactly: what they look like, how people acquire membership and how they are structured. The aim here is to help the reader build a picture of YSGs and become acquainted with all the structural aspects of the gang, how it is formed and how boundaries are established. The third section, on YCGs, and the fourth, on OCGs, similarly explore their membership, structure and organisation.

Recap: evolving gang model

Given that the Chapters 5, 6 and 7 are structured around the evolving gang model that I proposed in Chapter 3, it is perhaps helpful to once again touch upon this model in a more summarised manner. This will help guide the reader's understanding and prevent any need to jump between chapters.

I propose the evolving gang model as better capturing the evolving, and interlinking, processes that gangs tend to go through as they move from organised efforts of crime to outright organised crime. Situated in the recreational stage of development, the YSG is a youth group engaged in territorial violence. The gang can be divided into two sub-units: the 'outer layer' and the 'core'. Comprising a small number of persistent offenders who see criminality as integral to their own identity, it is the core body that tends to evolve along the continuum while members of the outer layer generally cease in accordance with the age–crime curve literature. Accessing pre-existing criminal networks (often via family ties) and drawing upon acquired status among local peers (often via YSG fighting), core individuals working with other core members now engage in organised efforts of crime. Criminality becomes part of group intent, behaviour and activity. If a YCG survives and manages to continue to professionalise, and relationships move from being socially based (with economic aspects placed second) to being economically based (with social aspects placed second), and the gang begins to engage

Figure 3: McLean's evolving gang model

RECREATIONAL	CRIMINAL	ENTERPRISE
Occupied by YSG;	*Occupied by* YCG;	*Occupied by* OCG;
Age range: 12–16	*Age range*: 17–25	*Age range*: adulthood
Relationships: social	*Relationships*: social	*Relationships*: economic
Terminology: self-labelling	*Terminology*: non-labelling	*Terminology*: non-labelling
Membership: open, residentially assigned	*Membership*: closed, assigned via friendships	*Membership*: closed, assigned via business arrangements
Group activities: recreational, occasionally delinquent and typically revolve around territoriality	*Group activities*: primarily delinquent and criminal. Wide ranging	*Group activities*: criminal and typically specific

in governance, then it becomes an OCG.[1] As OCGs typically occupy the higher echelons of their respective markets, they retain features akin to illegal forms of governance within their sphere of influence. Thus, OCGs engage in what can be deemed organised crime given that all official criteria for organised crime are met in addition to the added feature of illegal governance.

YSGs

Early socialisation and identity construction

Given that YSGs primarily arise in areas of deprivation (schemes), it is important to open up by exploring the early lives of participants and the roles of primary/secondary socialisation prior to involvement in YSGs. Likewise, as YSG membership generally begins in secondary school (McAra and McVie, 2010), this section draws upon earlier recollections. Furthermore, as noted earlier, YSGs are comprised of two units: the core body and the outer layer.[2] Most YSG members belong to the outer layer, yet the majority of interviewees here were core members due to the thesis research aims. Consequently, criminality was perceived as intrinsic to identity, although most recognised that early socialisation may well have significantly contributed to identity construction/reinforcement. Some participants likewise mentioned the immediate neighbourhood's urban ecology as also impacting upon identity. Such factors, and experiences, are inextricably intertwined and complex:

> *"Where I grew up [was] rough. Because you stay there doesn't mean you … grow up [bad]. Lo[t] [of] good folk from [Glasgow area]. No[t] saying am no[t] good, or people that get [imprisoned] aren't good. Can still be good [even if involved in crime].… I've done bad things [but] don't believe [I] am bad. [I] just [got] involved in pure shit. [I] think when you're always told you're bad, you can act up to it. I [got] in lo[ts] [of] trouble growing up [but I] had a lot of shit going on in my life at that time, at home. Acted up. It's like pure rage. Something would happen [in the house and] when I got out, it just comes out [like a release]."* (Jay, male, offender)

Jay notes that engagement in criminality does not necessarily equate to being immoral, but can occur as a consequence of other factors (Katz, 1988). Jay's recognition that household experiences may have affected his public behaviour was a common theme among participants:

> *"I guess they loved me. My mum … [she] struggled bringing up us four. Me and [brother X] were really bad. [Mum even] lost her hair through stress.… She would slap in at us but [we're] too big for her [laughs] … [dad], never seen him.… My mum's boyfriend, [he is] cool but I didn't meet him till 12, so [didn't build] that bond."* (Gavin, male, offender)

Gavin's childhood experience was unfortunately not uncommon. Most came from female-headed households, which were occasionally reordered from time to time when potential partners or boyfriends came along. This often meant occasionally living with potential siblings for various durations. Like Gavin, many discussed struggling to adapt to cohabitation and reordered family structures, not necessarily due to conflict, but simply due to inconsistency and the fear of building bonds. Roger (2008) suggests that the contemporary British family has become a never-ceasing negotiation based upon agreed cohabitation rather than finalised marriage.

While abuse (to varying degrees), neglect or simply poor parenting strategies from one parent (or both) were also not uncommon, most participants felt that they built decent relationships with potential siblings. Sibling conflict was, perhaps surprisingly, rare:

> *"Mum and dad split when I was a wee dude. [My mum] did remarry.… I was in primary 5.… We moved into [step-dad's]*

*house.... [I got] two older step-brothers. [They hit me a lot] but least
if I get in[to] trouble [outside the household] I can call on them for
protection.... I am close to them still."* (Henderson, male, offender)

For Henderson, the reordered family structure brought some positive
aspects. Having a stable family unit helped him settle and find supportive
relationship in older step-brothers. However, having older brothers
involved in YSGs did influence Henderson's own progression towards
gang involvement. While the street was a place of danger, Henderson had
his brothers to help protect him.

Often, the street is presented as a dangerous social space negotiated
attentively via unwritten codes (Anderson, 1999); yet, for some, it
simultaneously offers a haven from abuse. Several participants recalled
vacating the domestic space whenever feasible to flee abuse. As Tiny
(male, ex-offender and practitioner) points out: "I grew up on the streets.
Basically, my [parent figure] battered me every day. I thought fuck going
home [to be assaulted].... [When you're] out running the streets all the
time, it's easy to get into gangs. [I] look[ed] up to them. The bigger
guys and all that." As Tiny suggests, the streets could, on occasion, prove
to be a place of refuge. Yet, in some cases, the violence suffered in the
household became somewhat normalised. Tiny elaborates that he got
"used to getting hit". Consequently, this normalisation could, at times,
be projected out on the streets: "I was getting smacked about in the
house by [an adult], so fighting boys my age was nothing.... I was always
scrapping ... what happened ... in the home, aye, it did affect me outside.
I would say" (Tiny). Hanging about with 'troublemakers' as a result,
Tiny acknowledges primary socialisation as impacting upon secondary
socialising. According to Tiny, many 'troublemakers' were likewise
'acting out' because of abuse/violence, feelings of unimportance or
marginalisation. Indeed, along with other social characteristics, like ethnic
heterogeneity, deprivation and the lack of community cohesion, such
factors have all been identified as sharing varying degrees of correlation
with heightened rates of delinquency (Farrington et al, 2006).

Although participants generally have positive perceptions about
Glasgow's vibrant city centre, this changes dramatically when discussing
surrounding housing estates (Deuchar, 2009). These 'schemes' conjured
up imagery of dilapidated social housing, 'thugs', 'gangs' and 'drug
dealers/users'. Having, comparatively, one of the highest drug addiction
rates in the Western world, and an illegal drug market thought to be
worth approximately £1.4 billion (Scottish Government, 2009b), it is
evident that Scotland has an acute drugs problem. This is most visible
within schemes and impacts upon subsequent behaviour:

"No one calls cops where I stay.... Police always [labelled] us a gang ... we weren't at 10 [years old] ... [but] you couldn't go about yourself ... too [dangerous]. [Police] don't underst[and] that.... [Drug addicts] always hung about the main street ... if you passed them [yourself], they would defo given you shit." (Shaun, male, offender)

Even William (male, offender), who, at 13 years old, sold valium to addicts, states: "[Drug addicts] might want [to buy valium] off [me]. I wouldn't turn [my] back on them [though].... They would rob you if they got the chance ... that's why [I] always carry a [weapon] or go about wi' [my] boys."

The impact that urban ecology can have upon an individual's identity can be profound, affecting patterns of socialisation and behaviour, and penetrating the individual psyche. Despite negative connotations with their schemes, Miller (2015) found that young males will often internalise these factors, alongside local narratives and stereotypes. Street, or 'scheme', socialisation sees youths incorporate their territorial surroundings into their own internalised identity. This process may well be one of the main reasons why Glasgow has more youth gangs than much larger cities (for example, London).

YSG formation: territory and street socialisation

As mentioned, in the Glasgow conurbation, local narratives of surrounding territory, with which youths most affiliate, can become ingrained into, and part of, individuals' own subconscious identity. In many ways, the exterior environment becomes an internalised feature impacting upon identity construction and subsequent behaviour (see Vigil, 1988a). This is most evident during early to mid-adolescence, during which time identity tends to manifest around delinquent and aggressive behaviour (VRU, 2011):

"People say [scheme X] is a dump. [But at the] end of the day, it's my dump. Got to protect it.... [I] wouldn't get involved in [YSG] fighting nowadays, too old.... [But] I did in [secondary school]. [We] would fight [YSGs] from [surrounding areas]. Boys from [scheme X] have always fought boys from [scheme A]. Just always been like that. Even if you're not in a gang, [you] still can't just go walking about into other schemes. [The local YSG] would batter you for not being from there." (William, male, offender)

William's statement captured the general mood. While perceiving his scheme as a 'dump', William nevertheless felt a strong sense of attachment to it. In many ways, William had internally incorporated scheme identity as his own, as evident in fighting readymade scheme enemies in the form of 'scheme A' for reasons unknown to himself. Boundaries were learned subconsciously from a young age. In many ways, this is perhaps a softer version of institutionalisation within a concrete urban jungle.

Schemes are generally densely populated, small closed-off communities within imagined boundaries (for example, streets, signs, parks and so on). Traditionally, youths will all attend the same primary school (see Anderson, 1999; Kintrea et al, 2008).[3] Thus, early peer relationships tend to be formed with those from within and not outside the locality. Consequently, youths have few friendship groups to choose from or even avoid should they desire to. Therefore, placed in the scheme context, with numerous internal/external threats, youths congregate in large, age-appropriate peer groups for both social and protective purposes. Visibly grouping together in public space results in their being labelled by others as a potential, future, younger segment of or outright YSG. Due to close proximity and often kinship networks, the transition towards secondary school sees youths socialise more with existing, older YSG members. Gradually, these younger peer groups amalgamate with the existing YSG, being most evident during peak times for socialising (that is, at weekends and school). This process is further accentuated by the fact that existing local narratives have already created external enemies for upcoming youngsters, primarily in the form of neighbouring YSGs, recalling William's statement that "Boys from [scheme X] have always fought boys from [scheme A]. Just always been like that." This combination of push and pull factors creates a continual feed for local YSG formation regardless of which members come or go. This process creates a loop system for the local YSG. Yet, the gang can by no means be considered a cohesive unit.

As mentioned, coinciding with the last years of primary school and the first year of high school, a series of loose, independent peer groups with no structure or membership beyond that purely based upon selected friendship (often intertwined with kinship) will steadily become intertwined with one another as boundaries become blurred and socialising extends beyond traditional friendship groups. Usually, among such peer groups, one group particularly is already known as, or associated with being, delinquent. This amalgamation of peer groups in high school brings delinquents from other groups into contact with this main delinquent group. This tends to form the new upcoming core membership of the YSG:

*"Auntie [A] would say 'You [boys] are bad apples' ... 'Why can['t]
you [all] be like the other boys [in your primary school classroom]?'
I was like '[Aunt A] we're just gangsters' [laughs]. Me, [cousin A],
[friends B and C] [always] hung out.... I just liked them. I liked
other boys my age from [scheme A] too mind you. Got on with
everyone [but] most other lads were too quiet [for me]. I liked hanging
about with guys that liked [and did] the same stuff. [Once I] went
to [secondary school], [friend D] started [befriending] us. I knew him
anyways. He stayed [on neighbouring street] in [the scheme] [but]
went to [another] primary [school]. In high school, we started hanging
[out]."* (Steff, male, offender)

Steff states that, at this stage, prior to becoming or joining a YSG, the
foundation is laid for the future core membership in the coming years.
Steff, his four friends and another older member would form the core
of the YSG by the time he entered the fourth year of secondary school.
Ultimately, individual motives to socialise with like-minded individuals
saw Steff and his friends actively seek one another out. With entry into
the first year of high school, the friendship range increased and youths
had greater freedom, socialised more and ventured further. Furthermore,
as puberty begins, physical development increases, and males band ever-
more together when seeking females, who do likewise. Thus, youths now
encounter, and have greater and more significant interaction with, other,
older youths who likewise reside in the scheme, including YSG members.
Ties with the existing YSG are strengthened through kinship networks
and peer socialisation. Steff continues:

*"In first year ... [we] just thought they [existing YSG] were so
fucking cool [laughs]. I know I laugh but they hung about the park
smoking and drinking. Lassies always hung around them ... no cunt
fucked wi' them.... Me and [cousin A's] big cousin [censored name]
was [in the YSG]. So we could like talk and hang out with them ...
my other mates, aye, they were scared [but because of] our big cousin,
we were [fine] ... how we started hanging about actually."*

Steff demonstrates that YSG membership is gained not via initiation
processes, but rather through street socialisation. Steff notes that while
most youths could affiliate loosely with the YSG, deeper membership is
acquired via existing networks that facilitate safety. Yet, as members age,
one generation gradually replaces the last:

"The older ones stopped hanging about, like [members D and E].
Got jobs. Me and my mates already hung around with them before
[from first year in secondary school] ... [but as] the older mob stop
hanging about, it is like my [age-relevant peers] take over. [People]
don't really join the [YSG, the] older [ones] just stop hanging about
[and the] people my age start ... aye, some younger [ones], like wee
[member F] that were sound, acted older ... [and] hung about [as
well]." (Steff, male, offender)

'Hanging around' in public space, and, more importantly, in particular areas of social space already affiliated with the YSG, meant that those youths who socialised in this area tended to be labelled YSG members. Other rival YSGs, the public and the police would perceive youth as a YSG due to the visible space they occupied and associations they kept. This would result in tension, which served to increase cohesion. Tension was not always the result of violent confrontation, but could be subtler. Practitioner Clair recognises the role that official labelling can play in creating gangs: "Crowds of boys aren't criminal. They can be rowdy, but is that to say they are criminal, I think not. Young boys [socialised] in crowds when I was young. They weren't gangs ... [but] we make them a gang [via labelling]."

Tension meant that associating delinquents and non-delinquents were subsequently brought closer together. This could also result in the group adhering to gang labelling via linguistic slogans, graffiti and self-identification. This behaviour becomes further entrenched once youths actively seek confrontation. The behaviour described here effectively outlined the process as to how the YSG is created and continually recreated via intergenerational narratives. Yet, as mentioned, the YSG has varying levels of membership, with some members firmly embedded and others more loosely.

YSG structure and masculinity

A multitude of variables influence YSG formation; however, once peer groups begin (1) adhering to gang labels, (2) socialising with others who do likewise and (3) actively seeking gang confrontation, then they are by all accounts now a YSG. While YSGs have some basic structure (that is, core and outer body), the larger structure is fluid and under constant negotiation. This is primarily due to masculine practice impacting upon emergent structures, positions and so on:

"Hard to tell [how YSG position is determined]. There's always a popular group that everyone else [outer layer and associates] [socialise around] ... if they like someone, then suppose it gives [that individual] some rep[utation]. Boys look up to [others] that [fight well] ... [or] talk the talk, at least.... [But if someone is] good at sports ... [or] funny ... [then] they generally get on well." (Bucket, male, practitioner)

Bucket's statement refers to how young males determine status in relation to one another. Bucket notes how youths typically affiliate, drift or seek socialisation around more dominant groups, which tend to primarily comprise delinquent youths (YSG core). Consequently, status becomes primarily based upon delinquent attributes first, although other attributes such as humour and sporting capabilities also gain status. Peer status is based upon multidimensional aspects of masculinity. Yet, given that the core can offer status by way of recognition, it would seem that, at this age, the ability to fight well, display bravado and use lingo entrenched in 'tough' masculine narratives tends to elevate status best (see also Lawson, 2013). Numerous scholars (see Whitehead, 2002; Hughes, 2004; Deuchar, 2009, 2011; Holligan and Deuchar, 2010; Holligan, 2013) have found 'tough' or 'protest' masculinities to be somewhat culturally acceptable for acquiring status in the Scottish mainstream context. This may perhaps impact upon a reluctant 'acceptance' of gang culture[4] in Glasgow's most marginalised communities, as captured by youth worker Shrug: "[Of] course [young males in Glasgow] get into trouble. What boy doesn't, growing up. Boys fight. That's what they do.... Boys will be boys.... if my [own son] wasn't getting into trouble, I'd probably be worried to tell the truth."

The feeling that boys will inevitability engage with YSGs or violence at some point during their adolescent years does not mean that Shrug is accepting that this behaviour should be significant or become problematic; rather, like most interviewees, he is merely acknowledging cultural practices in the given context as the method used for acquiring status. Sometimes, recognisable marks gained during YSG battles could further demonstrate status and acquire a 'hard man' image. As ex-offender Boab illustrated:

"I got [the scar] from gang fighting. [The rival YSG] all punch[ed] fuck out [of me]. I did alright, [fought] a few off but one of them pulled a blade out and slashed [my cheek]. Just missed my eye... I didn't like it ... but see this scar ... it says who [I] am.... It does define [me].... people see it and [are wary]."

Boab did not like his scar yet noted that it nonetheless attributed him a degree of masculine status. By 'defining' Boab, the scar serves as a warning to others that Boab has proven himself in battle. It is symbolic of his willingness to engage in violence. Weapon carrying was unfortunately a common theme, and a significant proportion stated that they regularly carried weapons. While much media attention has been paid to knife carrying, participants discussed how weapon carrying often depended on circumstance. For example, during random fights, participants typically fought with their fists or lifted nearby objects (that is, bricks and bottles). During YSG fights, participants would pre-equip themselves with weapons ranging from sticks and golf clubs to swords, machetes and even balls and chains.[5] Yet, the latter were primarily brandished for show. However, should participants be involved in ongoing feuds, then they were more inclined to carry knives in case of being attacked unawares.

YSGs proved to be good outlets for acquiring masculine status as they offered opportunity for youths to 'big themselves up' among peers who accept cultural scripts and display bravery in battle. YSG position and status were constantly challenged by other members – verbally and physically. Thus, masculinity had to be continually (re-)proven (Keddie, 2003). This behaviour could result in various consequences, including heightened aggression and gang fractioning:

> "[I] h[u]ng about [with] a lot of boys in school. [It] was a good laugh, but too many thought they [had more status] … [and] get cheeky… [they] would say 'You scared, poof'…. Got me into a lot of fights [because I had] to prove [my]self. We don't all hang about now. [I] say ['Hello'] if I see them but couldn't hang about with them. [They are] alright in small doses." (Mitch, male, offender)

Inner group conflict could result in groups fracturing. In most cases, this fracturing meant that, on most occasions, members of the YSG will socialise in smaller groups and only on particular occasions will these segments re-merge. Sometimes, though, conflict could result in a complete breakdown of relationships, and subsequently one YSG could become two. Thus, although YSGs typically identify themselves with the scheme name, divisions, splits or even the formation of other groups of youths within the same area could see single schemes produce more than one YSG based upon territorial issues. Differences are recognisable in the terminology applied after the scheme name.[6] Gee (male, offender) explains:

> "The [housing estate] I grew up in didn't have one [YSG, but two]. We used to fight but then all started [socialising] till one guy from

[YSG A] got jumped by [YSG B]. After that, we all started fighting again.... was good no' having to worry about getting jumped in your own [scheme] ... while it lasted. Too many dodgy [dangerously unpredictable] cunts pure thinking they're [hard men] and starting [conflict]."

Contrary to the existing literature (for example, Fraser, 2015), YSGs could also occasionally merge with other YSGs, even if physically far apart. Within large official[7] estates, like Pollok,[8] streets and corridors were broken up and divided into a multitude of smaller, often unofficial[9] schemes. Yet, at times, smaller schemes could also accommodate more than one YSG. YSG structure can only accommodate a certain number of youths before becoming unmanageable, primarily via factors like intergroup conflict, as well as other numerous factors like lack of organisation, non-hierarchical properties, being developmentally too young and hyper-masculinity. Only on particularly organised occasions could numbers be significantly added to and retain feasible workability. Most YSG members would spend time socialising recreationally in those smaller groupings that they enjoyed best. Again, this often depended on their preferred activity:

"I like a wee toke [smoking cannabis] way my [closest] pals. We usually hang in mines, and get a smoke." (Del, male, offender)

"Mostly I [socialised] wi' my best pal. Only really seen the other lads if I got a [social media message] or [phone] call about a fight happening.... [Or if] I seen them at the [nightclub] ... I fought for my [YSG], so did a few [other friends], but I also [had friends] that [didn't fight]. No all my mates are [YSG] members." (Henderson, male, offender)

Del and Henderson explain how YSGs are anything but solid cohesive entities. Most of the time is spent socialising in smaller groupings and in activities that are more recreational than criminal. Likewise, gang members also befriend non-gang members, who may be labelled gang members given their associations. Consequently, a single YSG could be perceived as being in several places at once given members' tendency to disperse in smaller groups. While larger formations occur, in general, participants dismissed notions of YSGs numbering 50 members or so regularly grouping together and hanging out on street corners. YSG materialisation is relevant to occasion. Boab attributes this to practicality:

> *"[The YSG] could muster a squad of about 40–45 bodies depending [on] who [we] were fighting. If it was [another] local [YSG], then usually 20, but more if say a [YSG] had been arranging to come through from [a considerable distance] … [I socialised] usually [with seven others] … it's unreasonable to play football way 40 boys … [or] get them all in your mum's house to play the PlayStation at once."*

Like Davies' (1998) study of Glasgow's infamous urban razor gang, YSGs also typically consist of a core body of between two and seven[10] individuals who define their identity primarily via delinquency/crime, and a numerous loose association or outer layer of individuals for whom attachment to the core is primarily motivated through friendship, socialising, status, proximity and even, on occasions, 'fighting for fun' (Matza, 1964).

YCGs

Increasing gang organisation

As YSGs materialise out of street socialisation and territoriality, they have little structure beyond the core and outer layer. Yet, the same conditions that laid the foundation for YSG formation persist, and with the introduction of greater degrees of external/internal drivers, such division between the core and outer layer intensifies. Effectively, while the outer layer generally desist from crime altogether,[11] due to factors such as being of legal age to enter employment and attend adult social events (for example, pubs), developmental maturity, and raising families, those belonging to the core generally become ever-more entrenched in criminal activities due to the same factors, and thus undergo greater gang cohesion and pursue criminal careers.[12] Former police officer Iain explains:

> *"Large proportion of crime [committed] in the [community] is [due] to a handful of guys … happens with every generation … every young boy gets in trouble at some stage. Most are what I think of as good boys. They are more likely to get in trouble [when they associate] with the small proportion of bad ones [in the neighbourhood] … [from] bad families well known in [the neighbourhood]."*

Practitioner Clair further expands Iain's point, drawing reference to offender backgrounds in the process:

"Those who go on to become what we would deem or ... label career criminals usually have shown criminal intent, or behaviour, throughout their lives at various points. They often come from unstable backgrounds.... I have found domestic abuse and erratic lifestyles to be very common, unfortunately.... These kids grow up in this. Once adults [referring to mid- to late adolescent years], [society] expects them to suddenly become mature, but I'm sorry, that isn't going to happen. They have access to criminal networks, criminal friends and family.... what else do we truly expect when they and their friends become involved in criminal gangs."

Iain demonstrates how core members are generally responsible for the majority of crime, labelling them as innately 'bad boys' from well-known 'bad families'. Yet, Clair elaborates and points out that cause and effect may well be much deeper as certain youth are overexposed to 'risk factors' linked to offending and gang membership. Factors like growing up in 'unstable' households, having 'criminal friends and family' and pre-existing access to 'criminal networks' have been found to influence, but by no means determine, offending trajectories (Thornberry et al, 2003). While those conditions impacting upon gang organisation vary, several conditions in particular are pivotal to YCG formation: external threats; developmental maturity; pre-existing access to criminal networks; and ongoing commitments.

External threats

According to Densley (2012), gang organisation refers to a group's ability to organise in response to external threatening conditions that often impact upon group solidarity and cohesion. Consequently, this solidarity may serve to increase criminality in previously delinquent groupings (see Quinn, 2001). We have previously established how YSGs are formed through external tension around issues of territoriality, rival YSGs and the police. Yet, YSGs are very much recreational in purpose and intent. However, as core members mature and enter their mid- to late adolescent years, they form greater levels of solidarity while simultaneously increasing their disassociation with members of the outer layer. Given that YSG core members typically consider delinquency as intrinsic to their own personal characteristics, this process of increasingly looking inwards while severing, or weakening, ties with members of the outer layer results in greater levels of disproportionate association with like-minded individuals adhering to criminal identity and behaviour. Consequently, delinquent practices and delinquent identity become increasingly more recognised among members as acceptable (Thornberry et al, 2003):

> *"People [socialise] with their own. I wouldn't hang about with police, dafties working in social work. That lot … like teachers. I hang about with [people like me]…. [especially] when older. I just said to everyone that meant nothing to get to fuck. Hung about wi' them in school, but hardly spoke outside, so they can fuck off … [whenever] I get a friend request on Facebook, am like 'See ya', delete them. They only want to nosey in."* (Pete, male, offender)

As Pete aged, he socialised less with those who were not like him. Essentially, he saw their identity and practice as inherently different from his own. As he aged, he had more control over who he socialised with and thus strengthened bonds with those closest, while loosening them with others. Former offender Colin further elaborates:

> *"Get older and drift away from people [outer layer and associates] you used to [socialise] with, don't you! Different people, [I] suppose. Most my old [friends] got jobs after school…. [I] still hung around with my best mate [name censored]. We are kind of the same … like the same things…. [And regularly offended] together [laughs]."*

Having been core YSG members, Colin and his friend gradually relegated friendships with those of the outer layer and associates to a secondary position. This was because most entered employment while Colin and his friend did not, instead moving from delinquent identities to criminal identities as they began engaging in organised efforts of crime. In this smaller group, it was much easier to transmit individual identity to group identity, thus influencing practice much more than had previously been possible. Colin continues: "[We began] working together [in organised efforts of crime]…. My other mates, probably, wouldn't have been up for it, no…. [We eventually] got [imprisoned] together. [I know I] can pure trust him now." As most YSG members ceased offending, this left Colin and his friend looking inwards to one another in determining acceptable behaviour. As both viewed delinquency as innate, it became easier to gravitate from part-time delinquent behaviour to full-time criminal behaviour. Incarceration only served to increase their bond. Ultimately, external tension increased cohesion, which was based upon shared criminal identities, which is a process further aided by natural maturity as well as perceived external threats: "I only hang about way him [Colin's friend]. Got pure closer. You go through things and [it bonds] youse. That make sense? Police were looking for us … [so] was [rival gang] … [so my friend] ended up [moving in] wi' me. Basically" (Colin)

Colin illustrates that the presence of external threats (prior to imprisonment) brought a close friendship closer as members bound together for protection, perhaps also by a sense of only being able to trust one another. In addition, the ability to respond to external threats largely depends on available resources, which is itself tied to age. Being slightly older, Colin now had access to his own economic capital and living accommodation, whereas in YSG formation, where members are typically younger and reside within the parental household, Colin would have previously been unable to invite his friend to live with him. Having access to such resources is something that YSGs lack; thus, they cannot completely break with parental authorities (Hazani, 1986) as they rely on parental income. Decker and Van Winkle (1996) similarly argue that most gang members are simply too young to successfully engage in organised efforts of crime.

Developmental maturity

Age brings with it numerous variables that aid the potential for greater criminal engagement, including physical/psychological maturity, access to previously unavailable resources, employment, a driving licence, access to adult social arenas and access to social housing and welfare. Only with age and maturity are gang members able to gain access to the necessary resources for both independence and greater criminal participation. With age, YSG core members will generally move from primarily delinquent behaviour to criminal behaviour. This is because of differential association (Sutherland, 1939) among themselves, and even core members from other YSGs. This latter fact is only possible because, as youths move towards early adulthood, territory no longer holds the same degree of sway over identity construction. This is because individuals may acquire a driving licence, gain employment in other areas, relocate if offered – or they purchase – housing and socialise with others from further afield in natural settings such as pubs and clubs, all decreasing territorial significance. Allan states: "Fuck, my missis stays [in rival scheme], so if I move in with her, I would be living there. Doesn't make sense."

Territorial rivalry is the central component in YSG formation (Deuchar, 2009; Fraser, 2013; McLean et al, 2018); thus, as territorial significance declines, YSG membership unofficially ends. This does not mean that rivalry between members ceases completely – some vendettas remain lifelong (Deuchar, 2009, 2013; Holligan and Deuchar, 2015). At this stage, though, core members gradually begin to form YCGs unconsciously, largely due to the factors outlined earlier. While YSG membership ceases, individuals still associate with one another, continue to socialise in intimate gatherings and allow their own individual motivations to steer, reinforce and intensify consequential group behaviour, which, while socially rooted, is recognised as being beneficial for individual gain: "Gangs are simply individuals who [socialise with] other individuals [and work together] for their own benefit. Yes, [they] have loyalties, whatever ... [view themselves] as mates ... [but they organise] for their own benefit, [even if they] don't know it themselves" (Iain, male, practitioner)

Iain argues that gangs comprise of individuals who may socialise primarily for social purposes but, as a consequence of doing so, also organise – often sub- or semi-consciously – to better support their own personal circumstances. Working together has both social and economic advantages. Hagedorn (1994) likewise suggest that, more often than not, for youths who consider their own identity as intrinsically criminal and actively engage in profitable crime, such group behaviour is self-motivated and motivated independently of other group processes; yet, due to immaturity and inexperience, such ventures typically result in initial, and varying degrees of, failure. Former drug dealer, Brain, who attempted to engage in such criminality during YSG membership, only now recognises his flaws as a young adult:

> "[We] use[d to] hang about in big numbers.... [Getting into] fights.... [When I got] older, the group g[ot smaller].... think you're like the big man when you're wee [young] but you aren't. [You're] just a daft wee boy. I didn't start dealing proper till I was older [18]. I tried when I was 14 ... [but] was pure young [and] too stupid to do it. [I'd] tak[e] swedgers [ecstasy tablets] and falling about the streets. Giving them away to mates, [who] giv[e] [me] fuck all [in return]. Think [I] los[t] more than [I made]."

Brain recognised that with age comes greater refined mental capabilities, the ability to differentiate between social and economic relations, and engagement in organised efforts of crime. Previously being unable to distinguish between such relationships, and lacking the necessary self-control and experience to successfully sell illegal commodities, Grant similarly suggests that early to mid-adolescence is an inherently flawed age for operating in the criminal underworld:

> "[I was] doing no bad [selling drugs]. [Older drug dealers] came to my door one Saturday, about 1 [pm], before I headed out to the [Ran]gers game ... my mum invited him in[to the house]....

[Basically,] he let me know to [stop selling drugs], or there would be consequences. I was 15. What the fuck could I do … he could push me about [be]cause I was [young] … [now, at age 25], he works for me … funny how it works out."

Unlike Brain, Grant was relatively advanced, psychologically speaking, at 15. Yet, despite having the mental capabilities to engage relatively successfully in organised efforts of crime, he was nonetheless susceptible, and physically ill-equipped to deal with the full range of circumstances and hurdles that individuals must overcome when engaging in such occupations. However, as Grant developed physically, he was able to hold his own against other criminals. Grant was further supported because he could draw upon his own YCG, stating "if he came after me then he would have to come after all of us". There is strength in numbers in the criminal underworld. However, other factors similarly impact upon gang organisation.

Pre-existing access to criminal networks

A key finding from the research was that core members tended to come from households, or extended familial networks, with pre-existing ties to well-established criminal networks. Such access, which consequently went hand-in-hand with differential association, meant that individuals were more exposed to both criminal activity and opportunity. Having delinquent/criminal kinship, particularly within the immediate family unit (for example, dads), has been identified as strongly correlated with intergenerational criminality (Fader, 2016; Farrington et al, 2006, Thornberry et al, 2003). However, this study found that while parental engagement within criminality, generally speaking, was a good indicator for child engagement in general criminality, it was not enough to determine child entry into established criminal networks or engagement in organised crime. Rather, it was those who had greater access to such networks[13] who were more likely to partake in established/organised criminal networks. This was largely due to trust and common interest. As offender Geoff and practitioner Gregory explain:

"[Be]cause your da' was a bit of a hooligan in his heyday, doesn't mean that you are going to be like kingpin big baw's fuck sake. Maybe if he was like Tony fucking Soprano or that, aye you've more chance … [but even then,] no[t] if you're a fucking idiot." (Geoff)

"I would think [in those large criminal] syndicates, [they] already have other family working in them. That is how they gain entry.

They need to trust one another, don't they. Blood is thicker than water." (Gregory)

Geoff and Gregory indicate that while having kin who are criminally active may well heighten an individual's likelihood of engaging in general criminality, it is often the degree and type of criminality in question that is more significant for gaining access to established criminal networks. Kinship proved a key variable, yet this access was also extended to those closest friendships that such 'privileged' individuals held with certain peers. Jay, who initially gained a steady supply of drugs from his uncle, explains:

> "I had been selling [drugs] since I was a boy ... it was normal. [I] sold [cannabis].... My uncle [grew it].... I would get [supplies] from him. I did some [legitimate] work ... [but] wasn't for me like. Selling [cannabis] was easier. Was a career choice. I had a house at [17] so I could [eventually] grow my own ... [and] turned the spare bedroom into a [cannabis factory].... It's [risky] selling drugs. [I was] opening [my]self up for [being robbed]. You do need backup in this game. [I desired a] low [profile], but can't really, especially if business is booming. People aren't daft, they know you're selling and probably have a stash in the house ... [so] I phoned up my best mate, and said you want in on this? We had always [socialised], and he's [trustworthy].... So, I knew he'd be well up for a wee earner ... [and] can well handle himself. Had a bit of a reputation [from prior YSG involvement].... [Uncle] was cool with it."

Jay's uncle initially supplied him with drugs to sell and introduced him to various customers and suppliers. Thereafter, Jay was able to set up his own operation, but as business started 'booming' and after gaining 'the okay' from his uncle, he brought in his closest friend from his days in the local YSG. Mary, who herself heads an OCG, explains her recruitment processes:

> "[Family member X] got [me] into this line of work.... [Growing up,] I look[ed] after [my younger brothers]. Fell on me to [raise] them [because our] mum [didn't keep well].... I [did] everything for them. They respect me for it ... everything I do is for the good of the family. They know that.... So they do as they are told. My brother's [closest male friends do] some work for [me] but I can see they aren't happy when [I] ask them 'Do this' [because I'm] a woman. [But] they do what I ask because they know it is going to benefit them."

Both Jay and Mary indicate that trust is a key variable in accessing existing criminal networks, something that family ties help facilitate. After establishing their own operations, both brought in trusted individuals (see also Windle and Briggs, 2015; Von Lampe, 2016). While many individuals who are not core members may well still engage in crime-for-profit activities, like selling drugs, there is a glass ceiling when attempting to access higher echelons of criminal networks or move into existing markets. Mary captures this point: despite having her brothers and their closest friends working for her, she "only trust[s] those closest" who share 'blood' or considerable history in criminal ventures. It is for such reasons that she, and other participants, tend to utilise a glass ceiling for those who do not have access to pre-existing criminal networks. However, global changes, increasing technological advances, the dark net and so on have all contributed to considerably easing initial entry into illegal markets (something that we shall explore in Chapter 5).

Ongoing commitments

While age provides increased opportunity for criminal engagement, it also brings a greater sense of responsibility. Crime could be seen as a potential 'profession' or mechanism for supporting ongoing commitments. Crime was often driven by a complex mixture of innate features, external threats and a degree of rationality, more so when circumstances meant limited choice. At a young age, Wolfe sought local status through YSG violence; however, this led to him acquiring a criminal record. Since, he has struggled to gain legitimate employment. Wolfe is still subject, though, to those contemporary pressures of living within a consumer society where identity is increasingly defined by consumption (Bauman, 2005). Wolfe details how this process contributed to him forever rendering himself a criminal. Consequently, Wolfe used close gang connections to participate in gang business: "I didn't have an education and couldn't get a job. My [criminal] record was bad. I had no choice but to sell [illegal commodities]. [I] only want what everyone else [has]! Be comfortable and provide [for my] kids."

Wolfe's behaviour as a youth limited his options as he became a late adolescent, now with children of his own. Wolfe desired to engage in mainstream legitimate society; however, given prior YSG involvement, he, like most participants, acquired a criminal record. This record of his behaviour in his early years hindered his opportunities to gain worthwhile legitimate work in later life. After a series of failed job interviews and feeling the pressure to conform to wider social norms (that is, earning money, buying goods), Wolfe felt that he had 'no choice' but to engage in criminal coping strategies (Agnew, 2013) and utilised criminal identity, and connections, to do so. Drawing upon close relationships with like-minded individuals, who typically found themselves in similar situations, he engaged in gang organisation and business as a means of income, status and social participation.

Mary likewise points out how financial and family commitment influenced her own decision to engage in criminality in order to relieve the stress caused by wider socio-economic and political changes: "after changes in benefits [referring to recent welfare cuts], we literally were finding it hard to put a roof over our head…. [Family member A] helped us out." This need to provide was particularly evident among those participants who were themselves parents. This factor was something that was itself regularly recognised and exploited by others. Kim was initially brought into criminal networks through a long-term relationship with a partner, but after separating, and following the birth of their child, another member of a YCG capitalised on her vulnerable position to further their own business interest:

> "I didn't know [Steve] was selling [heroin] … [when] I found out, he stopped hiding it from me and just [brought drugs] into the house [openly] … [after] we split … [I] had bills and [a child], so … [Steve's supplier visited] me and said if I [wanted], would [I continue] to hold [drugs] … paid me £100 every week at first [but] also [bought expensive goods]…. Just [progressed] from there."

The growing sense of commitment and responsibility to others, the need to gain finances, and the desire to engage in society all impacted significantly upon the participants in the study. While participants generally viewed themselves as being intrinsically criminal, many were also risk takers and struggled to delay gratification. Subsequent actions had impacted upon their development and behaviour as youths, and had consequences (such as criminal records) that would be brought forward as they moved into young adulthood (16+). Coupled with other outlined factors, and having pre-existing access to established criminal networks (therefore being 'hooked up' with not only illegal goods, but protection, clientele and the removal of glass ceilings), ongoing commitments also contributed to individuals utilising criminal identities, networks and gang ties to engage in organised efforts of crime as a reputable means of income.

YCG labelling

While those factors outlined earlier impact upon gang organisation, as primarily YSG core members progress towards YCG formation, several distinct features begin to emerge that distinguish typologies. Wider literature (for example, Bradshaw, 2005; Deuchar, 2009; VRU, 2011) supports the notion of YSGs being self-labelling, early to mid-adolescent peer groups for whom delinquency, as opposed to criminality, is a potential outcome. Thus, key developmental differences between YSGs and YCGs are that: there is a decrease in territorial division; gangs become smaller; although gang membership remains based upon social relationships, gang activity becomes more centred upon criminogenic properties; gangs now engage in organised efforts of crime; and, most importantly, gangs no longer adhere to traditional, self-nominated gang labelling. Thus, no longer adhering to existing gang labels (that is, Young Goucho or Young Govan Team), or engaging in territorial-based violence, but instead crossing pervious scheme boundaries to engage in organised efforts of crime, means that a YSG has, at this stage, evolved into a YCG.

Gang labelling is a key distinguishing feature of YSGs as it demonstrates recreational behaviour, territoriality and identity bound to geographical residency. Thus, given that labelling undergoes a dramatic change, it is important to explore this process in detail. In the West of Scotland, gang labelling is steeped in history and has come to largely refer to delinquent youths in YSGs, particularly with the rise in (social) media. To break with such perceptions of being developmentally immature, gang members no longer adhere to these labels. This was a feature that recurred again and again in interviews for those who had moved from YSGs to YCGs:

> "No chance mate am I jumping around nowadays shouting [scheme] young team. Make me look like a daft boy, [you] know."
> (Henderson, male, offender)

> "Calling myself [and my] mates, young [scheme name] Fleeto, is immature man. People would just think we were fucking idiots."
> (Geoff, male, offender)

The quotes resonate with wider literature that labelling oneself a gang member and tying that label to territory is culturally perceived as something that 'boys', 'young teenagers' and 'kids' do (references to early to mid-adolescence), 'not men'. Having a long history tied to such labelling properties means that any gang formation outside YSG formation goes unlabelled in contemporary Scotland. Thus, hindering YCG prospects for being taken seriously and seem as 'real criminals' among criminal peers, such labelling is discarded. Unfortunately, in wider Scottish literature, this is where the trail ends regarding contemporary gang research. Yet, gang formation very much exists beyond YSGs – a fact referenced by numerous (auto)biographical accounts (see Boyle, 1977), media reports and practitioner services. Practitioner Bucket explains:

> *"The boys that deal [drugs] in groups don't label themselves by gang names or nothing. They don't call themselves like The Panthers or The Cobras [laughs]. It's not like that.... [They] refer to their [YCGs] or to other [YCGs] by the main guy's name. Or sometimes by the name of a guy they know in the gang.... [For example, they] might say something like '[I] get our [drugs] off of Boab', or '[Phone] Steg's team'."*

Likewise (ex-)police officer Iain continues: "Yeah, [there are] definitely adult gangs in Glasgow. Probably more than most places. We just don't call them gangs. Probably because when we say 'gangs', we automatically think of young hoodlums in [schemes]."

Bucket and Iain point out that how we label gangs is vitally important in their creation. That is not to say that gangs do not exist prior to labelling, but rather that how we label them affects how we perceive them, effectively rendering everything outside as something else, or to be looked over, even if differences are few and far between. To "get [drugs] off of Boab" or "Steg's team" is the most commonly used method for group identification at this stage. The term 'Boab' is not singular, but rather plural, despite only one individual's name being used. Windle (2013) similarly highlights that the terminology used to describe the Essex-based gang known as 'Tuckers' or 'Tuckers Firm' referred to a variety of those close-knit associates who sold drugs with the individual named Tucker. This use of language can give the illusion that one individual is responsible for a wide range of activities. Rather, all group activities are described under the umbrella term of a single individual's name. Sometimes, this name may have an 's' applied to it, for example, when referring to criminal activities committed by the Daniel family in Glasgow. The term 'Daniels' is used to refer to a wide range of criminal activities carried out by the immediate Daniel family, as well as looser associates and criminal partners. Gavin illustrates:

> *"This one guy tried slashing me. I grabbed the knife off him.... because he got done in [assaulted] off a boy I done business with a few times ... people started saying he was one of [Rav's] boys. I done fuck all. The guy that got done in didn't see it like that but [he] obviously thought I was something to do with it.... if people use your name [to refer to] a group of [us], it's you that ends up taking the derry [blame]."*

This lack of self-labelling can contribute to the misrecognition of individuals as members of organised crime, or even as single offenders, as Geoff suggests:

> "I done a drop for a guy I know. Well, don't know him that well mate, but he is pure well known through Glasgow's [criminal underworld]. Ended up getting [arrested] didn't I [during a roadside stop]. The police, [media], all that fucking lot, all got pinned on me. [Served several] years [in prison]. People think [I] am into all sorts of shit and wasn't like that at all."

That YCGs are primarily formed for the purpose of social relations, rather than for economic factors, contributes to the lack of self-labelling practices, which can have both positive and negative implications for those individuals involved. Practitioner Clair explains:

> "We tend to find they aren't a [YSG any longer]. Not in the way people tend to perceive gangs [in Glasgow]. They are more group[s] of delinquents ... [who band] together through friendship. You put these guys together in groups with the same mentality then ... they are going to commit crime. They commit crime outwith the group so what's so different when they band together! If anything, it allows more criminal opportunity.... crime is a social activity."

As discussed, as core members enter mid- to late adolescence, they generally become more tight-knit, cohesive units utilising greater access to a wider range of previously inaccessible resources. Being intrinsically criminal and socialising together results in a shift from mainly delinquent activity to criminal activities. Yet, crime is rooted in social relationships, and membership is not sought out for economic benefit. However, as YCGs mature in experience, some will become OCGs in their own right, though due to the glass ceiling effect and illegal governance issues, on most occasions, the most successful members are absorbed into existing OCGs, as we shall now explore.

OCGs

YCGs to OCGs

The transition from YCG to OCG is by no means a given. In fact, while few YSGs go on to become YCGs, even fewer YCGs go on to become

OCGs. Rather, the YCG stage of development occurs over a considerable duration. This is because YCG progression depends on YCGs learning their criminal trade, expertise and areas of specialism. This occurs through reputation and trust, which takes time to build, and experience, often through trial and error – some of which may involve mechanisms that lead to YCG dismantlement (that is, prison or being killed). A point that we have not touched upon specifically, but rather alluded to, is that these gangs are typically (and in all cases among the sample) involved in drug supply and/or other criminal activities tied to such activity (that is, money laundering, debt collection, firearm crimes and so on). These shall be explored in greater detail in coming chapters. Consequently, only the most successful YCGs are around long enough to reach the higher echelons of the criminal underworld to become, or more typically to be absorbed by, an OCG. When absorption occurs, it is often in relation to certain (not all) YCG members.

A key difference between YCGs and OCGs is that in YCGs, group relations are based upon social attributes first, and economic attributes second. In OCGs, the opposite is true. However, this does not mean that social attributes play no role whatsoever in group relations, but rather means that those relations that had been maintained that were purely social and proved to be particularly negative with regard to economic prosperity are no longer maintained for the sake of it.[14] Again, the degree to which economic relations are put before social relations varies group to group. Keddie (2003) points to how individuals who share similar interests are more inclined to group together. The same principle is applied in YCGs, whereby friendships are initially rooted in YSGs and continue thereafter to form YCGs. Where two or more YSGs come together when forming a YCG, this is because members bond with others due to liking the same things and sharing similar histories. As YCG members Allan, Boab and James explain:

Allan:	"I only knew Paul and Mark through Del, I didn't know [them] from like school or nothing.... Paul had actually slashed [YSG B associate] when we fought wi' their [YSG A] up the park, remember?"
James:	"Aye ... wasn't really a slashing, fuck sake."
Allan:	"I always thought you [two] were sound."
Boab:	"We were at a house party and Del came in [to the house] wi' [Paul and Mark]. [We] just clicked, didn't we?"
Allan:	"Every cunt was just closure [likable] mate."

The previous statement demonstrates that social attributes are what brought the two gangs closer in finally forming one YCG. Likewise, the main purpose of maintaining friendship, and gang membership, is the commonly held criminogenic ideology. Boab emphasises:

> "I wouldn't [personally label us] a gang. We didn't call ourselves a gang. Others [outside the group] might [do]. If hanging out, and [engaging in crime] at the same time, to make a living, makes you a gang, suppose we might be. Depends [on terminology]. [I have] known the two [members] since I was in nursery so would just say we were mates, who happened to do [criminal business] together."

Although making profit via illegal means is a central feature of YCG behaviour, it is nonetheless undoubtedly a secondary motivator behind that of socialising with like-minded individuals. This socialising can then be organised for effective gain of economic capital. Individually, the participants would most likely have engaged in criminal ventures, and often did prior to recognising the benefits of working together, but the coming together of individual criminal identities leads to YCG formation, and the existence of these social relationships steadily results in increasing and ever-progressive levels of criminal activity. As William explains: "[we] were a group. Course people had their roles, what have you, but [we didn't] say we [were] the [gang name] boys. We didn't hang out because we earned together. We earned together because we hung out."

Criminality is an intrinsic feature of YCGs and it is engagement in crime that binds them, bringing social and economic rewards in the process. Rooting gang relations in social as opposed to economic attributes meant that while boundaries existed, there remained an unclear division of labour (ever changing due to circumstance) and leadership:

> "[The YCG was] sophisticated in the way we [operated]. Everybody had their own tasks to do. Even had a guy that overseen the whole thing to stop bickering and shit among us, especially since, end of the day, we were all pals. No one [was] really in charge. It changes [depending on the situation]. I think [I] am in charge [laughs] but [others think likewise]." (William, male, offender)

Yet, here we see the evolving attributes of YCGs as they gradually move towards a professionalisation of crime. Roles and responsibilities become allocated, leadership begins to be formed and relationships begin to move from being socially rooted to economically based, whereby those who were considered 'bad news' or 'dead weight' had to be separated with, even if they were still likable individuals. Only by doing so could a YCG, or certain members, transit into OCG formation:

> "I basically kept myself to myself and [distanced] from [former YCG associates]. They were too wild and were always going to end up dead. I missed hanging out wi' them, still do, but they were bad news. [They] never grew up.... I [eventually forged an alliance] with a guy [we] had done some business with [previously]. He done alright and [propositioned me to] help him out.... [But] only if I ditched my mates." (Harold, male, offender)

This shift towards committing crime, rooted in economic gain, with business partners as opposed to only friends signifies a significant development in gang structure. OCG members may exist in networks of trust, but it also depends on what members can offer and bring to the table: "I only worked alongside one guy. No more than that. He arranged transport[ation] of goods into the country. I picked up at the other end. He had his connections over there [in exporting country], I had mine here" (Sean, male, offender).

Sean understood that at the higher echelons of organised crime, group dynamics were akin to a tight-knit business partnership rather than a loose-knit friendship. Business partners may well spend some time socialising, but the goal is to promote cooperation in business, much like how executives entertain their clients at corporate hospitality events. Should either party fail to uphold their 'unofficial contractual obligations' once terms are agreed, then relations cease. Moreover, if a better offer comes along, then business partners are easily replaced. Yet, it should be noted that these alternative 'offers' typically have to have some degree of social relation, or be vouched for by others who members share social relations with, given that trust plays a significant role in collaborative criminal ventures (Katz, 1988). As Sean explains, it is nothing personal, just business:

> "We weren't pals. I knew him through someone who introduced us. I liked the guy, but see if someone else came along wi' a better deal, then I would have forgot him in [an instance]. He'd have fucking done the same to me as well. There isn't no loyalty. Money doesn't have loyalty."

Sean's statements would suggest that the common image of the 'gang' (for example, Klein and Maxson, 2006) is not typical of the groups operating at the higher levels of organised crime, where relations adapt to match a change in activity (towards professionalisation). Yet, as mentioned earlier, true engagement in organised crime, as opposed to organised efforts of crime, can only come with specialisation, which, in turn, leads to potential monopolisation and the ability to conduct various forms of governance over either products or producers. Yet, monopoly by no means refers to the monopolisation of the whole market in which an OCG operates; rather, monopoly can be the monopolisation of a particular drugs market in a particular community. This will be discussed in much greater detail in the chapters to come, and more so Chapter 6 when discussing drug markets.

Becoming a professional: specialisation and blurring legal–illegal boundaries

YCGs undergo a fundamental change, whereby they shift from primarily delinquent groups to becoming primarily criminal groups. This means that they now begin to engage in an increasingly wide range of activities as they put new-found opportunities to the test (as we shall see in Chapter 5). Such activity was found to always include involvement in drug markets, either directly or indirectly, for all YCG members interviewed. However, such activity was always supplemented with a wide range of other activities and criminal engagements. As a result, YCGs are far from specialised, and even regarding drug supply, they typically deal in whichever drug types happen to become available to them. Supply, while steady, is still opportunistic in many ways. However, this gradually changes as suppliers higher up the supply chain become ever-more acquainted with the regular YCG distributors that they work with, particularly as YCGs build upon social, economic and symbolic capital (see Bourdieu, 1984, 1986, 1989). This gradual change and procurement of long-term resources results in a specialisation of supply, and crime type more specifically.

Using a particular OCG that had not too recently made the transition from a YCG to an OCG as an example, we see that the prior distribution of both Class A and Class B drugs decreases, and instead members now exclusively supply Class A drugs. This is because such drugs (that is, cocaine and heroin) are found to be 'the most profitable' and specialisation 'makes things easy' as established and developing resources become ever-more focused upon specific gang activities. At this stage, continuing to deal other drugs is now generally considered 'not worth the risk'. Effectively, gang members become professional traders within their respective fields and areas of expertise, for which they often acquire a reputation, not only among criminals, but also the general public more widely. This concentration of effort aids expertise. However, owing to their positions of dominance within illegal drug markets, and other types of criminal markets, OCGs will utilise to best effect established criminal networks to connect other distributers and buyers. Ewan explained:

> "We take nothing to do with [the sale of other drugs – often from unknown suppliers] … like, say, I don't know, Mr Jones, [but Mr Jones] has, say, £10,000 worth of E's [ecstasy], I would [say to Mr Jones] 'Hold on mate, I know a guy that might be interested' and then phone [criminal associate], cause that's his field man, he deals with that…. Course I take a cut but for doing that, don't work for fuck all … and basically making sure [Mr Jones] doesn't get bumped [by the criminal associate]."

For Ewan, a focus on one or two specific illegal goods allowed his OCG to operate more efficiently and retain a clear trail of thought and action. Diversification of gang activities would only result in "getting sloppy and fucking up". Yet, the fact that Ewan states, "I take a cut", as opposed to 'we take a cut', indicates that while Ewan drew upon the group's reputation to facilitate his business and still adheres to the wider gang manifesto – for example, stating that "we take nothing to do with [the sale of other drugs]" – he exploited such reputation to earn profit for himself as an individual. This is something well documented in studies of Mafia groups (see, for example, Reuter, 1983; Gambetta, 1993). This indicates a change in how group relationships work once they become more entrepreneurial, and how individuals negotiate interaction within and also outside gang boundaries.

This change towards professionalisation and specialism also results in a change as to how such criminals operate and interact with the illegal products/services they peddle. Extensive knowledge of the criminal underworld – the players involved, suppliers, customers and sources of financial and social capital – now allows OCG members the privileged position of being able to put some distance between themselves and the illegal commodities/services they once handled directly. Taking drug supply as an example, we see an evolutionary progression. YSG members purchase drugs and sell to customers directly; then, with time, experience and resources, YCGs purchase drugs in bulk and operate as low- to mid-level wholesalers, handling drugs during the initial cash–drug transaction alone. Finally, OCG members are now able to act as importers or, as often happens in Scotland, apex wholesalers (as wholesale from south of the border is often relatively cheap and it is easier to maintain logistics and product flow) (see Densley et al, 2018a); as such, they have enough criminal reputation, financial resources and connections to arrange the collection, transport and storing of such goods by other criminals and even non-criminals. Consequently, this means that while they arrange everything, they at no point handle such goods. Thus, to capture those at the top of the drug market on drug possession charges is nigh on impossible. Rather, there is a greater chance to capture such gangs by following the illegal trail of money, which they do handle, albeit often once it has been laundered. As OCG member Sean explains:

> "[People] that everyone reads about in the papers who get caught in possession of drugs aren't top blokes. Top guys don't even touch anything ... [they] have people running about doing that for them ... [they] only get the money that comes their way after it is all legit ... [illegal money] gets [washed through] fronts."[15]

This avoidance technique of removing themselves from illegal goods directly and instead only handling money once it has been laundered and made clean is something that helps OCGs monopolise criminal operations. This is because individual members will often have various roles in an OCG; thus, for example, in one gang of three, member A was responsible for the acquisition and movement of illegal goods, member B owned a series of fronts (not in his name) that laundered illegal money, and member C was responsible for the overseeing of the various workers that the OCG had in place. When other lesser criminals make efforts to do likewise, they often lack the resources, experience and connections (both in the legal and illegal realm) necessary to either establish such operations in the first place, or sustain them over a significant duration. The latter point is most notably due to the attention that this can bring to other criminals. As former offender Mark explains:

> "[We] cannot let that happen [other criminals in the area setting up legal premises]. It isn't, like, just about keeping up appearances [reputation] and all, [but simply] business strat[egy] mate. [The other criminal] buys this place and that, and we do fuck all, then, next thing we know, they are running the place, Getting our guys to flip [work] for them ... [and I] am no' going round getting new people in."

OCGs may not always intentionally set out to govern particular areas; rather, this occurs, as Mark suggests, out of necessity to retain not only criminal reputation, but also economic gains. Considerable effort put into finding and establishing working relations with trustworthy and responsible individuals is something that could be put at risk should the OCG not evoke their ability to govern the area and those within. Yet, the move towards operating legitimate businesses is also something that OCG members do with the intention of one day being fully legit businessmen. As Ewan and Stew explain:

Ewan:	"After I got out [of prison], I didn't want to go back. You miss so much inside, it's a canter but still. [I] don't want to be doing this shit my whole life. Want to go legit."
Stew:	"Right mate, too fucking right. Too old to be in and out of prison."
Ewan:	"No good for the kids."
Stew:	"We had owned the wee car wash up the road off of [street name] but looking to get [an] ice-cream shop up and running."

Many OCG members have the desire to leave the criminal underworld at some point in the future, although this is something that few achieve. The prior criminal reputation that they had acquired, which once aided their progression along criminal trajectories, now hinders their ability to leave. Rather, this mantle is often taken up by future generations, but only if the OCG remains successful and continues to progress along a more legal as opposed to illegitimate line, which is something easier said than done. As Ewan states: "Imagine running up an avalanche. That's what it's like staying [on top]. Everyone is out to get you."

Territory, structure and governance

Consequently, all these factors impact upon issues of territory and structure, which, in turn, affect governance. As OCGs are often comprised of adults in their late 20s and older, who work in gangs rooted in economic relations as opposed to social ones, with membership being based upon what one can offer, they are all too often imagined as largely independent partnerships. However, this is not the case and such imagery is often a veneer. Rather, using the 'Daniel family' or the 'Kray twins' as an example, we can see how these gangs often interact and 'do business' with others. Yet, such associations are not open to all and members can by no means freelance where they like; rather, they become affiliated with one particular OCG, to whom their loyalty is demanded. Should members or even associates operate with, often particular, others who are deemed to be rivals, they would be cut off, or worse. OCGs are professional criminals but they exist within the group, without whom they would lose support, resources, connections and so on. Therefore, while professional and having a fair degree of autonomy over individual behaviour, they are still tied to the gang, as trust, respect and loyalty (in criminal ventures) is to be upheld above all, which is a point often overlooked in academia. This gang behaviour means that OCGs still have some degree of interaction with territory.

We see that as various forms of criminal capital have been generated and criminal reputations are established over time, there is now no need to 'do gang' in the public arena, as with lesser group formations previously (Garot, 2007). As we saw earlier, YSGs are territorially rooted, and although moving from physical to conceptual territory, the business of YCGs is nonetheless very much still conducted in and around those areas that gangs have extensive knowledge of. However, for OCGs, territory is no longer important regarding business dealings, which extend well beyond the confines of the scheme, nation and even continent; yet, governing an area of physical territory for various reasons now becomes perceived as important to successfully maintaining and overseeing operations. This is because the OCG: seeks to control, sway and have influence over a given population – often tied to the territory that gang members grew up in, operate out of and are known in while in previous YSG and YCG formation; invest in legitimate business, which often requires physical premises and constant surveillance; and oversee transnational operations within a micro-lens (if possible). As Mark explains:

> "I wouldn't say having [territory] is important in the same way [as when I was a youth]. Fighting [in YSGs] for daft reasons. I know everyone here, they know me. [Previously] dr[a]nk in the [local pub name]. More, say, [I can] trust the people here. I know the place. The police even know me. They talk [with me] [laughs]. They [the population] see me as their own, that sound weird? [I can] make sure every[thing operates] smoothly here. I don't know Edinburgh. I don't know Ayr, do I? Why would I [operate from there]. Yeah, we might [work with] a few guys there. It is nice. I don't know it, in my bones."

Much like a transitional company, some degree of physical presence is often required. OCGs will purchase and sell illegal goods/services transnationally, yet they often seek to acquire a piece of physical territory to call their own, and where best than the areas they grew up in and have extensive friendships, peer relationships, childhood associates and a considerable criminal reputation. Yet, this territory moves beyond confined scheme boundaries to the more generalised area in question. For example, had OCG members grown up in the schemes of Linthouse and Drumoyne, the Govan district more generally will come under their control.

OCG structure is subsequently tied to this relationship that the gang shares with the territory, which likewise impacts upon the governance over it and the population within. While OCGs do not view territory in the same restrictive way as YSGs, having a base of operation within familiar surroundings means that the constant interaction and familiarisation of individuals has enabled a social hierarchy to be established in the community, built from childhood, which ensures that the local population happily protect OCG members from rivals, law enforcement and other threats. As OCG member Stew states: "We've [storehouses] all over. No[t] in just one place ... on the estate, cause no' wanting them too far [away] in case shit goes down."

At the apex of local (criminal) power and retaining intimate personal knowledge of local relationships and criminal networks, OCGs can (re)define the rules of the social field that they find themselves in to their own advantage.[16] In this way, they begin to acquire authority and then illegal governance of territory. To maintain privilege, OCGs ensure a covert presence supported by clear lines of intelligence and information. Adapted rules are learnt quickly by locals, who often witness sanctions taken against those who infringe the new rules of the social field, or who benefit by largesse, favours and gifting. OCGs can expand upon the properties they use as 'storehouses' for illegal goods. Marginalised and poor residents, in many cases vulnerable owing to age, gender or drug/ alcohol addiction, are easily exploited or enticed with 'extra income' to act as lookouts, store illegal goods, act as 'fall guys' for crimes they did not commit, be false witnesses, provide alibis, take out property or finances in their names to cover OCG members' paper trails, or even spread 'fake news'. Often, OCGs also put in effect a glass ceiling on criminal ventures, thus ensuring that local, often upcoming criminals have to gain permission, interact with or go through the established OCG should they wish to pursue their progressive activities. This ensures control over criminal activity in the higher echelons of illegal markets. This all affects OCG structure as the OCG, while a core of close-knit individuals, extends far and wide and has many employees, workers and ad hoc associates/benefactors. Such things further enhance the ability of OCGs to generate the dichotomous position of fear and respect in communities and to coerce legal businesses and influence official figures – all signs of extra-legal governance (Campana and Varese, 2011, 2018; Von Lampe, 2016).

Chapter summary

In this chapter, we have explored in detail the evolving gang typologies in the given context. We see how a complex mixture of internal and external variables creates both push and pull effects, whereby gangs progress from one evolutionary stage to the next. Formed via issues of territoriality, local narratives, scheme history and street socialisation, youths congregate in certain areas of local schemes to form YSGs, which are themselves largely recreational youth groups who engage in potentially delinquent behaviour as a consequence of peer socialisation. Yet, with physical and mental maturity, as well as access to a greater range of resources, some YSG members who view criminality as innate to their nature form closer tight-knit groups. As a consequence of individual motivation, innate criminality and coming together with – disproportionately – like-minded individuals, YCGs are born. Unlike YSGs, they do not adhere to traditional forms of naming and instead largely go by with no official terminology. Some YCGs in their own right, but in most cases particular YCG members, become part of local OCGs, who fully engage in organised crime on a transnational scale. Yet, by engaging in criminal behaviour like this and still maintaining some interaction with territory, this results in the monopolisation of power and illegal governance over the markets and communities in which they operate.

Yet, this summary neglects the activities in which these gangs engage and is thus only reflective of their structural properties. In order to get a more holistic, truer and more complete picture of these gangs, we also need to explore the activities in which they engage and also give more attention to context. Therefore, Chapter 5 will provide a descriptive account of the range of activities in which these gangs engage at their respective stages of development. Chapter 6 will then look at one activity in particular, that is, drugs, to provide a more detailed account and bring together structure, activity and context.

Notes
[1] While I argue that economic principles become key in the transition from YCGs to OCGs, social aspects nonetheless still play a vital part. Putting economic pursuits first and foremost allows YCG members who progress to put those friendships aside where they potentially hinder YCGs' existence altogether. Yet, friendship (and subsequent trust) is still important in forging relationships within OCGs (see Windle, 2013). Both social and economic aspects exist in YCG and OCG relationships; however, it is merely the ability for individuals to prioritise one over the other (where needed) that enables gang professionalisation to continue.
[2] It should be noted that other youths may well also share varying degrees of loose affiliation with the YSG but not consider themselves, or be considered by others,

as gang members. This is often due to socialising very little with the YSG outside a few members whom they perhaps know from early school years, family networks or living in close proximity with them.

3   In recent years, this issue has been addressed with the gradual amalgamation of schools. Previously, this had been an issue of controversy due to numerous factors, most of which related to religious practice.

4   While much has been done to combat YSG violence, YSG formation itself (not to be confused with knife crime) is still largely accepted as a given phenomenon in those areas most embedded with gang culture (see McCallum, 2011).

5   A chain is attached to a broken cinder block or a thick rounded piece of metal is welded to a bike/dog chain.

6   An example would be Pollok Bundy and Pollok Krew.

7   Recognised by the local council as an estate.

8   For example, the district of Greater Pollok has several YSGs, including 'Arden', 'Bushwhackers', 'Darnley', 'Nitshill', 'Pollok Krew', 'Scratchy' (AKA 'South Nitshill'), 'The Bundy' (although scheme now demolished), 'Tiny Priesty' and 'Young Team'.

9   Recognised among the local population but not by the local authority.

10 The former number and thereabouts being more common than the latter.

11 Although some may sporadically engage in petty offences and various forms of delinquency.

12 Some core members continue to offend outside gang settings, others desist, some move into employment and so on. Yet, when YCG formation occurs, it is primarily comprised of former YSG core members.

13 In addition to showing the necessary attributes (that is, calmness, patience, intelligence, likeability).

14 An example may be where a gang of, say, four members has a particular member who is regarded as being a high risk to gang duration, progression and sustainability (he may exert behaviour that potentially draws police or rival OCG attention time and again). Thus, while the gang maintain a friendship with this individual, as they move towards being an OCG, this member is gradually excluded from major future group planning. The excluded member is not excluded per se, but rather while still remaining in wider criminal networks, he is given a lesser, secondary role with regard to the actual future activities of the OCG in question.

15 'Fronts' is a term used to refer to legal businesses that are used to launder illegal money from other revenues. An example may well be a tanning salon, nail bar, car wash or ice-cream parlour.

16 OCG members do not usually reside in the area that they are most affiliated with, but often live in the upmarket estates close by, although they nonetheless socialise, purchase premises and 'do business' in the more deprived communities in which they were raised.

5

Street Life, Crime and (Dis)Organised Crime

Following on from the theme of Chapter 4, which highlighted the formation, membership process and other structural characterises of gang types in Scotland, this chapter will continue to present the gang within the current framework and will look to explore gang activity in a more generic sense. In doing so, the chapter will look to present what is essentially a descriptive account of the collective and individualistic behaviour that is most commonly associated with each level of gang typology. While structure and activity are always intertwined and feed off each other, the purpose of this chapter is nonetheless to be primarily descriptive, with structure largely being allotted a secondary role. This is largely because: (1) the chapter is aimed at a broad audience, and, in addition, Chapter 6 will look more specifically at gang structure and activity in the context of drug supply; and (2) the chapter is merely looking to attribute some degree of activity to the relevant typology, which can be vast at the lower end of the gang spectrum. However, a summary will conclude the chapter and briefly summarise the interplay between structure, agency and context.

YSG behaviour

As discussed Chapter 4, owing to their diffuse structure, whereby YSG membership is ascribed, typically via street socialisation and postcode residency, rather than achieved, I argue that it is more helpful to think of the gang at this stage of development as comprised of two subgroupings: the core body and the outer layer (McLean, 2017). Wider research also indicates such a distinction and finds that most youths who claim gang status during early adolescence will generally drift away from offending behaviour as they age and mature (see also Bradshaw, 2005). As only a handful of members retain what I term an intrinsically criminal identity, it is difficult at this stage of development for any identity to transcend the individual and become the overall gang identity; thus, YSGs are more likely to partake in acts that are delinquent or anti-social as opposed to criminal per se. As practitioners Yvonne and Stephen (who is also an ex-gang member) state:

> "The Young Teams are mostly [young boys] who hang out on the street corner, or over in the park.... they get in fights with [the other YSG] at the other side of the park. That's where it starts and ends for most, being honest." (Yvonne)

> "The boys [YSG] hang around with one another ... [they] get in[volved] in minor rubbish really. You know, sometimes hear them speak about getting a [drink] at the weekend. Some take drugs aye.... [Occasionally get in] fights, or smash shite up, when [intoxicated]." (Stephen)

As Yvonne and Stephen suggest, YSG formation is primarily the result of street socialisation rather than intended organisation, and when delinquency occurs, it typically revolves around boisterous behaviour that may lead to fights or vandalism, and more so when youths are intoxicated. Thus, YSGs, as a whole, are by no means inherently criminal; rather, they are recreational, with some features of their behaviour being delinquent. As such, delinquency is by no means a given, but rather a potential outcome of YSG formation. Sometimes, though, boisterous behaviour can have serious consequences. This is particularly true when gang fights occur. These fights typically occur during weekends, when youths are most likely to be on the street in number, and also more likely to have consumed alcohol or be intoxicated. Fights take place on the edge of scheme boundaries and often involve the use of weapons such as bricks, bottles and knifes, although it is not uncommon for swords, machetes and even knuckledusters to also be used:

> "You got to understand, these [YSGs], they are mostly just [young boys] out pure having fun wi' bravado.... The [YSGs] arrange to meet ... [or] just meet by walking into each other's territory ... they toss bricks and bottles and chase each other ...[occasionally youths get] hurt or stabbed." (Bucket, male, practitioner)

> "Aye it [gang fights] can get out of hand, aye. Wee guys chase each other about ... cause you've got blades but if you catch someone you

think 'Fuck man, what do I do now?'. You panic and cunts end up
plugged [stabbed], know. Stab or be stabbed…. You don't go out to
do it. Just happens." (Stephen, male, practitioner)

As practitioner Bucket and ex-YSG member Stephen state, while most acts
that YSGs engage in are largely benign, more serious acts do sometimes
occur. This is most common during gang fights and can be attributed
to a variety of factors, such as peer pressure, unintended consequences,
a need to display masculinity, intoxication or even simply peers 'egging'
one another on. Yet, vendettas sometimes occur, whereby gang fighting
becomes personal and individuals will actively seek out their rivals at their
workplace, home or school:

"It doesn't always stop [at the weekend]…. A cunt hooked me before
[during a YSG fight] and fractured my cheek…. I wasn't going to let
that lie…. Went to his door wi' my brother and my brother slashed
him for it, right there on the door step. Fuck you, knife down the
right side of his face. Tried to stab his dad [as well]." (Pete, male,
offender)

Yet, while such vendettas were by no means rare, they very rarely
manifested themselves in such extreme behaviour as that indicated
by Pete and his brother. Rather, general fights and 'bad blood' may
ensue for years, and in some cases even decades. This often resulted
in individuals being unable to travel into certain areas due to fear of
retribution, even as young adults. While YSGs are commonly associated
with gang fights in public space, they do sometimes partake in other
serious acts that blur the boundary between delinquency and criminality.
This may manifest itself in a variety of ways, one of the most common
being street robbery. Although occasionally planned and arranged, like
gang fights, street robbery is largely a sporadic activity that is based
upon opportunity, and most commonly occurs during peak times for
socialising and intoxication:

"We would get [the YSG] together and go [to the city centre]….
we would [walk] around the main streets, usually where the [most
popular nightclubs] would be. That way, everyone going there would
have to pass you…. We would rob them [as they] made their way
[to the nightclub]." (Shaun, male, offender)

Shaun indicates that he would regularly travel to the busy city centre of
Glasgow with his YSG during weekends. While this was primarily to get

involved in gang fights with other 'Young Teams' from around the city, the gang was open to the idea of committing other acts of delinquency and even criminality. These acts were often secondary to the main purpose of engaging in YSG fights. This often presented itself in the form of street robbery. Shaun and his gang would occupy those routes most frequently used by nightclubbers[1] to maximise the opportunity to engage in both fighting and robbery. Despite being more of a collective activity, though, robbery was largely opportunistic, not well planned, and carried out by the individual within the wider group context. Shaun explains how victims were selected and how robbery occurred: "We would [encourage] each other to [engage in acts of robbery]. We didn't care…. We would look for stragglers [and perceived weak individuals] …. stop them and [rob them]…. Never did it to birds [females], but if we had [females] with us, then they might."

Selecting victims based upon how they walked, dressed, talked and how segregated they were from their own peers allowed Shaun and his friends to use their own group as a means of intimidation, and by adopting an aggressive attitude, they were able to relieve the selected victims of their belongings. The degree of what belongings to take was typically minor, though, as while asking an individual for money would be met with little resistance, asking an individual for his trainers or clothing, for example, would be met with an increased level of resistance. As Gee explains: "[individuals] will hand over money, but even gimps [weak individuals] pure put up a fight if you start taking the piss and whacking their jacket or sneaks [trainers] off them, fuck sake [laughs]."

As mentioned, YSG robbery was largely sporadic, unplanned and individualistic; consequently, the distribution of the goods was also anything but planned, and rather than being distributed collectively, Shaun states that "anything I got I kept". Most participants disclosed partaking in similar activities, especially members of larger, well-appointed YSGs from areas closest to the city centre, where 'suitable targets' routinely converged with an 'absence of capable guardians' (Harding et al, 2018).

While YSGs occasionally engaged in other activities beyond gang fights in the form of robbery and knife use, which blurs the delinquent–criminal spectrum, more often than not, such crimes can be attributed to a handful of individuals typically belonging to the core body of the YSG, who are persistent offenders and perceive their own identity as intrinsically criminal. While the majority of YSG members cease offending as they mature, those who belong to the core body typically continue to offend well into adulthood and often become 'career criminals'. Next, I shall focus more upon this group.

YSG core body

Fighting and robbery

Members of the core body are disproportionately responsible for the majority of the problematic acts committed by YSGs. Part of the reason is that core members usually perceive their own identity as being intrinsically criminal, have stores of 'criminal capital' (Fader, 2016) and have ready access to sources of criminal socialisation (see Sutherland, 1939). Their criminal 'careers' were found to begin with minor acts of criminality among friends, associates and other YSG members, of both the core body and outer layer. In relation to those topics discussed earlier, that is, violence and robbery, Shaun and Gee explain how as core members, along with other core offenders, they were disproportionately responsible for many of the offences committed within their respective schemes:

> "I probably always thought I was like the top boy, you know. At my age group … [it was as though] I had to always prove myself…. [A number of family members] had all been in jail, know … was normal [to act criminal]…. [I recall] we had been fighting with a couple of the boys from [area X], this had been going on for years [growing up]…. [During that time,] me and [YSG member A] chibbed most of their boys…. [I] stabbed two of them…. Battered their top boy wi' a dog leash on the bus…. Kicked in [rival gang member's] door after he [had] got a [social] house in [area B], leathered fuck out of him and stole his TV [laughs]…. Few other things, but aye, I just loved it mate…. It was me, know…. [I] had around eight serious convictions by 17, 18, aye." (Shaun, male, offender)

> "Me and [YSG member C] would put up ads on Gumtree … mostly things that guys [our age at that time] would have bought. [PS2] games, slasher caps, mind them? Some things we never had but advertised anyway … like [jewellery] … always gave a fake address [when advertising] … [we wore] the old Bergus jackets…. They are good for pulling the hood up and hiding blades, [be]cause you had the inside zip pockets, mind!… when [the buyer] showed, we jumped out and robbed them. Did alright from it…. I wasn't into robbing women, but [YSG member C] did a few times … [also in another effort, we would] wait at the bottom of the hill [in area A], it is always quiet, but busy, know, people walk that way home from the town … [we would] stop them and put a knife to their throat. I always went behind them and put knife to their side but [YSG member C] held

it to their throat ... meant they couldn't run, and didn't know where I was standing exactly, [so] they were [unable] to react ... only took money, rings, [that] stuff. No point in taking credit cards or motor keys ... [did] that for about two years, until I got caught ... never got caught doing the crime ... [but] when I [traded] the [stolen goods] into the shop, they changed [policy], and you needed to give ID.... When we got caught, robberies around [area A] probably stopped [laughs]." (Gee, male, offender)

As demonstrated earlier, the level of crime that these individuals committed was disproportionate to the wider level of offending by other adolescents of similar age in the given community. Both Shaun and Gee mention committing such offences with a close friend. These offences were typically carried out not with the YSG as a whole, but rather in more coherent and smaller subgroups of two or three. Thus, while the larger YSG is used much like a hub where persistent offenders can come together and socialise with, and befriend, other like-minded individuals, it enables the formation of smaller groups to emerge within. In these smaller groupings, core offenders can project their individual criminal identities over the collective, and, as such, begin to carry out much more sustained patterns of offending behaviour, which also gradually increases in severity over time. This is seen in that these smaller groups move beyond gang fights and opportunistic street robbery, and also engage in other criminal activities. This often includes breaking into cars and homes before selling stolen property. Much of this behaviour is primarily for thrill-seeking purposes, especially in the case of joyriding:

"[I recall] breaking into about three houses a night at one stage when I was at my worst. Wasn't always houses but might ... be a shed or a car.... I did keep most of the stuff [I stole]. [Occasionally] sold [stolen goods], get me.... I didn't really do it for money, aye. I liked the buzz [excitement] it gave me.... [I] always [carried out such behaviour] wi' my best mate if it was a house. If it was a car radio or shit in the [car] boot, would just be me or whoever I [happened to be] with." (Gavin, male, offender)

As Gavin's statement suggests, residential burglary may have provided a good income or other material gains, but his primary motive for such behaviour was thrill-seeking. Much like Shaun, who mentioned that he 'loved it' when discussing engaging in extreme violence, committing crime for primarily thrill-seeking purposes is something noted in wider crime literature, particularly when it involves persistent offenders (see

Katz, 1988; Wright and Decker, 1997). As with the statements by Shaun and Gee, Gavin would usually involve his best friend, who, like him, could also be identified as a persistent offender. Yet, as a consequence of street socialisation, members of the outer layer, loose associates and even other non-gang-affiliated individuals could often become caught up in criminal acts, as Gavin suggests when he states "If it was a car radio or shit in the [car] boot, would just be me or whoever I [happened to be] with." Thus, by way of socialising, such individuals may be coerced into assisting Gavin in his crimes, for example, by "keep[ing] the edgy" or simply by affiliation.

Drug dealing

As a whole, YSGs tend to be primarily delinquent in nature as opposed to criminal. When crime occurs, it is typically due to core members. YSGs are primarily the result of street socialisation. Thus, most of their time is spent simply socialising with peers. Yet, the most common problematic activities that YSGs engage in tend to revolve around violence, with robbery often being a by-product of such behaviour. Involvement in drug supply is more aligned to consumption, as opposed to distribution, and is largely a consequence of socialising with young peers rather than being an economic-based activity. When distribution occurs, it is typically tied to social purposes as opposed to economic ones. Matthew and Geoff explain:

> "[The YSG would] meet up [in] the woods to take buckets.... People would take turns getting the [cannabis]. I used to get it [from an elder sibling], but they [peers] had to pay me back.... or sometimes we would all chip in [financially to purchase drugs]. I got it but, so didn't pay." (Matthew, male, offender)

> "Drugs are a big part of growing up.... I took [valium], only when mad wi' it [MWI] ... smoked [cannabis] from 13 [years old] man ... [usually] at [friend X] house, just wi' the boys. His maw was sound and let us all come in ... his maw actually got it for us [laughs], obviously she fancied me [laughs], kidding ... we liked to have a laugh.... I could get it as well." (Geoff, male, offender)

As Matthew and Geoff indicate, YSG involvement in drugs was primarily in relation to consumption as opposed to distribution. Distribution was largely social, yet even at this early stage, participants recognised that drugs could be used as a useful commodity to be traded:

"[As a young adolescent,] I didn't really sell weed, [like] how the cops think people deal [drugs].... [Was] more like my dad[2] sold weed man, and gave me some. Him and [uncle X] had a [cannabis] grow, going on.... He gave me the scraps basically [laughs].... I'd share it wi' me and my mates, [but] would sell the rest off, know, on tick [credit], or to pay for stuff I wanted [for example, clothing, shoes and so on] ... kind of like trading." (Mitch, male, offender)

Mitch's statement resonated with a lot of the participants in the study, whereby YSG members would access and distribute drugs socially as opposed to economically. The research found that even though core members typically had easier and fuller access to existing drug supply networks, and were often the main distributors among friends and peers as a consequence, social supply was by no means confined to core members alone. Small amounts of recreational drugs were easily obtained, particularly in deprived neighbourhoods, and did not require a great deal of, or in some cases any, criminal capital to access and purchase. Indeed, many participants spoke of even going to local street dealers trading on 'open markets' from an early age. Likewise, Geoff also indicated earlier that even his friend's mum would occasionally supply cannabis for them. Thus, drug taking and social supply are by no means wholeheartedly gang activities, but rather open to the wider community and population. However, as core members aged and matured, drug supply would come to play a much more significant role in their criminal activities, whereby the tradable qualities that drugs possessed were increasingly used to acquire financial and material gains. However, this process will be explored further and in more detail in Chapter 6.

YCG behaviour

As YSGs evolve towards YCG formation, the activities in which gangs engage change and broaden quite significantly. Likewise, those other activities in which the gang had already engaged also begin to change in that they become much more organised and the level of harm they pose increases substantially. This is largely due to the fact the YSGs consolidate around a few core individuals who see their identity as somewhat intrinsically criminal, while those of the outer layer generally drift off into legitimate employment, further education and so forth. Yet, faced with external pressures, the realities of adulthood, family and financial commitments, and so on, as well as often having acquired a criminal reputation and official criminal record, core members of YSGs thus begin to actively seek to make a living via criminal activity. In addition, the fact that YCG members are now becoming adults, both physically and mentally, means that they can begin to operate, and if need be challenge individuals, in the adult world. Nowhere else is this process more evident than in drug supply. Drug supply proves to be a major source of revenue here. Thus, pulling together resources (for example, finances, criminal networks, commodities, housing) and purchasing drugs in bulk before redistributing enables gang activity and structure to evolve simultaneously with one another. As Stephen and Micky summarised:

"At [16 years old,] I felt I didn't have any other options really, [having just] done a [brief] stint in [prison].... [I] had a criminal record.... Was struggling [to secure legitimate work].... My pal's dad was [selling] Pure [high-grade cocaine] back then.... Wasn't that easy to get.... He [Stephen's pal] knew I was struggling.... Had a wee boy to provide for [as well].... [My pal] came [to speak to] me, asked if I wanted to [work alongside him], sell[ing drugs]. Said 'Aye'.... Took off quick.... A few thousand a week [between the group], cash right in your hand, is big money at that age. Hard to stop once you start." (Stephen, male, offender)

"[Grew] up wi' the boys [YCG members].... [We] were muckers. They had my back.... Had fuck all growing up.... We [YCG members] were all in the same boat.... [Once an adolescent, we were] like 'Fuck this shit, let's just sell the smack [heroin], that's where the money is at, fuck it, who cares'.... My dad and my mate's mum were [heroin addicts] anyways.... Fucked up ... [be]cause we were destroying our own [community]. Fuck sake man, I even became my dad's dealer.... [We built] good connections.... After a few years, we had flooded [our local community] with [heroin]." (Micky, male, offender)

As both Stephen and Micky indicate, drugs are a useful commodity and can be distributed via market-based activities, whereby a future forecast of income, revenue, outgoings, debts and so on become somewhat predictable. This becomes tied to gang structure, and as a consequence, this enables the gang to evolve. However, as mentioned, this process in relation to drug supply will be examined in more detail in Chapter 6. Thus, this chapter will continue to give what is essentially more akin to a descriptive account of the range and level of criminal activities in which each gang type tends to most commonly engage. Thus, while drug supply is a vital part of gang organisation in the given context, it is by no means the only contributor, or the only activity in which YCGs are involved.

Cafeteria-style offending

YSG core members typically have well-established delinquent and upcoming criminal reputations not only among peers, but also, to a degree, even among younger and older generations, who are often aware of such individuals due to the generally small population and geography of schemes, the circulation of local narratives and stories, intergenerational and intertwined kinship and friendship networks, and YSG activities often being carried out in public (see also Deuchar, 2009; Fraser, 2013; Miller, 2015). Such reputations are used to engage in, and provide opportunity to partake in, a range of other activities as YCG members progress along criminal trajectories. In addition, enhancing already-established reputations through drug supply networks means that other criminal opportunities are often more likely to arise. As William explains:

> "You get a rep[utation] if you're doing well for yourself…. I had already had a rep from [YSG] fighting before…. The guy I was buying my gear [drugs] from asked if I wanted to do an earner on the side as well, know, extra [income]…. Was just to collect money that he was owed, know what I'm saying, pure fucking easy…. Most times, it went fine, just gave people a wee warning…. [On occasion, I] had to stab guys."

William articulated how a good name or 'rep' in the criminal underworld is typically built from a young age, and continual enhancement of one's rep is often itself rewarded with other criminal opportunities. Such opportunities often involved significantly riskier behaviour but paid well, particularly considering how little time and effort had to be exerted in their commission. Carrying out debt collection for other criminals and criminal outfits proved to be a popular activity among YCG members and not only involved the collection of drug money, but even spilled over into the legitimate sphere. As Reese explains:

> "I didn't know the guy personal. My mate [approached me] and asked if I would collect some money for his mum's pal, maybe his aunt's mate, can't remember exactly…. I thought it would be the usual [involving criminals and their clientele], until I got to the house. Belter of a house up the Mearns. Chapped the door and a pure gimp cunt

answers, asked if he was [name] ... [and] gave the cunt the whole
spiel [narrative script], 'You know who I am', 'You know who I run
wi'', that shit. Obviously, the cunt had no idea who I was, think he
was a doctor or something, [so] why the fuck would he know who I
am [laughs].... Soon clicked [why I was there] after I lifted my top
and showed a shooter, fake mind you but he didn't know that ... the
posh cunt [eventually] gives over about £3,000... I have to actually
drive him to his fucking dad's house to help him get it. Fucking sitting
in his dad's house, living room, while he is making me fucking tea
[laughs] ... turns out it was [an established professional] that had
been owed money for letting an apartment [to the debtor]. Only found
out cause my mate was out of town and had me drop it right to his
house. Wouldn't believe the cunts, fucking meant to be squeaky clean
as well ... [who would be] asking you to get their money."

As Reese states, it is not only criminals who use the services of YCGs; rather, this may involve members of the legitimate community, and may even include well-known public figures on occasion. When there is difficulty in having recourse to law, individuals may well pay for the services of YCGs to resolve the issue. In this case, Reese acted with another YCG member from another YCG that he generally does not affiliate himself with but knew through earlier years in the scheme. Thus, as evident, YCG members may well, at times, be part of one or more YCGs should a profitable opportunity arise. Thus, while YCGs generally align themselves to one YCG in particular, this is still fluid and is by no means fixed given that membership is based upon social purposes and engaging in criminality as a consequence. Furthermore, such recourse to YCGs is not confined to retrieving financial goods. Reese indicates that this may well include retrieving other materials, goods and even pets, stating on one occasion "no joke.... [We had to] collect a fucking dog, a wee Akita pup ... [from] her [his client's] ex-boyfriend". As with Reese's prior statement, indicating that he drove his victim to his "dad's house" to acquire the debt money, such behaviour was surprisingly not as uncommon as one might except. A number of YCG members in the study discussed 'abducting', 'capturing' or 'snatching' individuals and holding them against their will while contacting their family members and close friends to pay their debt in return for their safe keeping. These criminal acts typically revolved around the repaying of debts or, on occasion, for information. Jack states:

"Snatched the daftie right off the street ... in pure daylight mate ... [of
course] it was dodgy [risky] but the arsehole is a pure rat man ... was

in 10G [£10,000] ... need[ed] to grab him or he would have been off ... vanished ... put it this way, after spending a few days in our company, he paid up ... well, no' him directly ... say he was kind of incapacitated [laughs] ... few phone calls and you would be surprised how quick people get the money together for these scumbags ... if your son's a junkie, he's a fucking junkie ... wouldn't be me paying for them if it was my boy."

While Jack and his friend received a custodial sentence for their part in this crime, not solely for this act, but rather for taking part in a series of ongoing events between the victim and the victim's family, Jack and other participants in the study indicated that many similar events go unreported. Although participants like William and Reese engaged quite extensively in debt collection, others like Jack did so opportunistically, as outlined earlier. Yet, while Reese and Jack operated with other YCG members in carrying out these activities, William engaged in debt collection for a specific OCG and viewed it very much as a secondary activity that supplemented the income he earned from his primary activity: drug supply with his YCG. William kept this activity separate from his own YCG. William did not state why he did so, but it may be presumed that the OCG he worked with did not want others to become aware of his alternative business arrangements for fear of being exposed and thus increasing the likelihood for unwanted police attention. Like William, Reese and Jack, most YCG members participated in what Klein (1995) might call 'cafeteria-style' offending, meaning that, over time, a YCG has experimented with a number of criminal activities that vary widely. As Micky and Craig explained:

"[The YCGs acquire] a reputation [and their] name gets about.... A few cunts messed around wi' us once and got done right in.... People know no[w not] to fuck about.... That [incident] got us heavy known.... My pal got the jail for [that incident].... [Not long after which] a few older guys we spoke [with regularly] suggested doing some drop offs for them. Was a canter [easy].... if we got stopped [from police], it might have been different." (Micky, male, offender)

"[Our YCG] mostly shifted coc[aine], ecstasy, some weed, types of amphetamines, well anything really, anything we got passed our way.... wasn't all we done. [I] wouldn't say that. Get bored, don't you, always wanting to make a faster buck here or there, aye.... getting older, [we were] on the scene a lot.... Tried armed robbery,

> *was too fucked up man.... Tried [fraud involving third-party delivery services].... [Was] a good earner for a [while].... [Also sold cigarettes] we'd got [smuggled] in, well no' us directly like, more through a guy, for a bit.... [Carried out false] insurance claims as well, know, with the mobiles.... Just meet people in this game that are into all sorts. End up giving it a try and see if it works for you, don't you?"* (Craig, male, offender)

It should be noted that Micky failed to specifically identify what objects or items were being 'dropped' exactly, but firearms are likely included because when asked to elaborate, Micky motioned with his hands in a manner that could be interpreted as 'firearms', and shortly afterwards stated that a 'shoot-out' would have ensued should they have been stopped by the police or anyone else. Micky did explain that the opportunity to transport valuable commodities within the criminal world only came about because he was 'known' for prior delinquency and a particular incident in which rivals "got done right in", which is another example illustrating that latent criminal structures create 'criminally exploitable ties' (Von Lampe, 2016: 110). In addition, Craig pointed out that his own gang experimented with a number of criminal ventures, all very different, as they sought to secure income, establish a reputation and discover other types of criminality that may have proved to be more profitable. Both statements would suggest that criminal opportunity often arises from time spent 'on the scene', as well as by virtue of a change in the level of gang organisation:

> *"The boys do get more sophisticated in what they do, yeah. [I] would say that. Over time, they may start with selling drugs, but quickly are involved in lots of things.... Some of the stories they tell, I think 'How did they even get into that?'"* (Yvonne, female, practitioner)

> *"It's like playing football, mate. More they played it, [the] more they get experience of their position.... They also get chances to try out new positions as well."* (Bucket, male, practitioner)

These statements by practitioners Yvonne and Bucket imply that, in agreement with (ex-)offenders themselves, while more gang organisation brings more criminal opportunities, realising these opportunities tends to bring about an increase in gang organisation. The process is reciprocal: both causes feed into one another. Bucket's sports analogy regarding the acquisition of specialist skills is important here as he states that entry into the criminal underworld, that is, 'the game', often comes via the most common and culturally practised crime type, which, in Scotland, is drug supply. Those 'playing the game' will gain a firm understanding of how the rules work, and thus how best to gain advantage over other players. With time and a holistic understanding of the game, experienced players (that is, those involved in YCGs) will be asked by others to try out 'new positions'. These new positions operate on the same principles as the game overall, but they are unique. While playing these new positions, some criminals find that they are, in fact, well adapted to them (see Harding, 2014). Others learn that they are not. In the latter case, they reject other roles to take up another position or, in most cases, the original position that they are most familiar with: drug supply.

Robbery, extortion and bribery

Several of the activities outlined so far are relatively new to YCG members and go beyond the traditional fighting and street robbery carried out previously in YSG formation. This is because as YCGs become more established and, with age, begin to acquire access to more resources, such as housing, cars, social welfare, adult relationships, entry to adult-only establishments (that is, nightclubs, pubs) and so on, they begin to expand and try out new criminal ventures. In many ways, the expansion in criminal activity simply mirrors the expansion in activities by the wider mid- to late adolescent population. Yet, many of these activities are nonetheless simply a refinement of those previous acts carried out regularly while part of YSGs, namely, those that revolve around violence, weapons and robbery. Robbery moved beyond street robbery, though, and took on a more organised role. Given that YCGs typically operate in illegal drug markets, they often have extensive knowledge of those other dealers, gangs and various individuals involved in such networks as a consequence. In addition, through experience and criminal connections, they become aware of how others' operations work (that is, the location of drug storage, regular customers and distribution networks). This enables insider knowledge to be established and helps a YCG select or identify potential victims who they can rob or steal from, or muscle in on. Concurring with the work of Decker and Curry (2002), Harding et al (2018) likewise found intra-gang violence to be a common occurrence among gang members. In the given context, this often materialises when one YCG exploits their relationship with another YCG, for example, when one member who blurs[3] the membership between both gangs begins to align himself more strongly with one gang in particular and, in the process, uses built-up knowledge and established trust to rob the other gang.

Gangs robbing gangs and other dealers is very common, and while lone individuals do engage in such practices, more often than not, this type of robbery is largely practised by gangs due to practicality. Sole dealers are particularly vulnerable to YCGs, who will use their collective capabilities to exploit and victimise the individual. This is another key reason for dealers operating in gang contexts as opposed to remaining sole dealers. While there are undoubtedly individuals who work solo and are able to progress via the various market levels, all participants in this study who moved from retail-level dealing to wholesaling and beyond discussed a need to align themselves with others, most commonly, to pull together resources and avoid victimisation. Mitch explains the need to work in gang formation, and recalls his own experience when he had been doing well as a sole dealer moving from retail-level supply to wholesaling practices:

> "It's [risky] selling drugs. [I was] opening [my]self up for [being robbed]. You do need backup in this game. [I desired a] low [profile], but can't really, especially if business is booming. People aren't daft, they know you're selling and probably have a stash in the house … [so] I phoned up my best mate, and said you want in on this? We had always [socialised], and he's [trustworthy].… So, I knew he'd be well up for a wee earner … [and] can well handle himself. Had a bit of a reputation."

Thus, while motivation for partaking in drug dealing is largely self-driven, it typically expresses itself in the group context, and more so when looking to operate beyond retail-level supply. Robbing dealers was usually well planned and was a far cry from the sporadic street robbery carried out by YSGs. 'Raids' were often aimed at specific dealers and at specific times (often when drugs storage was at its peak at the given location):

> "We would usually steal drugs, aye mainly drugs, from like other [dealers].… no' like ounces … needs to be worthwhile.… that's why we hit it when it's housed, know.… [Therefore, robbery] depends [upon] who has what, and when they have it, know.… people might know you are into that game but see if they can prove it was you that [robbed] them, they'd wan[t to] fucking kill you, for serious.… fact, more time goes into planning.… [when] robbing other crews then ramming the locals [shops]." (Ken, male, offender)

Yet, robbing dealers could be risky and unpredictable, even for those carrying out the robbery, as Allan's statement suggests:

"Fucking right it's dangerous man, know? See, you can hit a place and the cunt's inside are heavy Ricky Maroo'd [armed] right up, no joke.... aye, we would defo be tooled up, [as well]. Aye ... take a shooter [firearm] if you can get your hands on one, but that's more like shit you read about happening down England.... we always had blades, case shit gets close and personal know.... [YCG X] always carried a machete on raids.... they aren't the best in truth mate, but they scar the fuck right out of cunts.... you really want to hit the place when its empty.... [Recalling one occasion] [YCG member Z] was pure mad with it [intoxicated] [on this particularly robbery on another YCG], fucking coked right out his eyeballs.... [he] was [only] to watch the [hostages] ... we use' to always put them in the bathroom crouching down [Allan does motion].... It's no[t] like in the movies ... tying cunts up.... No time.... Plus, you start that shit and the cunts are going to fight back. No chance they are going to let you just tie them up.... [Anyway YCG member Z] starts thinking he has heard one of the guys saying his name, pure para, fucking para, so [he] fucks this cunt right in the head with the [hatchet].... we had to fucking bail.... left with fuck all [except] an attempted murder wrap on our hands, well on [YCG member Z's] hands. I wasn't taking no derry [blame] for that."

Yet, YCGs also took part in other types of robbery that carried less immediate physical risk and yielded potentially greater profit. Some spoke of regularly stealing vehicles for more established criminal organisations, including other more experienced YCGs and OCGs. The desired vehicles would be identified and then stolen before being brought to 'chop shops' where they would be dismantled, with some parts being sold and other parts being used for existing vehicles that required repair. However, it was also not uncommon for YCGs to simply carry out such activities at an individual level to help improve their own vehicles. Some YCGs, though, move from robbery towards fraud, bribery and blackmail. Steg explains the perceived benefits:

"[I had previously] been in [jail] ... for robbery. One of them was bad, and the guy ended up in hospital. Got out of hand ... didn't like that.... It wasn't worth it.... [I] learn[ed] from [previous experience] ... more money in blackmailing nuggets on the net ... get them to send you the money. It is much easier than taking it."

Steg's statement is in reference to an ongoing criminal operation that he and his friend set up. Following two spells incarcerated for robbery,

Steg learned from his errors and instead began to blackmail individuals, whereby money is extorted from them in return for Steg's silence. Steg and his friend would use his friend's girlfriend to talk on online chatrooms with males and carry out a series of pornographic acts upon herself. The spectators watching these acts would often relieve their sexual frustrations online for her viewing also. Yet, Steg's friend would record this event and, if possible, also store any other personal details that he could. Afterwards, Steg would contact the individuals and threaten to release these explicit pictures online or, if such details were acquired, send them to the victim's family, neighbours, work colleagues and so on. In return for Steg's silence, a fee would be paid by the victim. However, while Steg stated that the material would be destroyed after payment, on occasion, the victim was held to ransom several times over. The financial gains would be split between the group of three. Steg shows criminal learning from his previous errors, adapting his technique to carry less risk and less effort, and yet yield greater profit.

While YSGs primarily engaged in acts of delinquency that occasionally blurred boundaries with criminality, such as gang fighting and occasionally street robbery, YCGs tended to move away from gang fighting altogether but nevertheless refined their techniques and engaged in violence in a much more organised manner, whereby it becomes much more symbolic as opposed to actual. Similarly, while YCGs still engage in robbery, it is refined and becomes much more sophisticated. Robbery also becomes a much more collective activity, whereby planning, organisation and communication are required. Goods are also distributed among members collectively. At this stage, the YCG will also expand their activities and try out, or experiment with, a range of other activities, many of which they had little experience of beforehand. Yet, engaging in drug distribution is the central activity in the formation of YCGs, as we shall see in Chapter 6. Gang structure and gang activity are intertwined, and as the gang becomes a more cohesive unit and the internal dynamics change, allowing individual criminal identity to become part of the collective identity, gang activity changes and becomes more refined and less sporadic. While the other activities are largely predatory crimes, the ability to engage in a market-based crime, such as drug supply, is a central component in allowing organisation to take place and to continue. Yet, this behaviour is still far from being organised crime as there is little effort to control any particular market whether by monopolising power or the products or actors involved. Rather, activity gradually progresses towards organised crime and can thus be termed 'organised efforts of crime'.

OCG behaviour

As gang organisation continues to increase as both a method for, and consequence of, distributing illegal drugs, and occasionally other commodities alongside this such as fake goods (see Bjerregaard, 2010), it becomes ever-more difficult to verify where a YCG, and organised efforts of crime, ends and an OCG, along with organised crime, begins. Indeed, this is indicative of wider gang research and not just problematic in Scotland (Varese, 2001). While YCG activity certainly fits the criteria for 'crime that is organised', YCG members are still far from being 'organised criminals' (see Schelling, 1971). A number of variables differentiate the YCG from the OCG, but the two key features that distinguish one from the other are: (1) the purpose for establishing and maintaining relationships; and (2) that the gang begins to engage in organised crime as opposed to organised efforts of crime or disorganised crime, whereby some form of governance takes place.

Moving towards professionalism

As YCGs progress to become sustainable and durable, and their members become more experienced with crime, some will become OCGs in their own right. On other occasions, the most successful members of one YCG will merge with those of another YCG and form a single OCG. More common, though, is that YCGs will disband or dissolve, for numerous reasons, leaving members with what amounts to the most 'criminal social capital' free to associate with pre-existing OCGs already operating at the higher echelons of the drug supply chain. Often, the reason they dissolve is that the most successful members are absorbed by prior existing OCGs. With this progression along the gang continuum, it was found that while YCGs tend to engage primarily in drug supply (involving a wide range of drug types), as well as a range of other secondary activities, OCGs tended to specialise in one particular criminal activity, usually drug supply, at the expense of other activities that are unrelated (for example, robbery and extortion). Stew, a convicted offender involved in a highly publicised drug seizure, explained:

> *"Was purely the moving of [drugs], nothing else. I had been doing this in one form or another as far back as I can remember.... Got a record for some daft crap when I was a teenager like most [people].... Fights, stealing cars.... I eventually just concentrated on moving*

stuff.... I never sold directly, too risky, no' worth my time. The one time I got involved [directly], I got arrested."

Stew stated that he had always been involved in the supply of drugs to various degrees since what can be assumed as either late childhood or early adolescence. While his teenage years saw him become involved in what he now considers "daft crap", Stew graduated on to concentrate solely on the illegal supply of drugs, at which point, other activities, even retail-level dealing (which necessitates the direct handling of drugs), were "too risky" and no longer "worth [his] time". This proved to be true because the one time Stew handled drugs directly, as an adult in an OCG, he was arrested and subsequently incarcerated. Experience of drug supply and avoiding police detection, as well as the financial profits to be earned via the high-end movement of drugs, were both factors that steered Stew and those he worked alongside to become specialised and focused on one specific activity. Offender Harold expanded on the need for specialisation of criminal skills and activities: "Like anyone who does anything, do it enough and they become an expert. Same wi' us [the OCG]. Bringing [drugs] in[to Britain] takes heavy efforts, you know.... Can't be running fingers in every pie going, just get nowhere."

Harold argued that in order to advance to the higher echelons of organised crime, it is highly advantageous to become specialised in one or two areas, as opposed to having "fingers in every pie". Even then, secondary activities are typically closely related to drug supply (for example, drugs and money laundering). Trying to engage in a wide range of activities would only lead to energy being expended on diffused efforts, consequently resulting in "get[ting] nowhere". Regarding other sources of income during his criminal career at this time, Harold stated:

"The [prosecutors] said I made six-figure sums on a regular basis from 'the illegal supply of narcotics' in the high court. That was bullshit mate.... I had three [legitimate] business. They all brought in good income.... Aye, fair enough, the first property I might have started out [by purchasing] with dough [money] from drug [sales]. After that, but, most, aye most, the cash was [legitimate], honest mate.... Fucking judge was having none of that. They fucking [unfairly brand] people."

Like Harold, most of the participants who could be considered as being involved in OCGs (in accordance with McLean's model versus Police Scotland's definition) blurred the legitimate and illegitimate spheres via the (co-)ownership of businesses. Often, such businesses would be purchased with income secured through illegal activities. However, while participants spoke of desisting from crime to become 'legit' business owners, or knowing of, or having worked with, others who likewise disengaged from gangs to become legit business owners, this was often only the case after several businesses had been purchased or somewhat of a monopolisation of the legal market had been achieved (on security firms, see, for example, McKay, 2006). Yet, greed, declines in financial revenue, 'owing favours' from prior criminal life or attacks from still active rivals more often than not combined to pull people back into criminal activity:

> "Once you're in, you're in. You don't get out of this life that easy.... I tried to leave all that rubbish [organised crime] a few times. I had a good thing going with a couple of tanning salon I bought, well co-owned wi' others.... Enemies get jealous but if they see you doing well.... A few of my premises ended up being vandalised.... I know who fucking did it. Bastards." (Stew, male, offender)

Former offender Dale, who made his initial wealth from drug sales before purchasing and operating a small, yet successful, construction company, added:

> "Cunts [the public and police] might have been saying I was doing this or that [criminal activity].... [But] years went by without me being involved in fuck all man. I wasn't a crook man. I always had wanted to be straight.... My company was doing pure well.... [The economic] recession fucked that.... Still have bills now.... [Eventually,] I got back into the game [criminal activity].... No[t] that I wanted to be. I planned to leave after I got enough money to get me back up and running."

The ideology and realities of involvement in organised crime created a dichotomous position in many of the participants. As for both Stew and Dale, involvement in organised crime was often initially a natural process but always with the end goal of leaving a life of crime and going 'straight'. Yet, involvement in organised crime brought with it rivals, pressure to increase profits and criminal connections, among other things, which would ultimately act as pull factors in hindering any efforts to desist.

The ability to enter the legitimate market at a position that participants considered worthwhile, such as company owners, managers and so on, meant that in addition to acquired criminal knowhow and a criminal skill set, those involved in OCGs were able to become highly specialised in one area of expertise. This primarily involved the movement of drugs, as well as secondary activities to a lesser extent, most often revolving around fraud, tax evasion and manipulation, and money laundering.[4] Yet, while this was the case for participants in this study, participants did speak of other OCGs that specialised primarily in other types of organised crime, with drug supply playing a secondary or even non-existent role:

> "Most of the people I know are in the drugs trade in one way or another. Don't think most people would disagree with that mate. I have known of a few guys that do other stuff, like that's their field mate, get me [speciality].... [One group], right fucking hard bastards from [housing estate in Greater Glasgow], have a heavy rep[utation] man [for sorting] shit [out, with disputes], know.... Like, take care of problem people." (Dale, male, offender)

> "Met a boy that [friend X] introduced me to. Guy seemed sound [nice] enough. No problem.... Then my mate turns round [after we left his company] and says 'That's [name]'. I was like 'Fuck man you might want to have said, 'cause I'm slagging the cunt off and all that [laughs]'.... [The person in question] runs a prostitution ring up [Greater Glasgow area].... rumours his mob are into human trafficking, that shit .... working with [overseas OCG X]." (James, male, offender)

These statements would suggest that regardless of the niche within the given market that OCGs may operate in, it is one in which they are, or make an effort to become, experts. The findings in this study would support current views by academics, the media, the police and the political establishment that in Scotland, the primary form of organised crime pertains to drugs. However, there is some selection bias here, which means that more 'hidden' crimes like human trafficking remain precisely that. Other highly specialised OCGs outside the involvement in illegal drug markets tended to be affiliated with foreign OCGs, while in the Scottish context, the illegal drug market is primarily operated by indigenous OCGs. Moreover, while other types of crimes exist and are carried out by gangs (primarily YCGs), drug supply remains a mainstay largely due to its accessibility, demand and the way in which it is conducive to a businesslike approach.

Governance activities

OCGs largely differ from YCGs in that they engage fully in organised crime. This involves activity pursuing some form of governance over either products, services, criminals, the local population or the wider community. In relation to the illegal drug market, in the given context, there was little effort to control the flow of product. This may be attributed to the fact that the unprecedented rise of the global drug trade in recent decades, and the flow of goods from so many sources being accessible to the wider population even outside traditional criminal networks, has consequently meant that drug supply cannot be stemmed and thus efforts to do so would only prove futile. In addition, given that most OCGs usually deal specifically in one or two drug types at most, the control of drugs as a whole is impossible given that user–supplier connections may, to some extent, be dependent upon drug preference.

OCGs typically sold those drug types deemed to be 'the most profitable'. Interviewees said that other drug types, particularly those not in the Class A or B categories, were generally 'not worth the risk'. Yet, owing to their established reputation within the criminal underworld and influence in the market, they still used established networks to connect distributers and buyers, even outside the products they themselves most associated with:

> *"We take nothing to do with [the sale of other drugs – often from unknown suppliers] ... like, say, I don't know, Mr Jones, [but Mr Jones] has, say, £10,000 worth of E's [ecstasy], I would [say to Mr Jones] 'Hold on mate, I know a guy that might be interested' and then phone [criminal associate], cause that's his field man, he deals with that.... Course I take a cut but for doing that, don't work for fuck all ... and basically making sure [Mr Jones] doesn't get bumped [by the criminal associate]."* (Ewan, male, offender)

Reiterating a point made earlier from Ewan, we see that Ewan's OCG focuses on one or two specific illegal goods, which allows his gang to operate more efficiently and retain a clear trail of thought and action. Diversification resulted in "getting sloppy and fucking up". The fact that Ewan stated, "I take a cut", as opposed to "we take a cut", indicated that while Ewan drew upon the group's reputation in his business, he exploited this reputation to earn profit for himself, which is something well documented in studies of Mafia groups (for example, Gambetta, 1993). This may indicate a change in how group relationships work once they become more entrepreneurial. Ewan demonstrates that as part of a well-established OCG, he is able to exert power and some degree of governance over others, using reputation and criminal capital to do so; thus, he can take a cut and tax others wishing to partake in criminal networks. YCG member Allan likewise discusses how OCGs may still take a more active role in offering criminal opportunities to others – for a fee of course:

> "[When] we done [robbed] [OCG A's] stash over at the flats [in Glasgow area A], we got about a kilo in Chico [already cut cocaine], I would say so. Aye, think about that. Probably just over to be honest, [be]cause some was already bagged to go…. I got [paid] about eight G [£8,000] for that hit. Same wi' the [other YCG members], more or less, aye. It was worth more but we had to punt it on fast [for an associate to sell]…. I kept the weed I took, wee [YCG member A] took the speed we got off [victim A]…. think there was around £13,000 [in cash]. That went to [OCG B] … [because] that's [YCG member A's] brother, well step-brother [a member of OCG B]. Was him that tipped us off."

While, for Ewan, such taxing was opportunistic, according to Allan, other OCGs take a more direct role in connecting criminals to potential crimes. Yet, still other OCGs exerted a more direct influence, and consequently taxation, upon those criminal networks within their domain, as offender Shuggie explains:

> "[If crimes for profit take place] in my old [scheme], then we [OCG A] need to get paid first. I don't like everyone doing anything …. We never bother with wee guys, scheme jumpers, know what I mean…. [But if] like [highly profitable crimes], or like it's ongoing … then we need to get paid … simple as, [or] it does happen."

While Ewan used his OCG membership as a mechanism for exerting power and governance via reputation and established criminal connections, Shuggie and his OCG used direct intimidation and an ability to instil fear in the community to govern the physical territory that they are most affiliated with. Yet, while Shuggie taxes other criminals involved in highly profitable crimes, other OCGs use their ability to instil fear in the community to employ coercion tactics and thus govern not only criminal, but also legitimate, aspects of local life. This may involve 'pressuring' vulnerable individuals to store drugs, money or goods in safe houses. Yet, it may also involve buying people off, with fear of retaliation for refusal of the bribe, in order to employ official members of the political establishment to work for them, such as housing officers, concierge officers and employees of local councils. Fear (of the OCG), being socially excluded or marginalised, and even having grown up alongside OCG members[5] all play a part in this process. As offender Andrew states:

"You can always get someone to [store the drugs] for you. Better having them close [as well]. Just on the off chance. Plenty of cunts owe money ... [and] need that wee extra bit of [income], you getting me?... [Those that don't] are better to take the [money] than not [doing so]."

Bourdieu terms this as a 'conservation strategy' aimed at retaining the benefits of power and privilege (Swartz, 1997). Having reached the apex of local (criminal) power and retaining intimate personal knowledge of local relationships and criminal networks, OCGs are now in the position of defining, or redefining, the rules of the social field in which they operate to their advantage. In this way, they begin to acquire authority and to govern a given territory, most often that with which they are most strongly affiliated, usually stemming back to their time in YSGs. To maintain their privilege, the OCG will ensure a covert presence supported by clear lines of intelligence and information. Adapted rules will be learnt quickly by the local community, who may witness sanctions taken out against those who infringe the new rules of the social field, or who may benefit by largesse, favours and gifting. An OCG's reputation could also be enhanced by demonstrating their influence over the territory or environment (for example, opening new bars, shops or premises, owning multiple properties, and so on), thus 'making it theirs'. By investing capital acquired via crime into legitimate, localised businesses, criminals secure 'legitimate' reputations as 'businessmen' and 'not thugs'.

Overall, OCGs differ from YCGs primarily in that the purpose for the relationship undergoes a drastic change in that membership is based upon what the individual can offer other gang members as opposed to being based upon pre-existing socially rooted friendships. This means that the gang has now become a means to support the individual, and, as such, the gang is the mechanism used to achieve individual ambition. Thus, membership is based upon what the individual can get from being part of the gang. This economic objective allows the gang to undergo greater organisation in that the activities of the gang are now solely aimed at acquiring profit for the individuals involved. This means that the gang now moves from engaging in organised efforts of crime to partaking in organised crime. It is typically only those reputable criminals who are 'business-minded' and have a 'level head' that can operate in successful OCGs, although the odd 'crazy' individual is by no means uncommon. Consequently, to help achieve their objectives, OCGs generally cease taking part in high-risk activities, and predatory crimes altogether if possible. Rather, market-based activities are preferred. This is because these activities offer steady income and little need for continual planning and improvisation. In the contemporary era, drug supply is the most profitable crime meeting this criterion, although other counterfeit commodities may often also be distributed. To maximise profits, OCGs will become experts in certain drug types and have extensive knowledge of their given market. In many ways, they are almost professionals in that they know their product and market. This dedication and time is also another factor for seeing a reduction in other crimes. Coinciding with these market-based crimes, though, is the need to conceal finances, which often means that there is a need for money laundering. Consequently, OCGs purchase and operate legitimate businesses, in some cases, very successfully.

When OCGs take part in predatory crimes, and other riskier crimes, this is often indirect and the result of acting as a middleman in connecting other criminals to relevant and well-suited criminal opportunities, or taxing criminals operating in their area. No set rate of tax was identified in this study; rather, the rate set was often dependent upon what the OCG could get away with, which, of course, varied from criminal to criminal. This means that income comes not only through their own crimes, but also through governance over others, which is a process that often penetrates legitimate society.

Chapter summary

This chapter has presented a largely descriptive account of the behaviours that the various gang types identified engage in at their relevant stages of development. The chapter has explored how, during the early stage of gang development, most acts committed by YSGs that are assumed to be problematic are largely delinquent as opposed to criminal. This is because the gang is large, and membership is assigned to youths as part of scheme socialisation. Yet, some YSG behaviour can blur the sphere of criminality. When this happens, more often than not this revolves around violence (most frequently, gang fights, occasionally involving knives) and robbery. The majority and most severe of these acts are generally carried out by core members. The chapter then explored how as YSG members mature, most fall by the wayside, leaving only the core.

It would seem that strain impacts quite significantly upon these youths in particular, who already retain certain personal traits and characteristics favourable to delinquent behaviour and are likewise exposed to certain environmental circumstances, and begin developing and refining those coping strategies that are likely to be associated with criminality in subsequent years (Agnew et al, 2008). Criminal identities are ones that are reinforced not only by the self, but also by wider society by way of reputation and criminal records (De Coster and Heimer, 2001). For the core membership, the criminal identity often means that individuals either cannot enter the legitimate world of work (or find great difficulty in attempting to do so) or, at times, are not willing to. Rather, in response to growing strains placed upon the individual and the group as a whole, members solidify. Cohesion increases and the criminal identity that is innate to all now transcends the individual and becomes part of the group's identity as a whole. While group relationships are still primarily social in their purpose, individuals – now young adults (legally if nothing else) – respond to the need for finances through the resources most readily at their disposal. For those with access to prior existing criminal networks, drug supply is found to be a profitable activity. The YCG now partakes in what can be deemed organised efforts of crime, although still a far cry from being outright organised crime. Yet, involvement in the drug trade, alongside a prior reputation and criminal connections, means that YCGs will be given the opportunity to partake in other criminal ventures. These range significantly from bribery to motor theft and extortion. YCGs also refine those other previous criminal activities that they once engaged in as YSG members to greater effect. Consequently, violence becomes symbolic as part of debt collection and robbery becomes organised.

For those YCGs that manage to avoid detection, withstand the strain placed on them from rival outfits and retain a degree of self-control over their hyper-masculine nature, the possibility to progress further towards becoming an OCG beckons. OCGs become highly specialised, although much of this generally revolves around the drug trade to one degree or another. Yet, OCGs will also begin to enter the legitimate sphere as they purchase, rent and co-own (or often own via other legit members of society) businesses and premises. OCGs engage in organised crime and exert power over their sphere of influence, yet this is not confined to criminals alone, but also involves legitimate members of society. Having now outlined a descriptive account of the range of activities that gang types generally become involved in at their relevant stage of development, Chapter 6 will look more specifically at the interplay between context, structure and agency. This will be in relation to drug supply given that all participants in the research had been involved in the drug trade to some extent at one time or another, and that it was the key variable in gang organisation as persistent offenders move along criminal trajectories.

Notes

[1]   Shaun is making reference here not to adult nightclubbers but rather the 'unders', which is where popular nightclubs open their door early, typically from 4 pm to

10 pm, and allow individuals who are under 18 years of age to enter for a small fee in order to socialise, meet members of the opposite sex and listen to music. Yet, no alcohol is sold at these venues, although youths typically got drunk before leaving their schemes.

[2]   See Van der Rakt et al (2008).

[3]   An individual may blur membership between two YCGs, or even in some cases more, for various reasons. However, the more common reasons may include the fact that the individual had previous experience with and membership of several YSGs while growing up (perhaps due to moving residency, relocation, moving school or having separated parents with homes in two different locations).

[4]   Having legitimate premises also played an important role in helping account for otherwise unaccountable sources of revenue.

[5]   While many local to the OCG members in question may fear the OCG, they also nonetheless usually feel some sense of security from them, and loyalty to them, having been raised alongside them from youth in the local housing estate. Even though OCGs do not confine their criminal operations to the local estate, they often nonetheless still strongly affiliate with these areas as they have strong ties to and a shared history with them, and often even live close by if they relocate.

6

Gangs and Drug Supply

Before proceeding with the aims, purpose and intent of this chapter, it is perhaps important to briefly recap on the developments of Part III of the book as a whole so far. Chapter 4 began by proposing a gang typology, previously outlined in a succinct way in Chapter 3, which most accurately reflected the majority of, although by no means all, gangs operating in Scotland's criminal markets, particularly the illegal drug market. Gang typology was conceptualised as existing on an evolving continuum, whereby gang organisation occurs as a response to/means for gang business. Three stages were identified and explored that accurately reflect key points of evolutionary transition. Chapter 4 focused significantly on structure as opposed to activity or descriptive context. Chapter 5 then made largely a descriptive effort to outline and encompass those behavioural aspects that gang types tend to participate in the most. The chapter concluded, in summary, by identifying that YSGs were largely delinquent in behaviour, and when criminality occurred, it could largely be attributed to core members or persistent offenders. YCGs' behaviour ranged considerably and was criminal as opposed to delinquent. OCGs, however, drew upon previous experience, knowledge, connections and so on to become specialised in one criminal arena, although some overlaps existed in other areas. Regarding other criminal activity, OCGs were involved indirectly, often via illegal forms of governance.

Yet, a consistent theme is that despite differences, all gang types were involved in and around drug supply. Likewise, drug supply has been identified as the main form of organised crime in Scotland (Scottish Government, 2015), and the one the public are most concerned about (Scottish Government, 2013). Around 70 per cent of organised crime in Scotland has been identified as taking place in and around the Glasgow conurbation, with 65 per cent of this activity being directly related to drug supply, as well as other types of activity often a consequence of drug supply itself, that is, money laundering, debt collection, illegal businesses, firearm crimes and so on. The growing illegal drug market has coincided with responses in gang organisation. One tends to feed off the other and they are deeply intertwined. Therefore, given the key role that drug supply plays in gang organisation and the importance that the public and political institutions alike attribute to the activity, this chapter shall now focus on drug supply and how it is the key factor in aiding gang organisation and gang proliferation – although it should be noted that while the key and most consistent factor, it is by no means the only one. Thus, this chapter will retain the same structure as the previous chapters in Part III by examining the topic (drug supply) within the presented typology in a chronological manner. The chapter will go beyond a descriptive account and look more specifically at the development of gang organisation and the interplay between activity, structure and context, which may be particularly useful to practitioners and insightful for academics. A summary will conclude the chapter.

The first main section will look at YSGs and how core and peripheral members engage in drug dealing and drug use, as well as how the YSG responds to those outside the gang who also operate within the gang's vicinity. The next section will then look more in-depth at YCGs and how certain members of YSGs, and occasionally rogue/solo dealers, become intertwined with one another and engage in the distribution of drugs at low to mid-wholesale level. The chapter will also look at how the gangs at this stage of development respond to other dealers in their operational proximity. The final section will look at OCGs and how they engage in the distribution of drugs. Yet, it is perhaps first of all important to open up with a general discussion of Scotland's illegal drug market, and, in doing so, to explore some of the changes that have occurred, in order to help the reader get a better understanding of the supply process and move away from all too often imposed stereotypes.

Illegal drug market(s) in contemporary Scotland

Nowadays, illicit drugs are big business and, consequently, an even bigger public health problem, yet research on the 'realities' of drug markets is surprisingly thin (Antonopoulos and Papanicolaou, 2010: 3). This is especially true in Scotland, which has been identified as having a disproportionately high drug problem when compared to the rest of the UK (Scottish Parliament, 2017). Taken as a whole, drug harms are thought to cost the country's economy approximately £3.5 billion annually (Casey et al, 2009). In addition, drug supply has been identified as the main form of organised crime in the country, with other organised crime categories typically linked to it directly and indirectly (Scottish Government, 2015, 2016).

Studies seeking to conceptualise the country's illegal drug market as a whole have been few and far between, often being either neglected/overlooked by drug scholars or subsumed under studies of UK-wide drug markets (for example, Matrix Knowledge Group, 2007). Yet, when such studies have emerged (see Preble and Casey, 1969; Coope and Bland, 2004; May and Hough, 2004; Cyster and Rowe, 2006; McLean et al, 2018), similar to those within the wider UK context, they tend to adopt one of two models. The hierarchy model (see Figure 4) compartmentalises supply into distinct international (importation), national/regional (wholesale or middle market) and local (retail) levels (for example, Pearson and Hobbs, 2001). Local retail markets are further differentiated as open, semi-open (for example, pubs and clubs) or closed markets.

Yet, McPhee et al (2009) note that while hierarchical models are found to be the most applicable to the Scottish drug market, there is a distinct lack of empirical evidence for such assumptions. The second model type is therefore one that is perceived as highly differentiated, with no unified market, but rather a series of loosely interlinked local and regional markets (Coomber, 2006). Ultimately, though, Scotland, and Britain more generally, is an end user of drugs, with the exception of cannabis, which is imported in some cases and produced locally in others. As Delph and William outline: "[Imported cannabis is] brought up from London. My guy says it comes [into Scotland] from when we pick up … at [particular service point midway]" (Delph, male, offender); "Cannabis is just grown in [homemade] factories [throughout Scotland]. Fuck, everyone going has a grow, even if it's [only for] their [personal use]" (William, male, offender).

The saturation and normalisation of use and cultivating techniques have arguably contributed to changes in the cannabis market (see also

Figure 4: Hierarchy model

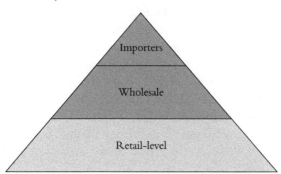

Silverstone, 2011; Silverstone and Savage, 2010). However, consistent with United Nations Office on Drugs and Crime (UNODC, 2016) data, interviewees said that other drugs, such as heroin, come to Britain predominantly by land routes from opium fields in Afghanistan, via Turkey and the Balkans; or by sea via boat from Pakistan. Cocaine likewise came in by sea routes, going through South America via Jamaica, North Africa and Spain. Ecstasy and other synthetics were often transported from The Netherlands (SOCA, 2009). Yet, international importation into Scotland was uncommon, with typical points of entry coming from England or Northern Ireland. Thus, this contrasts with the hierarchical model suggesting importers to be at the apex of local drug markets. As Sean explained: "Not everyone can import stuff.… [When this occurs, importers] sell large to a few guys who [then] move it on to people who sell it in smaller bulks … not everyone buy[s] the same amount. Depends [on circumstances]." Rather, in Scotland, large wholesale distributors were thought to have greater sway over the illegal drug market. As Sean continues: 'High-end drug distribut[ors] basically control the market. [Lower dealers] work for them, [but] no[t] always directly. Most don't even know [who supplies them]."

Overall, though, studies have identified that while the majority of drugs in Britain are distributed/sold by non-gang-affiliated dealers who often supply socially, working within friendship networks (Parker et al, 1998) or by 'going solo' (Hales and Hobbs, 2010; Windle and Briggs, 2015), commercially motivated 'real dealers' (Stevenson, 2008) and those who operate, or seek to operate, beyond retail-level supply are significantly more likely to be organised into 'criminal structures' (Von Lampe, 2016), which are partially sustained via kinship and ethnicity (Pearson and Hobbs, 2001), and/or criminal drugs gangs for whom illicit enterprise is integral to collective identity (Densley, 2014; Densley et al, 2018a, 2018b; McLean et al, 2018). Exploring drug markets in several Scottish case-study areas, Cyster and Rowe (2006) found heroin to be so widely available and geographically widespread that conventional wisdom about illicit drug markets required substantial revisiting and overhaul. To this end, McLean et al (2018) and Densley et al (2018a) sought to shed light on the role gangs play in drug distribution and the changing nature of the illegal drug market itself. Both studies found that traditional supply processes have changed dramatically in recent years due to a number of factors, including: the increase in digitalisation; the rise of the dark net; and other technological advances. The internet not only enabled respondents to source drugs from further afield than was possible in years past, but also fed consumer demand for new illicit products now flooding the market:

"Too much risk in dealing heroin [in contemporary Scotland].... [People] aren't interested in being junk balls now. Everybody [wants to] look pristine, hitting the gym. People are selling steroids and melan-o-tan more than ching [cocaine] now.... I go online. You could type it into Google shopping right now and it will come up. I order it ... [and receive] it about three days [later].... [Ste]roids are good sellers, [if] you [know what you] are looking for. Tanning injections as well. Girls buy them.... I could sell more tanning injections in a week than [cannabis]. If [I] get caught, it's a fucking slap on the wrist, whereas heroin, you're talking serious jail time." (William, male, offender)

Patterns of globalisation have enabled greater diversification in both drug types and routes to access, which has consequently also increased the role that gangs have come to play in distribution and supply chains, not only in Scotland, but also in Britain, Europe, the US and other continents (Alonso, 2004; Harding, 2014). Gangs have evolved to not necessarily control drug markets per se, but rather facilitate supply within, and benefit from territorial control and governance of a marketplace when doing so (see also McLean, 2018a; McLean et al, 2018; Robinson et al, 2018).

YSGs: the blur between drug use and supply

YSGs and drug consumption

Having briefly outlined some of the challenges faced in relation to both uncovering intimate supply processes and the evolving nature of Scotland's illegal drug market, we now turn to analysing the role that gangs have increasingly come to play in such activities. All participants in the study were found to have been involved in drug supply, directly and indirectly, at various points in their criminal careers. Yet, this did not mean that drug supply could be termed organised crime in all cases. In reality, supply is far from black and white and, like gangs, also exists on a shifting continuum. Despite drugs being very much a consistent feature of the YSG 'scene', the role that YSGs had in relation to supply itself was far from organised. Given that YSGs have been identified as the consequential result of various combining factors, including street socialisation, external/internal tension and local narratives, it is recognised that they are primarily recreational, age-relevant outfits for whom delinquency, as opposed to criminality, is a potential outcome, and not a given. This means that they have no identifiable structure, leadership or division of labour. Rather, the only identifiable structural feature they retain is that they predominantly comprise a core body and outer layer. For this reason, it is first important to consider the role that drugs play in relation to the YSG as a whole before then exploring each unit independently of one another.

Drugs do play an important part in YSGs, and while not all members consume them, they nonetheless often equally feel their effects in other ways. As with a substantial body of work on drug taking and alcohol consumption more generally, this research similarly found that during early to mid-adolescence, the risk of consuming drugs and alcohol increased quite significantly. As delinquency is a regular outcome of YSG formation, the role that drugs, and alcohol alike, often play can be quite significant. Regarding alcohol consumption, participants Stacey and Brain reflect upon their time socialising in, and with, YSGs:

> "I [recall getting drunk probably] every weekend, maybe every second weekend. [Myself and friends] would always [purchase the alcohol drink] Merriedown. Silver or gold [label]! I preferred the gold. [However,] as [we had to ask] people [of legal age] to go in [to the shops and purchase drink] for [us], [we] never knew what [we] would get. We took bets on it. Who would get what. Not for money, for fun." (Stacey, female, offender)

> "[People are] more likely to get in trouble at the weekend weren't [they? Because they're] steaming, mad wi' it [intoxicated]. Think you're pure untouchable and heavy brazen as fuck aye. End up punching dafties, know. End up in tussles [fights]." (Brain, male, offender)

Both participants highlight the role that alcohol regularly plays in socialising during this turbulent age. Both highlight consumption to occur most frequently at weekends and often in specific locations. It is assumed that this is largely tied to the fact that school, and most forms of employment, take place throughout the week. This allows for a sufficient recovery period from any consequential 'hangovers'. Likewise, in a number of cases, parental figures would also be intoxicated at weekends, allowing for a decrease in supervision, thus making it easier for youths to consume alcohol without being caught.

Drug use, however, differed slightly, with consumption being dependent upon a number of factors, including time, drug type, drug need, socialising patterns and so on. Like alcohol, Ecstasy, and other associated 'dance drugs', were most likely to be consumed at weekends.[1] Cannabis – 'hash', 'weed', 'grass' or 'skunk' – like buzzing gas, was found to be consumed on a more consistent basis, often occurring throughout the week. Other drugs may blur both spheres though. For example, some participants discussed consuming prescription drugs such as valium during the week, while others would only take valium or 'jellies' at weekends, often in conjunction with alcohol. Addicted, recovering or recovered drug addicts – typically heroin addicts – mentioned how valium was good for 'self-medicating', easing waiting or recovery periods. Speed was perceived as being good for weekend partygoers but also those who simply had busy work schedules. As Henderson, Jay and Gavin explain:

> "[Myself and friends would] pop [take] eccies. They are cheaper. If [we are] heading into town and want a good time on the cheap, then eccies are good. [They] get you fucking buzzing ... [and] feeling on top.... [I] never [consum]ed during the week [be]cause of the come down. Fucking make [me] want to kill [myself] if [I] had work the next day. Tried it once ... never again." (Henderson, male, offender)

> "E's and speed, all the same shit ... for the [clubbing scene].... Cunts do take speed to get up and out. I know some [people] ... mostly housewives pure stressing wi' the wains and running about hunners' [laughs] [that do this]. [I] smoke grass most days ... can't function if I don't do it every day. Buzz[ing] [gas] ... was great but fucks you right up mate. Can die from it. It is pure dodgy." (Jay, male, offender)

> "I did [regularly] take jellies [when] ... getting steaming up [park A]. A couple of jellies afterwards and [I would be] fleeing [feeling good].... I take them [at present] as they help me [self-medicate] my [heroin] addiction.... I don't like them now." (Gavin, male, offender)

As youths' drugs were perceived as playing a particular role, and to be consumed at set times and often in set locations, such consumption practices inevitably changed over time. Various factors, such as increasing levels of stress, drug addiction, social position, employment status, peer socialisation and so on, all impacted upon the changing nature of consumption. While some drugs were to be consumed at weekends, others, like cannabis, played a much more consistent role in the lives of individuals. As youths, participants' drug choice was also often limited due to issues such as accessibility, regularity, financial constraints, peer acceptance/exclusion and so on. This meant that drugs like ketamine, meow-meow, crack, heroin and cocaine were almost exclusively for, and available to, adults. However, it is important to note that while participants called upon their own consumption patterns, most did not take drugs with any great deal of frequency during this period. Rather, most consumption was experimental. Furthermore, participants discussed how during early to mid-adolescence, most of their peers, and more so those outside the YSG, did not consume drugs either experimentally or at all. At this stage, drugs, and alcohol alike, are a key feature of YSG formation and subsequent activity in that youths socialise and have camaraderie with one another around such substances, and that ensuing delinquency and violence may also be a direct result of such consumption.

YSGs and the social supply of drugs

Drug supply among YSGs members is very much akin to what Coomber and Moyle (2014) term 'social supply'. This is where the line between drug user and drug supplier becomes significantly blurred. This is because drugs are shared, traded and sold for finances and other commodities without any degree of predictable consistency or organisation. Likewise, the motives and reasons for social supply may differ significantly from those that engage in 'drug dealing proper'. Drugs are generally procured from retail-level, solo and (other) social supply dealers by YSG members, to be consumed and redistributed for social purposes. McLean (2017) found that the social supply of drugs was by no means limited only to gang members,[2] but rather a wide variety of youths could, and did, engage in such activity within their respective communities, and even within YSGs, both core or outer layer members alike engaged in social supply:

> "Anyone can sell [drugs]. I know loads a gadgies [people] that sell drugs to their close mates. Trade them know, like sharing. Mates rates, ken. [Most of these suppliers] can't go big time or nothing like, but don't take much to walk round corner to your dealer and get [drug type] to share wi' mates." (Svenson, male, offender)

> "My nana [grandparent] use to get high as a kite. Her and her old mates [A and B] would get stoned to fuck on Tuesdays. Like they pencilled it into their diaries [laughs]. Don't know if that makes her a dealer [laughs]." (Tammy, female, offender)

As Svenson and Tammy state, low-level dealing was typically social dealing, where drug use was seen as being a social event. Yet, where YSG members sold drugs with any degree of regularity, more often than not, it was core members who did so. This was because core members had established pre-existing access to criminal networks of drug supply and thus 'never ran out' and were 'always in business'. This steady access meant that they quickly built reputations as 'go–to guys' for drug procurement among fellow gang members, associates and other local youths. Practitioner Clair explains drug supply within YSGs:

> "[Local youths] usually get their drugs from one or two of the [YSG core] members … [who, in turn,] get them from their family … or the families of their best friends. You know, the ones they are always with. It is difficult to get them to stop this behaviour. [It is] easy money and [steady access to] cheap drugs. You give that to most 15-year-olds, from anywhere, and they would snap it up. Even more so when it's normal[ised in] their own households."

Clair concurs that because core members often have steady access to established networks, often facilitated by close kinship, this allows drugs to be purchased at a cheaper rate, which, in turn, can be passed on to the customer. This gives considerable strategic advantage over other would-be dealers. In addition, as differential association enables this behaviour to become somewhat normalised, and consistent profits are good (in relation to age), such behaviour becomes difficult to eradicate in later life. However, YSG core members do not have the mental capability, experience, physical stature or maturity to oversee successful, ongoing drug operations (see Hagedorn, 1994; Densley, 2012). Thus, while some degree of consistency exists, supply is still at this stage sporadic, unplanned and often carried out for the purpose of covering their own drug habit and expenses, or to provide income when needed. As Steg explains:

> "Most [individuals] start [off by] selling a bit of weed. I started with [selling] val[ium] [be]cause I could get from my bro[ther], who was [a heroin addict and] he sold val[ium] anyways. I got them and used to [distribute them] among the troops [YSG] … for laughs really…. Suppose it gave me a bit of a reputation. I liked that. Wasn't 'till I was older I thought about [selling drugs] for a living."

While drug supply occurring within YSGs is primarily in the form of social supply, as opposed to drug dealing proper (Coomber and Turnbull, 2007; Coomber and Moyle, 2014; Moyle and Coomber, 2016), it provided the gateway for criminal progression. If left unchecked, typically core members may progress towards more serious forms of drug supply, which is a process that would lay the foundation for evolvement into a more cohesive criminal gang. McPhee (2013) notes that if allowed to do so, and resources are available, those who have been involved in social supply are more likely to engage in drug dealing proper in the future. Matthew, who had been involved in social supply, reflects upon his progression towards drug dealing proper:

> "[Progressed] from [sharing drugs with friends]. [I] was getting nine bars [a large weight of cannabis] quite a bit at the time from [relative]. He was giving me them. Well, no' giving me them. [I] had to pay, course, but was getting me [nine bars] if I asked. On tick [credit] … [a lot of] my mates had left school and had jobs, so had money to get ounces, whatever, aye. I [began selling] them [cannabis in larger quantities].… Wouldn't say [the progression] was intentional. More, I could get it and they wanted it. I needed the money."

Matthew's story epitomised the way in which most participants began selling drugs. With access to extensive friendship networks facilitated by YSG membership, Matthew was able to utilise to best effect those pre-existing criminal contacts. As such contacts were kinship, they would be lenient with Matthew and aid/facilitate his ambition and opportunity to sell drugs at a decent level. At this stage, the gang is used not so much as a cohesive vehicle for aiding and supporting dealers, but rather as an established network facilitator for accessing (potential) customers. Yet, YSG membership could be exploited further in some cases. Ben, now a low to mid-wholesale distributor, outlines how he utilised gang connections to stop other upcoming dealers during his days as a YSG member, which is a tactic that he still deploys whenever feasible:

> "[I didn't] make loads of paper [money]. Couple of hundred a week more or less… [But] I didn't have much growing up … [so] every penny was a prisoner mate. It made a difference to me at that age [16] … the way I seen it was they were taking my money. Well, what would have been coming my way [had I been the only dealer on the estate]. I have never been the biggest. Heavy fierce [though]. [In addition,] I had my [YSG members] as [well].… [Even today,] if I see [anyone] trying to take a piece of my pie, in my district, I tell them 'Get to fuck', 'You'll get fucking done.' [They] might be young now [but] they aren't young forever. I pick what wee guys are selling, and who isn't. Need to show who's boss. There are [people] above me, am above them."

It was not uncommon for a variety of youths, YSG members and other segments of the local population to all engage in various aspects of social supply. Drugs could be peddled for various types of profit, reputation, status and reasons. Yet, core YSG members were found to have significant advantages that they regularly exploited. This only further embedded potential criminal trajectories. As with any business model, customers like cheap and reliable sources of supply, which are best facilitated by core members. Supply was very much individual, although the close bonds that would aid gang organisation can be seen as being put into place here, whereby close friends and kinship networks are brought into the fold, while simultaneously excluding others. This is further facilitated by the fact that some YSG members, like Ben, discuss how they began to monopolise supply within their community at their relevant age group, which is something that was supported by gang affiliation. These factors would sow the seeds for gang organisation and increased involvement in drug supply networks as youths entered mid- to late adolescence and early adulthood.

YCGs and drug dealing proper

Bringing together commercially motivated 'real dealers' via gang organisation

While drug supply within YSGs was primarily in the form of social supply, it was by no means an activity confined to core members alone. Yet, as core members had pre-existing access to established supply networks, as well as the support of esteemed peers and criminally renowned kinship, they had significant advantages to progress upwards within the illegal drug market more rapidly and with less hurdles to overcome. As we saw in Chapter 4, as these members aged, they, like their peers, faced increasing sources of tension and external/internal threats and pressures. Aided by natural physical and mental maturity, and coupled with a delinquent identity (within themselves and among peers who also favoured law violation), they were much more likely to utilise existing resources to engage in greater levels of criminal behaviour in order to further their own position, status and situation. This was further aided by years of being labelled, and known, as a criminal and often an 'official' criminal title by acquiring a criminal record, typically through YSG–related violence.

Criminal behaviour would continue to progress and become even more refined with gained experience, secured sources of revenue and widening networks. For many participants, the normalisation of drug use extended to the normalisation of drug supply (see Chatwin and Potter, 2014) regarding the basic principles behind drug use, social supply and drug dealing proper:

"They want [the drug in question]. They are going to get it whether I do it [sell] or don't do it, so why no[t] do it. Everyone I know does it [consumes the drug]. I [used to socially supply] it when I was taking … [so] it's really the same thing [now that I sell it]." (Micky, male, offender)

As Micky states, the logic behind moving from a social supplier or user to drug dealer proper is natural in its progression, particularly when any obstacle stops alternative (legitimate) pathways being taken or explored. As with any activity at this stage, while supply is, and arguably always has been, driven by individual motivation, circumstances and identity, to a degree, core members are already plugged into existing 'associational criminal structures' (see Von Lampe, 2016). These structures exist in a very loose manner at this time and are accessed via kinship or the kinship of close friends. Yet, now moving beyond mid-adolescence, and with increased tension, commitments and resources, individuals bind tighter to like-minded peers with whom they already have a prior extensive history as YSG core members. Disproportionate association within this close-knit, inward-looking group means that as gang organisation occurs, it does so as a means to engage more deeply in gang business (see Chapter 4). Although overlooked in the Scottish context (McLean, 2018a), English scholars have firmly established links between youth gangs and organised crime in the English/Welsh context (for example, Pitts, 2008; Densley, 2012, 2013). Likewise, the National Crime Agency (NCA, 2013: 9) also recognises that 'areas high [in] gang activity … tend to be areas where organised criminals are most active'. These links are found to be true in this research as one is often facilitated by the other. Combining access to prior criminal networks with gang formation involved in drug supply, Gregory states: "[My dad] didn't want me doing what he did. He used to say that. [It was him though that] gave me a couple of gram first. Said 'Sell it, get yourself off your arse'. I think he thought fuck it. Took it to [my friends and] we sold it."

As Gregory illustrates, by capitalising on 'criminal learning and criminal association' (for example, Sutherland, 1939), he was able, and wilfully encouraged – despite contradictory utterances adhering to mainstream value systems – to sell drugs as a way to help him 'get off his arse' and be able to stand on his own feet financially. Gregory then turned to his closest friends, who had prior knowledge of selling drugs, and they together engaged in drug dealing proper. While this potentially reduced his own profit, Gregory recognised that by finding support in his friends, he was able to utilise to best effect their collective criminal know-how and sell the drugs quickly, which enabled the profits to go to purchase a greater quantity of cocaine for future sales. The potential reduction in individual profit is something that many participants had to weigh up when considering gang organisation. Yet, the need for support, in the form of peers and kinship, was something that was 'not an option' given the risks involved in ever-progressive involvement in drug supply:

Evens: "[It is more effective] working with mates. [Dealing individually] can be pure hassle. More likely to get [robbed].... We [friends from the YSG core body] had always ... [been] thick as mud [shared close relationships] ... can trust the boys. [Working] together is easier."

Interviewer: "Can you explain how it is easier [to work in groups]?"

Evens: "Aye, it's like, if you pure fuck up a payment, [for example, be]cause sometimes you end up snorting half the gear on a weekend binge, getting the hookers round and having a coke party [laughs]. [Then] you still need to pay for what you've [been] given. If your mates have your back, [however], then they can [assist financially]. [I'd] do the same for them. Everybody fucks up now and then ... selling and having an addiction can be a bad recipe."

By working together, Evens' YCG reduced the chances of 'fucking up', for example, by being robbed, attacked, 'bumped', 'conned out' of goods, consuming all the goods or missing payments. In addition, working in gangs enabled collective resources to be pulled together, and safety nets for 'rainy days' to be set up. As Evens found out, working with trusted peers who are similarly criminally inclined has significant benefits, and more so when drug suppliers are simultaneously drug users.[3] Supplier–user overlaps often affected the ability of a gang to evolve along the gang continuum. For example, YCG relationships centre on social aspects first, and economic aspects second, meaning that relapses in drug addiction prompted other group members to use their accumulated wealth to pay for their friends' habit and debts. Interestingly, interviewed OCG members acknowledged that although, at one time, they too felt a moral obligation to their peers, once evolved, economic goals gradually took precedence over social ties. Thus, they were no longer obliged to 'bail out' other members when they 'fucked up', with responsibility being seen as the individual's rather than the gang's.

Further defining a YCG: retail-level and wholesale dealing

Efforts to gauge precise definitions of market levels, and wherein dealers are situated, have been a difficult task for scholarly researchers, to say the least. As models of the country's illegal drug market are conceptual representations, levels within are by no means an exact science or a precise tool for measurement. It is helpful to perceive OCGs as operating at the apex of the illegal drug market. While there are two primary illegal drug market models, in reality, OCGs operate a hybrid system that blurs both. This is because they generally have well-established trafficking routes of their own, and are therefore importers, as well as purchasing drugs in considerable bulk – more so in the case of Scotland – from other UK-based OCGs. While OCGs are to be considered apex-level distributors, YCGs are thought of as operating within the middle-market niche, connecting top to bottom. In the middle market, YCGs operate primarily as wholesalers, as well as often taking on a number of simultaneous lesser roles, such as runners, high-end retail-level distributors or acting as 'faces' (see Pearson and Hobbs, 2001). YSGs, like most dealer typologies, operate within the retail-level and social-level dealerships. While each typology has key structural distinctions (which we explored earlier), there are also a number of behaviour distinctions with regard to how gangs operate, and where they are situated within the illegal drug market.

However, while we can identify that YCGs primarily operate within wholesale-level drug distribution, exactly what wholesaling looks like, and detailing the precise functions within, can be difficult for several reasons. Four of the main difficulties in constructing a unified categorisation of behaviour in the illegal drug market are that: (1) as YCGs mature, they often merge with other YCGs, or specific individuals, and considerable periods emerge in this process where there is a crossover of activities as two gangs become one, or certain individuals are incorporated into existing gang structures; (2) given that wholesaling is situated between retail-level dealerships and importing, while one YCG may blur the boundaries of the former, another YCG may blur the boundaries of the latter, with other YCGs only concerning themselves with wholesaling in its purest form; (3) market levels change with regard to drug type sold, and while YCGs in their early development are more opportunistic and sell "whatever comes [their] way",[4] more developed YCGs gravitate towards being 'specialists' in one or two areas; and (4) where exactly a YCG operates within wholesale practices, when compared with another YCG, is largely subjective. This means that the response given by interviewees will often depend on who is being asked, their own position within the gang, their own knowledge of other suppliers/market levels, the drug types that they distribute and the efforts they may deploy to either conceal or enhance their activities (see Pearson and Hobbs, 2001). Evens details the difficulties in gauging the precise levels at which a YCG may operate when compared with another:

> "[I] wouldn't say [my YCG] were big. We were well known ... brought in a couple of G [£2,000] from sales ... [earnings varied for] drop offs.... Moving [heroin] brought [good income]: £10,000–£20,000 for each bulk shift[ed]. We didn't sell it ourselves. Fuck that. Been there, done that. Would [sell] to [others] to do that. [If] we earned £10,000, it's no[t] as though you get that yourself. [It] get[s] [divided] up [with members].... Am sure there are boys out there earning much more, but anyone we worked with never earned the kind of money [media outlets suggest], £1,000,000 here and there, bollocks. Never know [I] suppose [because] people always talk shit [regarding earnings]. If they have a good earner, they keep it quiet so cunts don't muscle in. If they [claim] they bring in [particularly large sums], then they are probably talking pish, wanting a rep."

Evens highlights that position and activity are largely subjective phenomena. This is particularly true when also taking into consideration media portrayals. Such portrayals of gang earnings are often inaccurate and may contradict with what gang members themselves claim to earn. According to Evens, the majority of YCGs rarely brought in more than five-figure sums. Evens attributes much of the myth surrounding drug supply and high earnings to factors such as dramatisation, or people "talking pish" to earn a "rep". However, Evens recognises that even should others, akin to his own gang formation, earn considerably more, they often took precautions to conceal their true earnings. This secrecy significantly hinders efforts to precisely locate gangs at specific market levels. Furthermore, dealers themselves are often unaware of the restrictions that they potentially face as, and should, they continue to progress up the supply chain. As Evens explains, this as a key way of distinguishing between who is 'talking the talk' and who is actually doing 'what they claim'. Evens elaborates on supply and sale:

> "[When we] sold ecstasy at the [nightclub], [one] pill would go for a couple of quid. Start of the night, a pill went for a quid. [We increased] the price towards the end of the night [because buyers] were [more likely to be intoxicated] then. [They] would pay more. If they looked like a newbie [new consumer of drugs], I would say the [pill] were tenner shots. Make ten times as much on it. [I

> *thought] it would be the same [once I became a wholesaler], know,*
> *a quid a pill. It isn't [however]. See, the pills actually go down [in*
> *value] the more [I] bought. I could never have sold them [all], we*
> *[arranged for others] to sell. They don't buy at the going rate per pill*
> *[but]. Drop the prices. Street sale [prices] are not [simply replicated*
> *at wholesale-level] buys. [So, for example, if I have] 11,000 pills,*
> *that doesn't mean I make [£11,000]. Don't [realise that] when*
> *[beginning dealing]."* (Evens)

Evens points out that financial profit is typically reflective of market-level distribution, with sale technique and commodity prices being affected within. Coomber and Moyle (2014) likewise suggest that methods of measuring supply value may differ considerably between suppliers/users, the political establishment and public perception. However, 'bulk-buying' and 'bulk-selling' practices are the most common traits shared by YCGs, despite discrepancies within. Police Scotland similarly ascribe drugs traded in metric measures as a way of determining those involved in the higher echelons of the supply chain from those at the lower end (Pearson and Hobbs, 2001; Murray, 2016). While Evens' YCG had no intentions to operate at retail level, but rather only high-end wholesaling, this was not a unanimous consensus among all those involved in YCGs. As discussed earlier, practice often reflected the duration, and beginnings, of the YCG in question. As Donald explains:

> *"[We] take what [we] can get. If the opportunity is there to get cash*
> *coming in, do it. I don't like [selling drugs individually]. Can be*
> *dodgy [and time-consuming]. [When working in a group context,*
> *we] always stash elsewhere at a [female associate's] house. But when*
> *[drug supplies] dry up, it's no[t] like she has anything to keep. She*
> *isn't going to take risks for fuck all [so that is when] I keep [a lesser*
> *quantity of drugs] in my own house and [sell individually at retail*
> *level]. Still need money."*

While Donald's YCG prefers bulk-buying, retail-level distribution is by no means beyond members when required. Donald indicates supply techniques to be largely driven by opportunity and the overall ebbs and flows of the illegal drug market. Unlike, Evens, who has "been there, done that", Donald's YCG may need to engage in retail-level dealership when necessary due to not having established regular, and trusted, access to high-end suppliers. Evens' YCG is no longer interested in the risk involved in retail-level distribution, and given that YCG formation occurs over time, it is likely that Evens' YCG is much more developed and has greater longevity and more experience than Donald's YCG. The ability to consistently undertake wholesaling practices takes time to develop. Like Donald, Sheba reflects upon his own YCG's early development, and outlines the efforts, and additional techniques, that they had to take to make their product go further, particularly when certain commodities are in short demand:

> "[When we] started off…. [We would] cut and sell [cocaine into smaller] packages. [We didn't get bulk in] every day or nothing. Sometimes, this kind of thing comes in, other times it doesn't. That's when you end up selling to people you know, [cutting] grams [further], here and there, shit like that fella."

Sheba points out that when he began selling drugs, his YCG turned to the most popular products on the market as an entry point. Yet, even then, at times, access to product alone was not enough. They were thus subsequently required to reduce product quality at times in order to make the product itself go further and undercut the costs of competitors, as well as resorting to sole distribution when needed or dealing in other types of commodities/drug types. However, as the gang expanded their business efforts, accumulated resources and capital, grew in self-confidence and specialism, and gained greater supplier–customer connections, they were able to reduce risk, retain a steady flow, keep product quality high and, when possible, deal with the products that they were most comfortable with handling. This theme of entering illegal drug markets from the bottom was a common one among participants. Yet, it was in this field that competition was at its fiercest. As well as appealing to a limited pull of consumers, and competing with a number of competitors, certain products themselves were often considered to be saturated. These factors combined make it difficult for would-be commercially motivated dealers to progress up the career ladder. As Wolfe, Sheba's fellow YCG member, points out: "The [cocaine] market is [saturated]. It's not as though people could not get coke. It's everywhere man. More to do wi' the purity people can get it. Everyone sells council, Chico as well. It is harder to get pure, pure [cocaine] but."

Less developed gangs are more susceptible to markets' changes and environment settings, and often have to engage in riskier behaviour to progress as a result. In the early stages of YCGs' development, the pulling together of economic capital to bulk-buy is vital. Similarly, working with trusted friends, as opposed to business associates, enables them to build upon common grounds. Yet, other more assertive YCGs take different initiatives when seeking to progress up the supply ladder:

"Initially [sold] Eccie's [ecstasy tablets] [at 15 years old] because we use to take them. My pal knew a guy who done pure good [cocaine], so got some and a few of us just sold it for this guy, who was a so-called gangster, supposedly, he was an older cunt. We got a cut for mostly selling to other people we hung about wi'. [After a while,] we thought '[Let us] cut him out. He's not doing the work.' [We] went right to [the source after he revealed source name]. If you don't want cut out, don't tell who your source is." (William, male, offender)

William and his friends recognised that they would be unable to progress up the criminal ladder working as retail-level dealers; thus, acting shrewdly, they found out the source of their supplier and cut out the middleman. By drawing upon the strength of his gang, and an aggressive nature, William's YCG was able to avoid retaliation for this perceived 'backstabbing'. William's statement highlights that there is often a valid reason for lacking trust within such networks, which is something Evens also alluded to earlier. It is an industry where trust is lacking; individuals will only trust those who they share kinship or considerably close friendship – and often history – with. Now, progressing up the ladder, William reveals how this new-found connection and source of responsibility increased gang organisation, and enabled the creation of a division of labour:

"[One member] would drive to Inverness to meet the [importer or wholesaler].... he was my cousin's pal, that's all, he put me in touch, don't know the guy other than that.... [We] would pick the [drugs] up and bring it back [to Glasgow].... At first, we had to mix it with other ingredients to get more quantity. [We] could [thereafter] sell it on in small batches [to other distributors] or just sell [as a group].... after a while, we thought fuck doing all that all the time, [and] just started to buy more.... [Allowing us to] move it right on [after collection and short-term storage]. Means you're no hanging about wi' it [for an extended period of time]. Or having to deal wi' [customers directly]. Way less fucking hassle."

Discussing the division of labour, William reveals how the gang's new role typically consisted of not only purchasing drugs in bulk, but now also arranging transport and storage, as well as 'cutting', 'mixing'[5] and repackaging the product (prior to selling solely to other wholesalers). Gang organisation and gang business tend to go hand in hand, with structure impacting activity and vice versa. Increased access to the illegal drug market has arguably also aided gang evolution in Scotland, opened up previously censored markets and enhanced gang proliferation. While there are now more gangs than in previous decades involved in organised efforts of crime and organised crime, the growth of the drug supply on a global scale has undoubtedly proved to be a key contributor. Yet, one of the key questions that has all too often been overlooked is how those in well-established intergenerational OCGs have responded in kind to such developments. While access to the higher echelons of criminality is still controlled by the most prestigious OCGs, in prior years, access was even controlled at the local level. Yet, this has been gradually eroded due to numerous changes and contemporary developments, including the growth of kinship networks (via reordered family structures), the decline of direct kinship options to help in criminal networks (due to birth control), extensive friendship networks rooted beyond locality, the growth of globalisation and increased access to knowledge at the click of a button (for example, YouTube), all of which have impacted upon changes to OCGs' structure, behaviour and governance.

OCGs and drug supply

Before continuing, it is perhaps helpful to set aside a brief paragraph to recap on what has been covered as this will help to better understand the traditional and more contemporary role of OCGs in illegal markets. We have so far been exploring how complex processes apropos globalisation have impacted upon the accessibility for populations to tap into such supply chains (many of whom were previously unable to do so or were denied access by existing criminal organisations). This, in turn, has enabled more young gangs undergoing early development to continue their criminal progression well beyond what was possible in previous years. Greater accessibility to a globalised drug market has significantly enabled gang organisation as a means for gang business. As mentioned, where many YSGs would have had limited capacity to evolve, this is now possible. As such, YCGs have emerged that, in many ways, play a vital role in filling a substantial void between apex suppliers and retail/ social-level dealers/users, a role previously facilitated by highly specialised individuals or employed runners (often typically working for apex-level dealers directly).[6] Consequently, traditional supply chains were much more susceptive to intervention strategies. Yet, the increasing role of the gang in such supply lines has made these supply chains much more robust (see Gootenberg, 2007, 2011).[7] While OCGs retain many of their traditional roles, involvement in the illegal drug market, and the evolving nature of the illegal drug market itself, has meant that there has also been a need to adapt to these changes. These changes inevitably affect OCG structure, behaviour and strategy. We shall now look at the role that OCGs have come to play in the illegal drug market and how the illegal drug market has affected how OCGs operate, and adapt their roles, within it.

West Coast theory?

Participants discussed how the country's West Coast drug traffickers had a significant strategic advantage over those in the east, south and north of Scotland due to geo-proximity, shared history, established criminal networks and social/familial ties to major distribution 'hubs' in the north of England (in the form of Liverpool and Manchester) and Northern Ireland (in Belfast). Such links have arguably afforded OCGs in the west of Scotland a consistent supply of first-hand freshly imported drugs. Police Scotland supports such perspectives and has similarly identified significantly elevated levels of drug supply, organised crime and OCGs situated in this region of the country (Scottish Government, 2009b, 2013, 2015, 2016). Media reports of successful police operations targeting traffickers likewise support such a stance. It is therefore important to look in more detail at OCG supply in Scotland, and in particular the West Coast. This 'West Coast network theory' (see Densley et al, 2018a; McLean et al, 2018) argues that it could, or should, be considered a very real possibility that two wholly separate methods of distribution now operate in Scotland, with West Coast distribution differing from that of East Coast arrangements.

It helps to think of OCGs as operating at the apex of illegal drug markets. This viewpoint has traditionally meant that apex-level gangs were thought to engage in apex-level supply. Yet, this is not always the case. It is true that OCGs are apex-level gangs that do engage in apex-level supply, but this is not in alignment with traditional supply perspectives or models. What I mean by this is that while British-based OCGs do engage in importing drugs into Britain, in Scotland, a number of factors, including practicality, the robustness of supply lines, passive responsibility and so forth, have meant that most of the country's OCGs typically prefer to engage in apex-level wholesaling:

> "[Most drugs] that come into [Britain] come in from the main ports, and other [land] routes … [and] go through London or Liverpool, even if it goes on to like Birmingham, Essex, where else, Nottingham. London is the capital. A lot of migrant routes are already established there." (Iain, male, practitioner)

"Some guys bring [drugs into Scotland] themselves, directly, [but] most get their shit from the [most densely populated English cities]." (Summer, female, offender)

As Iain and Summer state, in Britain, drugs being imported tend to head to several key destinations in England. Importation was generally secured into one of four cities that operated as national supply 'hubs'. These included London, Birmingham, Liverpool and Manchester (NCA, 2016). Iain attributes this to both the economic and situational importance of these cities, as well as the fact that they tend to have well-established, intergenerational, ethnic networks. From these destinations, other OCGs would bulk-buy from importers. Yet, these OCGs are not to be considered lesser OCGs; rather, they often play a substantial part in the importing process itself. For example, while they may not have directly made importing arrangements, they may have 'fronted the money', or allowed for their 'own men' to be used, to help facilitate transport if needed. Typically, goods would have been paid for in advance. From these major hubs, imported drugs would be transported onto smaller regional hubs. These regional hubs were often major cities themselves in their respective country or county (for example, Glasgow, Cardiff, Sheffield). Once at these destinations, drugs would be sold by OCGs to other, and in this case lesser, OCGs or to high-end YCGs, which, in turn, distribute to lower-level wholesalers, retail-level dealers (Matrix Knowledge Group, 2007) and even 'user-dealers' (Moyle and Coomber, 2017). Thus, most drugs that enter Scotland come primarily via the English border. Participants talked about making 'runs', 'collections' or 'pickups' from England. Liverpool and Manchester were the most frequently cited collection points. It was not uncommon for wholesale dealers to mitigate risk by employing (both directly and indirectly) young people loosely embedded in criminal networks to travel to make 'pickups' for them and drop money in return:

"[Individual X] always meets me once there.... No, they don't meet us halfway or nothing. I have to drive right to [Merseyside area].... [We don't always rendezvous] at same place.... I hand over the bag [of money], no[t] to him, in his hands ... put it somewhere ... mostly [in his] car trunk ... [or] leave it for him under table if we are at [restaurant X] ... [and] he leaves with it.... [Once back in Glasgow,] I make a drop-off to [an associate], and they hold onto it." (Craig, male, offender)

While Glasgow and the West Coast retain the vast majority of drug supply in Scotland,[8] and have particularly strong links with Liverpool and Manchester, it is important to note that not all drugs from England go directly to the West as the capital, Edinburgh, on the East Coast, also has its own well-established traffickers and supply routes. Several participants spoke of these alliances, with the strongest links being with the English Midlands, many of whom were labelled 'Yardies' by our white respondents because they conformed to stereotypes of black criminality (for a discussion, see Karim, 1999). Stephen describes making large collections from Birmingham:

> "Quite a few boys from around [Scotland's East Coast] had strong [ties] with [censored group name] from Birmingham … [they] put me in touch [with this gang]. Most [of] the pickups used to come from around Liverpool, but for a few years there … [significant] amounts of like pure [potent drug quality] was coming in from there [Birmingham].… especially Skag [heroin] … from Pakistan and [Afghanistan].… Was a heavy outfit [sophisticated organisation] going, [which] ran a lot of the shit coming into Scotland for a while … dried up a good bit … few guys making strong connections back with the Liverpool [gangs] again."

After Stephen, who resided on the West Coast of the country, was 'hooked up' via connections on the East Coast, he started dealing directly with these Birmingham connections. Owing to globalisation and immigration patterns, Birmingham had emerged as a source of a better and more consistent supply of heroin for Scottish customers. However, when the Birmingham pipeline 'dried up', Stephen stated that he, like many West Coast importers, was forced to go back to more durable, traditional supply lines from Liverpool and Manchester. Like these latter cities, OCGs on Scotland's West Coast also have strong ties to OCGs in Northern Ireland. After the 1998 Good Friday Agreement, the province witnessed a significant rise in drug markets and the consequent emergence of trafficking networks (McElrath, 2004; Coomber, 2006; McSweeney et al, 2008). Allan and Mark state:

Allan: "[My family member] was heavy moving [supplying significant amounts of drugs].… He was working wi' cunts from all over Glasgow.… [Even] Ireland, going over to [Irish city]."

Interviewer: "How often do you think you go over [to Ireland] then?"

Mark: "Catch the ferry around couple of times a month to meet [individual Z].... aye few at least, I would have to say."

OCG members, and some high-level YCGs, spoke about regularly wholesaling and distributing drugs out of the regional hub of Glasgow to other major Scottish cities in, primarily, the central belt, the East Coast and, to a lesser degree, Northern Scotland (for example, Aberdeen and the Western Isles). However, an overarching theme of the study with regard to apex-level wholesaling from Scotland's OCGs was that OCGs in the major English hubs arranged for large-scale drug importation, often aided by OCGs from these regional hubs, to be collected thereafter by OCGs[9] from these regional hubs. In Scotland, this primarily related to the apex-level OCGs on the West Coast. The majority of drug supply in Scotland tends to originate from the West. However, these OCGs also very often have their own importing supply lines from within the country, albeit to a lesser extent than those OCGs in England. This hybrid model of supply has seen substantial changes to OCG structures occur in recent decades.

Importation, wholesaling and faces

As discussed earlier, the West Coast of Scotland has a disproportionate number of OCGs who engage in drug supply. These OCGs are involved in both importing and wholesaling practices. While direct importation into the UK primarily occurs from OCGs in England and Northern Ireland, before being directly wholesaled onto major OCGs in Scotland, as their preferred method for creating and maintaining reliable supply routes, a number of these OCGs usually still engage in the direct importation of drugs into Scotland themselves, albeit to a lesser degree – and typically less profitable when compared with their wholesaling activities – than that of their English-based counterparts. Importing often involves carrying out illegal operations within legal business activities, for example, using legal shipping companies to transport illegal drugs from one destination to another. This is achieved when OCGs are able to corrupt key players in, or who work in conjunction with, these companies. Thus, the majority of employees of these shipping companies are oblivious to the illegal operations that they are involved in. Another example is that of using young impressionable holiday-goers as 'mules', who are given incentives, such as fully paid, all-inclusive holidays, in exchange for smuggling drugs back into Britain. Again, legal airlines are used, but of all the individuals on board, only the smugglers themselves are aware of the illegal activities taking place. James uses both examples to explain imported supply techniques, and outlines how preferred techniques have evolved:

> "[It] use[d] to be popular for [an OCG employee or lone affiliation] to travel to Columbia, [or] the Caribbean ... and bring [drugs] over on flights. That isn't really done now. [It is easier to] pay ... someone to do it. Like daft wee boys. Offer them holiday[s], a week away, and set them up to meet [OCG representative(s)] while there. Mules basically. If they get caught, it's them that gets [apprehended]."

With only two international airports in Scotland, such use of drug mules was highly risky and restricted to small amounts of high-quality drugs at any one time, usually from Spain or The Netherlands. To mitigate the risks, international importation directly into Scotland was now more routinely undertaken via sea routes. Scotland has a significant number of ports, and the West Coast in particular has multiple sea lochs, making small levels of importation comparatively easy. Moreover, OCGs have sophisticated networks of contacts remunerated for ease of importation:

> "Smuggle that shit in from everywhere.... Say, gear [cocaine], right, is coming in on a particular boat. The guys getting their hands dirty aren't the ones arranging it all, no.... takes a bit more brains than that.... If it's coming in on a ship, there will be, say, inside guys, working the dock, emptying containers, that know, HGV drivers ... they get a cut [paid] for just moving it along.... Most of the workers don't know what's going on.... Might not be the best [wage for those transporting], but you don't bump these guys arranging it.... [Or] they will get you fuckin' done in, if you get caught dipping goods."
> (James, male, offender)

Shipping is outlined as now being the preferred method for importing drugs into Scotland. Both financial incentives and fear of reprisals played a significant role in accessing, and keeping, these infiltrated players in place (see Densley et al, 2018a). Regardless of how drugs were brought into Scotland, once drugs entered British shores, OCGs would arrange collection. As James states: "Once [in Britain], [drugs] might be transported right to [a] yard, whatever, or sometimes, depending on bulk, someone will collect directly." Traditional OCGs often used certain family members or hired hands to act as their front, or symbolic power. This is something that OCGs still do today. As Sheba elaborated: "I've only met [the individuals who] bring [drugs] in, but they won't be the actual guys arranging the smuggling ... they are like representatives ...

obviously working for [traffickers] ... probably [extended] family or something."

Speaking from the perspective of a 'runner', Sheba has little, if any, direct contact with those OCG members who arrange for drugs to be imported or collected from England/Northern Ireland as part of wholesaling practices. Sheba's direct contact is with the designated representative(s), who Pearson and Hobbs (2001) refer to as 'faces'. Over the decades, OCGs have learned a variety of techniques that have continually put more and more space between themselves and the criminal activities in which they engage. With regard to the direct collection of drugs or debts, they will use faces, although these faces have increasingly become ones that share little, if any, degree of kinship.[10] This is a role that high-level YCGs have come to increasingly fulfil, with the most successful members graduating into the OCG itself, often having continually proved themselves time and again by overseeing such transactions, OCG operations and allocated responsibilities. A key reason in the increased role of using certain YCGs, and specific members, as a face for the OCG is that as the illegal drug market has grown, the roles involved in the supply chain have also increased and subsequently evolved. OCGs have simultaneously made considerable efforts to, on the one hand, limit their own role in transaction processes while, on the other hand, also increasing profitability and efficiency. Much like legitimate multinational companies, whose business models they seek almost unconsciously to emulate, OCGs now outsource much of their previous held responsibilities to other independent gangs and partners, that is, lesser OCGs, YCGs or occasionally specialised individuals. This has meant that while imported drugs tend to come via the efforts of key players operating in legitimate companies, the handling of imported drugs thereafter, or drugs directly collected from importing OCGs in England or Ireland, has now become an outsourced responsibility, often allocated to well-established and highly trusted YCGs, or specific members. These YCGs may themselves also employ others to collect on their behalf when supply lines are over some distance or considered overly risky[11]:

William:	"[I or other YCG members] usually go [ourselves]. [Whenever I collect] from [city in Southern England], we just send [YCG loose associate]."
Interviewer:	"Why [YCG loose associate]. Cause you said he was always [missing owed payments]?"
William:	"Aye, well, he is fucked up, aye. I can't do that drive but. Dodgy. I would well be stopped [as William is well known to police]. They [police] aren't fucking

stupid…. I phone down if [YCG loose associate] is
meeting with [known smuggler]. Anyone else but
we don't go. Aye, [I] get raging phone calls and shit.
I just get him [the unknown smuggler] told, 'I don't
fucking know you'. Make him wait, till I go and meet
him first, scare him know, sus him out. If [I think]
it is cool, I get [YCG loose associate] to make [the
pickup] a couple of weeks later. I know it slows shit
and [the OCG who have arranged for my YCG to
collect] do get pure annoyed, but you can't be too
careful. [They] just need to wait."

William's statements, which are found in earlier subsections and chapters,
firmly demonstrate that he and his YCG are an independent outfit, yet
they work for rewards with OCGs (and anyone else who is willing to
pay their fees) on their behalf, much like a quasi-style collection agency.
This means that OCGs have gradually outsourced the collection of
drugs to others. William's YCG is used as a trusted and reputable outfit.
Upon 'drop-offs', William and his YCG take the drugs either directly to
storehouses, other wholesalers/buyers or to their own storage facilities
until further arrangements to collect are made by the OCG in question.
William's YCG either takes its own payment as a percentage of the drugs
it collects, or retains a percentage until the OCG in question exchanges
the agreed monetary fees. Should these fees not be paid, William's YCG
would simply retain the percentage of drugs they held onto.

By outsourcing roles that were the responsibility of the OCG itself
in prior decades, supply chains have become more extensive, robust
and yet increasingly flexible and resilient to those efforts that seek their
dismantlement. This has created a greater degree of space between OCGs
and their direct involvement in criminal activities. Likewise, it is also a
way in which OCGs can place a glass ceiling over upcoming criminal
outfits and, as James states, "throw a bone" to certain individuals within
as an incentive to become a part of their own OCG. In doing so, they
therefore defuse potential future rivalries in the process (with YCGs that
may have otherwise become OCGs in their own right) and maintain their
own position of power over both the legitimate and illegitimate spheres
in which they operate. It is easier to control those operating within the
illegal drug market rather than seeking to control the flow of product,
particularly as the product has become increasingly accessible. As James
states, contemporary OCGs have learned significant lessons from their
earlier predecessors: "Back in the day, [OCGs] were killing each other to
stop each other dealing. That is just fucking daft man, too many dealing

now. [Easier to] make [the most successful dealers] part of the team, know, [rather] than fucking killing them all." This adaptation to their business strategy is one that, alongside the growth of the illegal drug market, the digital age and other impacts of globalisation, has also impacted upon OCG structures, and subsequently illegal governance.

OCG structure and governance

While contemporary OCG structure somewhat differs from that of traditional OCGs, many of these changes go by unnoticed, or are not immediately obvious at first glance. Traditional OCGs were thought to be largely family-based firms who acted in an ad hoc manner, employing or working with others who had specialist skills as and when needed. Yet, membership was largely based upon kinship, extended only to the closest family friends. This was true of Glasgow OCGs led by the likes of Arthur Thompson, Walter Norval or Tam McGrew, to name but a few, towards the end of the 20th century and early years of the 21st century. Yet, while such stereotypical perspectives of these earlier prototypes still exist today, in reality, this is not quite accurate of contemporary OCGs. It is true that many OCGs are still considered as, or deemed to be, primarily family-based outfits,[12] yet the lines of kinship among members now extends further than ever before possible and typically include many who are considered kinship merely through once-reordered family structures. In addition, these OCGs also now include many non-kinship individuals, who are likewise no longer to be thought of as employees, but rather retain varying degrees of partnership and membership.[13] These adaptations can be attributed to numerous social, economic, political and cultural influences. Yet, while these changes affect gang operations, the illegal markets in which they operate are simultaneously affected by the changes that such markets themselves impose upon those operating within them. The gang is forced to adapt and change in order to survive an ever-changing market, which is itself changed due to not only macro-level influences, but also the micro-level adaptations undertaken by these OCGs as they continually strive to control and exert, whenever possible, their own influence over markets. According to practitioner Tiny, this power is very much in the hands of the few:

> *"[Those involved] in high-end drug distribution basically control the market. A few ... run it all. That is why you always hear of one or two names running the show. Everyone works for them, no[t] always directly. Most people don't even probably know they get their [drugs]*

off them.... The guys running it basically can [be]cause they get a
wee foothold, bring their family, [friends and other trusted criminal
partners] in and start using [their power of governance] to keep anyone
who tries to muscle in out of the picture."

We have discussed some of these changes to OCG structure in Chapter 4,
and even earlier in this chapter with regard to outsourcing. In Chapter 5,
we touched upon the fact that OCGs tend to be specialists and only deal
in those drugs that are most profitable, typically Class A drugs. Yet, OCGs
do deal, albeit indirectly, in the sale of other drugs outside the sphere in
which they have influence:

> *"Suppose, you could say that [we deal indirectly] with [other drug*
> *types]. Same as [a parent] take[s] dig money [from their children]....*
> *[We] take our dig money [from lesser dealers in sphere of influence].*
> *It is only right to take what is owed"* (Ewan, male, offender)

Ewan points out that while his own OCG has no direct involvement
in either the importing, wholesaling or distribution of other drug types
that they do not specialise in, they nonetheless utilise their power of
illegal governance to still indirectly intervene in criminal transactions.
Ewan justifies this as his OCG's 'right' given that they allow space for
other criminal gangs to operate and earn a living, stating that "if we
wanted, we could own the whole [illegal drug market] in [our own
sphere]".[14] Therefore, this method of taxing others has impacted upon
the structures of those lesser gangs operating as they seek to keep up
with the fees. Monthly fees tend to be negotiated between OCGs and
lesser gang typologies directly below them, as opposed to a fluctuating
percentage, given that the OCG does not know the exact amount that
another gang earns or want to draw attention to themselves by getting
involved in feuds.[15] Jay reveals how his own YCG has responded in kind
to meet the demands:

> *"[We] have bills to pay. Not just bill, bills, but like [criminal] bills,*
> *hear me? [YCG member A] and [I], every month, hand out £4,000,*
> *well £4,655 more precisely. Fuck knows why the fiver, something to*
> *do with the account it's paid into.... That's just to [OCG A] ... it's*
> *good, easy to live by, know mate. It is fair.... Have you watched that*
> *programme The Wire? Its good.... I watch it because I like it, that's*
> *all. Gave me the idea of ... [using] runners. Like stashing gear and*
> *collecting it.... work[s] so so. [Can] only [employ this method] in your*
> *own scheme. Doing that up the town [centre] would be too [risky]."*

Jay mentions that his own gang have had to evolve and become more efficient in order to meet the demand of monthly taxed income. Yet, Jay accepts this position as 'fair', almost like an unwritten criminal code (see Maitra et al, 2017). Jay uses a similar method when dealing with his own 'runners', who tend to be young boys on the estate who he likewise 'taxes'. Like other YCGs who use a similar method, Jay tends to use boys from the local YSG. This is because they can be trusted to work in criminal networks and are less susceptible of being robbed and losing Jay's product. OCGs' gang boundaries are very much closed off (see Rafanell, 2013; Rafanell et al, 2017), yet they nonetheless use their financial resources to extend their structural influence to those they pay (as opposed to employ), such as William's YCG, to engage in their criminal work. OCGs likewise use financial incentives, as well as drawing upon their criminal reputations, to directly employee key players in legitimate companies to aid their supply networks. At the same time, they solely use their criminal reputation to exert influence and capital from other lesser criminals, whom they 'tax' on a regular basis. These criminals, in turn, tend to tax those below themselves in many cases. OCGs likewise exploit those marginalised individuals, legitimate business owners, members of the political establishment such as council workers, concierge staff and those who are indebted to them (or even the family members of indebted individuals) to further benefit their control over the supply chains in which they operate (see McLean et al, 2018). A further and more recent example of this is the development of what is known as 'county lines' (see Robinson et al, 2018).

While most OCGs were very much male-dominated outfits, Mary was one of two exceptions among the sample. As a female, Mary used her matriarchal position over kinship to develop the internal gang structures necessary for her to engage in successful gang business. Mary rarely dealt directly with non-kinship members and instead did so through her closest relatives within the gang (her siblings). Having found Glasgow a place saturated in OCG activity, and variety of drug products, as well as also being high in police attention/surveillance, Mary relocated her operation to the southern regions of Scotland, which are dominated by various interlocked villages and towns that have small populations and are spread out over a vast geographical area:

> "[It's] good here. Quiet, so no' much hassle. Hardly any police ... loads a' wee villages round about as well ... well, basically [Brother C] or [Brother A] usually go scope [a neighbouring village] first and if it is cool, then they start dealing ... get a feel for the place."

Here, Mary's OCG had little competition, and she states that after her brothers 'scope' neighbouring villages, they then begin dealing drugs. Once a regular drug user, typically an addict, had been identified, s/he would be propositioned to 'stash drugs' in their property on behalf of Mary's OCG. In addition, this individual would then be required to sell drugs on behalf of the OCG. In return, they had free access to the drugs that had been stashed. As Mary states:

> "They get an allowance from what we put there so don't need to [source drugs elsewhere]. They take what they want, but we don't allow them to have parties ... [or] they [may] come up short [with payments]. [If they do, we] give a warning. [Brother C] might tax them ... like interest. Fuck, [he] even puts the girls out [for sex] work if it's a good bit."

As Mary states, users occasionally run up debts and when they do, they are required to repay with interest or by being exploited and used in other criminal activities until the debt is paid. Note, once the user is selling drugs from their home, the OCG has little contact beyond the collection of money. Other customers are made aware of where sales can be purchased either through social networks, word of mouth or a text-messaging service that original customers and associates are put onto after an initial buy. Contacts are synced to a phone held by the OCG, or an associate, which are then placed within another mobile. In this way (potential) customers are made aware of OCG 'one-time offers'.

As evident, OCGs have continued to adapt to an ever-growing and ever-changing globalised drug market. Responding in kind, OCG structures have evolved to become less directly involved, yet more efficient. Membership has become based upon what others can bring to the table, and with regard to drug supply, OCGs now focus more on "making [money] clean" as opposed to getting involved in the everyday 'nitty-gritty' scene of drug dealing.

Chapter summary

In this chapter, we have explored how activity and structure are intertwined processes that equally impact upon and, in turn, influence one another, a process that is always relevant to the given context. The chapter began by exploring YSGs and found that the growth of the illegal drug market, alongside a variety of complex processes apropos globalisation, has enabled greater potential for gang organisation as a means for gang business. The changing and growing nature of the global drug market has likewise impacted upon traditional OCG structures, creating more space for evolving and proliferating gang typologies to operate within and fulfil outsourced roles and responsibilities. Yet, in contemporary supply chains, these outsourcing organisations retain their own independence, thus making supply chains much more robust and flexible. This has arguably been a key factor in the growing illegal drug market in the West Coast of Scotland, along with the number of actors involved. Yet, while context is always unique, we see that trends emerge that see gangs become more and more like one another. For example, in the last section looking at Mary's OCG, we see the description of her activities – that is, the relocation/extension of criminal activities to rural regions of the country, working through others and exploiting young people and adults to "stash [drugs] in their house and sell from there" or "set up in their house" – to be reminiscent of the 'county lines' and 'cuckooing' operations (see Coomber and Moyle, 2017), which originated in Southern England.[16]

Notes

[1] This often occurred alongside alcohol consumption.

[2] In several cases, participants even mentioned that their own mothers, aunts and grandparents (in one case) would procure drugs for them, or engage in wider social supply within their own friendship groupings.

[3] This was a consistent finding among most participants, from those at the lower end involved in social supply to those engaged in large-scale wholesaling and importation practices. Often, though, key differences between those gangs at the top and those at the bottom related to how they practised consumption (that is, time, place, quantity, addicted or not, and so on).

[4] This study found little evidence for 'shopping lists' like those described by Pearson and Hobbs (2001), yet this may reflect the Scottish context of the study as opposed to overall market changes.

[5] The product was typically mixed using Benzocaine.

[6] For example, when cocaine was flooding the streets of Miami in the late 20th century, Columbians were the producers, importers (though specialised solo importers also occasionally facilitated such roles) and retail-level dealers. The whole supply chain began and ended with Columbian cartels. A number of scholars, including Alonso (2004), McLean et al (2018) and Venkatesh (2008), to name a few, discuss the role that home-grown gangs helped play in making these supply chains more effective, robust and profitable by utilising turf, territory, existing networks and criminal reputation to aid drug supply chains.

[7] For example, say one or two gang members are removed as a result of being incarcerated, in reality, this affects the contemporary supply chain very little given that other members will fill the void. In addition, those incarcerated members will often continue to receive financial rewards for ongoing distribution, thus having little impact on the individual and their household, while maintaining strong incentives to continue in such activities upon their release.

8   See also media reports on the Gillespie Brothers who, being from Glasgow (Rutherglen), are thought to be responsible for the vast majority of cocaine that has entered and been distributed throughout the country.

9   YCGs were typically used as runners or for collection purposes. Sometimes, individuals closely aligned to the OCG themselves would be used, or even employ runners, although the latter are being used less as part of anti-detection strategies.

10 For example, gangland enforcer Robert 'Piggy' Pickett is a key 'face' for the OCG contextually known as or referred to as the Lyons family, despite having no direct or indirect kinship. Piggy had been a key player in a former YCG and subsequent OCGs in the neighbouring town of Paisley, having been involved in illegal drug markets before and after the 'Paisley Drug Wars'.

11 YCGs may make most collections themselves, but over considerable lines, where the risk of apprehension is at its highest, they may employ a lone individual (often someone owing a debt) to collect on their behalf in order to reduce the direct risk to YCG members.

12 This is most prevalent in media circles and, consequently, much of the general public. How these gangs are labelled – by way of using the primary known individual as a point of reference – also affects how gang structure and membership is perceived or assumed to be. For example, a not-too-recent media photograph captured three completely non-related individuals together from apex OCGs situated in Glasgow, Paisley and Edinburgh. Yet, the media labelled, and referenced, this grouping of individuals with the family name of the more notorious individual from Glasgow, despite not sharing any degree of kinship. This gives the impression that they not only all belong to the one OCG led by the individual from Glasgow, but are also somehow distantly related.

13 A recent example would be the OCG labelled Scotland's 'most sophisticated gang ever'. No member was directly related and membership was largely established through personal and business exchanges that occurred around a well-known OCG that is now largely dismantled.

14 This is highly doubtable, yet such views are projected in order to emphasise a sense of omnipotence and a charitable nature by giving other criminals a corner of the market to earn a living.

15 When feuds do occur, YCGs and certain members who act as 'faces' when required tend to take up the feud on the OCG's behalf, although further down the supply chain, at times, those embroiled in feuds over outstanding debts, on both sides, may not even know who the orchestrators of such feuds (the OCGs) are. This is because 'taxing' tends to work down the supply chain, with each part acting independently of one another for their own benefit in order to meet their own negotiated payments.

16 This is a recent and developing phenomenon whereby OCGs, particularly from London, set up drug operations in rural towns and villages nearby in which the homes of vulnerable adults are used as an operational base for drug sales.

PART IV

7

Tackling Gangs and Organised Crime, and Rethinking Drug Policy

The book began with two main objectives in mind. The first was to provide insight into contemporary gang organisation as a means for gang business. While the research was conducted in Scotland, in many ways, it resonates with ongoing processes occurring throughout the length and breadth of Britain, albeit taking its own unique form, as it would in any region of the country. This first aim of the book was catered to a large audience, ranging from academics, practitioners and students, to those with just a general interest in gang activity, and to a lesser extent organised crime (more specifically in relation to drug supply given its relevance). Ultimately, the first objective was to present a somewhat holistic picture of gang organisation in contemporary Britain that is accessible to all. The second purpose of the book was more specific: to re-engage Scottish scholarly gang literature back into the wider scholarly UK gang debate. This is because while the gang as a whole has been significantly researched by scholars in the English/Welsh context, this has not been the case in Scotland, where scholars have become overly fixated upon the gang at the embryo stage of development. This is not to suggest that this research is in any way the be-all and end-all with regard to gang studies; rather, it is hoped that the book will be used as a foundation from which others can build, refute, draw comparison or cherry-pick when undertaking research in similar areas, such as research into criminal careers, youth offending, gang/group criminality, organised crime and drug studies, to mention but a few.

Thus, in seeking to achieve the aims and purposes of the book, I began by opening up, in Part I, with an introduction to the topic of gangs, the context and those involved in the original and follow-up studies. I proceeded in Part II of the book to provide what is essentially a literature review of gangs in general, organised crime (to a lesser extent) and gang literature in the Scottish context. Part III of the book then presented, in the voices of the participants, an analysis of gang organisation and gang activity before looking in more detail at the activity of drug supply and how this is intertwined with structure and context. This final part of the book consists of only one chapter. This chapter will seek to: give a general summary of the book; address whether the aims have been met; discuss some of the factors contributing to gang organisation; and outline how the research could be used in practice and policy. Within the discussion on policy and practice, I will draw attention to potential predictors that see 'core' or persistent offenders progress towards organised crime. This section will also bring attention to the fact that gang organisation can only truly be addressed by tackling the root causes of crime. The chapter finishes with a short reflection of the study as a whole and, in doing so, draws attention to various limitations.

Achieving the book's purposes

The book sheds much-needed light on gang organisation as a means for gang business. How exactly gang organisation occurs, how subsequent gang business is carried out thereafter and how criminal careers progress are analysed in a specific context, as is the case with most research. Yet, the book is still applicable to the British context as a whole. The same can be said of all gang scholars in the field, including the likes of Briggs, Densley, Deuchar, Hallsworth, Harding, Pitts, Windle and so on. All research is both specific and applicable to the wider socio-economic, political and cultural context to varying degrees. To look at gang organisation, this book essentially took a two-pronged approach. The first was to look at the structures of gangs. To help aid conceptualisations, a range of group typologies were placed on an evolving continuum under a single umbrella term, that is, 'gangs', as opposed to using typically unhelpful gang/group variations, which are contained within. This adoption of umbrella terminology helped us address the second approach, which was to consider gang activity. This is because the growth of various illegal markets – not only drug markets – has essentially meant that activities previously situated in the realm of OCGs alone have been outsourced. As a result, various gang typologies, previously distinct from those OCGs engaged in organised criminal activities, are now engaging in similar types of behaviour, albeit on a somewhat reduced scale. Yet, this again varies considerably. Thus, while, in previous years, gang/group distinction was perhaps helpful in separating those delinquent youth groups from adults carrying out high-level organised crime, this is no longer the case and the distinction between both has steadily become ever-more blurred. Thus, to help address this issue, as well as an umbrella terminology for various group types, activities considered to be organised crime, in addition to the four mandatory points outlined by the 2000 Palermo Convention, were given an additional feature of illegal governance. Only when gangs are conducting illegal governance over their area of influence, as opposed to being the illegally governed, can such gangs be considered as being involved in organised crime. Everything else meeting the current Scottish Government's (2015, 2016) definition of organised crime,[1] which does not retain illegal governance, is to be considered as organised efforts of crime, whereby progression is being made by criminals towards organised crime itself. This was used as the key indicator for separating those gangs involved in criminality from those who operate at the higher echelons of their respective arenas. This is a much-needed feature, particularly given that organised crime has continued to move towards market-based crimes as opposed to predatory crimes (Scottish Government, 2016).

The book has also revealed that while gangs exist on an evolving continuum, there are certain features and criteria that occur at key stages of development. This helps us to identify typologies within the evolving continuum. Thus, although during transition from one stage to the next, a degree of overlap may exist, and slight differences within typologies may also occur due to duration and the context in which they evolve, it is helpful to conceptualise the continuum as comprising three key stages of development. These stages are characterised by essentially three different gang types or variations: the YSG, the YCG and the OCG. The book contributes significantly to shedding light on the latter two typologies, and in particular the YCG. This is because while a number of scholars have discussed and spoken of similar gang types in the English/ Welsh context, often using a variety of labels, terms and acronyms, which typically include the word 'gang', this has not been the case in Scotland. Thus, to simply use the word 'gang' would only confuse intended audiences given that the term has come to be used to specifically and almost wholeheartedly to refer to youths in their early to mid-teenage years who are undergoing street socialisation and, in the process, engage in recreational violence over territorial, and occasionally other, issues related to securing masculine identity. Therefore, the book moves beyond this and using the prefix 'young criminal' to indicate the transition from delinquency to criminality, while still making reference to the relative youthfulness of these gangs at their mid- to late teenage years and early adult years. The book looked specifically at the use of terminology and how, in this context, evolving gang structures do not require gangs to self-label or even be labelled. The book then continued to contribute to shedding light on gang organisation as a means for gang business by moving from exploring emergent structures to progressive activities, first from delinquent to criminal, and then from criminal to organised crime.

This, of course, aids the book in achieving its second purpose, which is to successfully re-engage Scottish gang literature back into the wider British gang debate, itself seeking to identify whether or not gangs are truly organising and proliferating across the country, and, in the process, often taking on similar attributes/properties of those found, or assumed to be found, in the North American context. The book achieves this by continually underpinning those structural, activity and contextual factors that see gang organisation emerge and develop. Therefore, the book helps to fulfil this literature gap by linking Scottish gang literature – undertaken in the excellent works by the likes of Bartie (2010), Bradshaw (2005), Davies (2007, 2013), Deuchar (2009, 2013), Fraser (2013, 2015), Holligan and Deuchar (2010), McAra and McVie (2007, 2010), Miller (2015), and Patrick (1973), to name but a few – to that of scholars in the English/ Welsh context (for example, Pitts, 2008; Densley, 2013; Harding, 2014). This work is to be considered not as the totalising study of Scottish gangs, but merely to act as a basis which other research can emerge from, build on and even refute. As with all research, limitations and flaws are always evident (I shall consider some particular points later on).

Further contributions

In addition to the two main objectives of the book, that is, undertaking a contemporary study of gang organisation in the Scottish context, and re-engaging Scottish gang literature back into the wider UK gang discourse, the book has hopefully made other contributions. There are potentially several. First, as mentioned earlier, by highlighting inconstancies between (1) gang/group terminology and (2) the use of the term 'organised crime', we see that simpler and more universal definitions are required if the gap between academia and practitioner services is to be bridged, making best effect of the research carried out in the field.

A further contribution of this book, however, and the research more generally, is that it highlights the evolving nature of the illegal drug market in the country (again, it must be remembered that this is just an umbrella term as drug markets vary according to context, level, drug type and so on), and how this both influences and, in turn, is influenced by gang activity within. The research makes efforts to chart recent changes and adaptations to drug distribution networks in Scotland. Owing in part to adaptive risk mitigation on the part of drug dealers, it is evident that Scottish drug markets are in a state of flux, and risk mitigation is essentially a form of displacement that produces, at times, unintended consequences. Therefore, the research contributes to a significant body of work on drug market displacement and the unintended consequences of drug enforcement (see Caulkins, 1992). Historically, primarily white, working-class criminal families with extensive access to criminal networks controlled the Scottish market at all levels, as directed by kingpins in Spain and Portugal (Matrix Knowledge Group, 2007). Distribution was conducted by middlemen leveraging criminal networks to shift product via the commercial club scene and door security staff. However, law enforcement action, along with a variety of other factors (for example, advances in technology, evolving production methods and so on) changed this, disrupting traditional distribution networks. Market diversification in supply and demand, and enhanced competition, compounded this disruption. For example, one participant identified the rapid growth of steroids as a result of the huge rise in interest in bodybuilding and body image (McVeigh and Begley, 2016), and its concomitant dearth of enforcement compared to other drugs (for example, heroin), thus influencing his economic decision to switch products.

Likewise, product diversification has also brought further adaptive distribution methods, including online sales and 24-hour dial-a-deal delivery services. Such diversification offers new points of entry into the market, often for those who previously had no chance of access. Here, traditional methods of selling and dealing count for less. In this new marketplace, value is given to telephone databases of users rather than the networked knowledge of domestic markets alone. In turn, this feeds into another driver for change: the emergence of 'county lines' (Coomber and Moyle, 2017). This new distribution model is foregrounding several key changes to drug distribution in Scotland, not least because of the violence associated with it. Yet, with the expansion of English-based OCGs searching further afield for new pastures, this has gradually seen such gangs extend their lines into Scotland itself, as evident in the Woolwich machine-gun attack by London gangsters in Edinburgh in 2013.

While those involved in drug distribution will often work with anyone (who is trusted/established in criminal networks) to turn a profit, these changes nonetheless represent a challenge to Scottish police, who might find traditional lines of intelligence no longer effective, and new arrival communities under-researched and unfamiliar – a position that gives these new players a short-term advantage. Likewise, the progression of disadvantaged young men from the 'social supply' of cannabis into the retail and wholesale supply of Class A drugs should be noted. Research has found that economic factors can account for such decisions (for example, Windle, 2017) and we are mindful that the current study was conducted in the aftermath of the 2008 Great Recession that affected our respondents in ways beyond the scope of this book. Further, the emergence of newer markets centred on steroids and psychoactive substances requires updated policy to address online purchasing and street-level distribution among young people. Moreover, it is worth asking the question as to whether or not, in what is essentially a globalised era, the emergence of new arrivals and new players in the market, with many self-starters from diverse ethnic backgrounds, will spell the end of the ethnically homogeneous family-centred distribution networks of Scottish cities.

Practice and policy

With regard to practice and policy, this research has numerous implications. Yet, given the limited scope of the book and the restricted word count, I shall only focus on one aspect here: identifying linchpin areas and intervening appropriately.

Linchpin areas

The scarcity of information regarding interrelationships between Scotland's, and more so Glasgow's, gangs and organised crime is regrettable, particularly given that both have generally been viewed, and approached, as distinct and unrelated phenomena in Scotland. This has resulted in YSG progression towards organised crime continuing to go by somewhat unchecked. Not properly identifying those youths at the highest levels of risk allows persistent offenders to slip through the net undetected until it is too late, when they have consequently already become entrenched in criminal lifestyles, often unopposed or even reluctantly (see Pitts, 2008). In addition, when developing a gang typology for the Metropolitan Police in 2006, Hallsworth and Young similarly noted that gang types will generally respond differently to intervention programmes depending on what stage of development a gang may be situated in. Thus, intervention may prove irrelevant to some, yet to others, it can prove to be a factor in fostering group cohesion and criminality (see Klein, 1971). Therefore, identifying the gang correctly and intervening accordingly has to be accurate given that choosing the incorrect intervention method may produce counterproductive results.

The research here goes some way in allowing correct gang identification to be achieved more effectively. This is because YSG membership was previously typically allocated an either/or status. Yet, this research can inform policy and practice by, first, demonstrating the different levels of YSG involvement, with identification of core members and the outer layer. Thus, given that members of the outer layer have been shown in this research to gradually disengage with the YSG, and criminality more generally, as they naturally mature and age, it is advisable to simply allow such members to carry on their loose affiliation with the YSG since they will naturally desist from participating in delinquency and subsequent criminality (see Klein, 1971; Klein et al, 2006).

It is also advisable that YSG core members equally be allowed to carry on with YSG involvement, even though they are at high risk of having a criminal identity firmly embedded as one that they view as intrinsic to their own nature. This is because, like Klein (1971), this research found the presence of external threats to only further solidify group cohesion and transfer individual criminal identity onto the group as a whole. Thus, it is recommended that while some level of intervention should be introduced to core members, those agents who do so must adopt a soft approach and seek to engage with individual gang members at the individual level, as opposed to addressing the gang as a whole. I recommend that intervention agencies need to show a considerable focus on nurturing those natural turning points that may arise and seek to aid core gang members in taking on role transitions towards one that is more socially acceptable (see Carlsson, 2012), and evidently beneficial for themselves (Deuchar et al, 2018). However, these turning points need to be supported in a very practical manner, whereby core gang members can be encouraged to actively pursue and engage in activities that nurture the formation of a new identity.

Decker et al (2014) likewise argue that desistance from gang membership often requires a new role to be readily adopted. For example, in relation to the Scottish context, it would only prove futile for intervention agencies to discuss with already-marginalised individuals – which many of the core members are – to seek, let us say, a professional career, or one that requires some form of higher educational achievement, without providing those means to do so. Individuals must be provided with the means to engage (see Merton, 1938). However, as noted by Sweeten et al (2013), even once gang members leave the gang, any existing ties may correspond with serious consequences; thus, it is important that new roles be ones that aim to completely sever gang ties altogether over time. Yet, a significant source of criminal stigma, identified throughout the study, was that of a criminal record. Hlavka et al (2015) similarly point out that the acquisition of a criminal record can prove particularly hindering to those who wish to desist from crime, or take on a new non-criminal identity. This is an issue that needs to be addressed immediately. An Enhanced Disclosure will reveal any crimes committed, regardless of how long ago a conviction may have occurred. This is counterproductive to the rehabilitative process (see Holligan, 2013). For the core YSG members in the study, a criminal record merely gave an official stamp to an already-embedded criminal identity.

A further key strength of the research is that it goes beyond contemporary Scottish gang literature in providing a gang typology where the link between YSG membership and organised crime is made known. Previously, YSG members would often remain unknown and be allowed to progress towards organised crime, or become more entrenched in criminal lifestyles until too late. In contrast, this research details the progression of gang organisation as a means for gang business and, in doing so, allows gang/group types to be addressed more effectively.

Yet, the findings reveal that most YCGs fail to progress on to becoming SOCGs because members are often incarcerated, or issues of hyper-masculinity break down gang workability. Therefore, it is recommended that YCGs be addressed in a much more punitive manner than that for YSGs. Once YSG core members have solidified and adopt criminal identity as intrinsic to group practice and nature, then soft intervention policies will be unlikely to prove effective. Rather, greater degrees of gang suppression are required. Yet, this is a difficult area to negotiate because while gang activities typically resemble organised crime, they are more akin to organised efforts of crime. Usually, gang activities are rooted in issues related to positions of advanced marginality and the social aspects of gang lifestyles.

Likewise, another issue of YCGs is 'age'. Given that members are very often still adolescents, heavy-handed gang suppression may only prove to aid criminal trajectories in the long run, even if the gang itself is dismantled. Therefore, it is recommended that gang suppression and gang dismantlement be undertaken by police, along with other agencies that simultaneously offer gang members alternative routes out of the gang along the way. This may involve assisting in desistance programmes aimed at helping offenders cease offending patterns, or even working with the police on future issues. This is a type of restorative justice, as opposed to simply dismantling the gang and simply imprisoning gang members with no longer-term objectives (see Braithwaite, 1989; Barton, 2000). Rehabilitation must be put at the forefront when dealing with YCGs following efforts to dismantle the gang. Gang member imprisonment can by no means be the end goal. While YCG networks require dismantlement, members themselves also need to be given the chance to effectively re-enter society without being continually criminalised. Mandatory assignment to back-to-work schemes and further education, which offer real career prospects as opposed to dead-end jobs, while inside prisons may go some way to helping offenders re-engage with wider mainstream society upon release.

OCGs, on the other hand, are firmly entrenched criminal groups and the nature of the relationships within are purely business. Thus, it is recommended that police are used to dismantle the gang. Given that OCG members are persistent adult offenders who have firmly adopted criminal identity over a considerable period of time, they should be subjected to the full force of the law. Additionally, this is also done in order to reflect the serious nature of the organised crime that they engage in. Given that such activity has the potential to cause significant socio-economic harm to the communities in which they operate and also wider society more generally, strict sentences should be used as a deterrent. Yet, it must be recognised that this is unlikely to actually deter the majority of these individuals; thus, efforts must also be made to disrupt those networks, areas of social space and illegal markets in which they operate (Paoli, 2000). This requires an intelligence-led approach to policing (see Ratcliffe, 2008). Given that YCGs have often begun to affiliate or have loose associations with such individuals, YCG members can be used to help provide information and intelligence, which, in turn, can be used to dismantle and disrupt OCG operations. The SSOCS (Scottish Government, 2015) already works on a similar premise regarding the necessity of disrupting organised crime networks. However, where this research can significantly aid policy and practice is in providing inside information as to how these illegal markets operate, and how individuals and gangs engage within them. There is a significant lack of literature that accurately reflects the largely amorphous Scottish illegal drug market; yet, while insights are limited, this research nonetheless offers a foundation from which future research can be conducted. Arguably, a key method for apprehension is to trace the money as opposed to the drugs, particularly given that OCGs rarely, if at all, handle such commodities directly. In addition, money is often laundered by the time OCGs handle it directly; therefore, it may prove more effective and worthwhile making efforts to capture such criminals by investigating benefit claims (either as claimants of welfare or non-claimants living high lifestyles with no, or little, explanation for their sources of financial income), tax evasion or legitimate revenues of income (comparing reported with actual figures).

Identifying differing criminal trajectories

A central theme to emerge from this research is that the study here presents, and traces, in detail the criminal pathways and trajectories that career criminals and chronic offenders who seek to engage in organised crime take. This makes the book unique in many ways given that such offender trajectories are tracked both individually and in the wider social group setting. A consequence of carrying out research exploring criminal trajectories and how criminal identities and practices are developed and refined over time is that those facilitators that aid and influence such behaviour can also be identified. This, in turn, allows for subsequent recommendations to be put forward that can help remove and reduce the impact of particular factors that may aid criminal trajectories. Likewise, by also accessing participants, at least initially, through desistance-based outreach programmes, those facilitators that aid the desistance process can also be highlighted and evaluated. First, though, it is important to outline those main facilitators that the research identified as having a particular impact upon criminal trajectories.

The study found that personal traits/characteristics innate to the participants were of significance in the early development of delinquent coping strategies (see Agnew, 2006, 2013) and delinquent identities (see Eysneck, 1947). Quick recourse to the emotion of 'anger', in particular, was found to be strongly linked with delinquency (Agnew, 2006). Yet, this by no means certified a criminal identity. Rather, such coping strategies were also reinforced through a number of other factors. Early socialisation was found to be particularly important in the development of subsequent delinquent identity. Factors like poor, abusive and inconsistent parenting styles/techniques aided criminal coping strategies. Likewise, the local urban ecology was also found to be important in developing proactive responses based upon aggression and even violence. Adolescent years in themselves proved to be particularly stressful periods of time for a multitude of reasons; yet, peer influence and identity seeking proved to be significantly important in embedding a criminal identity as somewhat intrinsic. If favoured by the participant and established from an early age, this would, in turn, be developed and reinforced over time.

A number of longitudinal studies (see Glueck and Glueck, 1950; Gottfredson and Hirschi, 1990; Laub and Sampson, 1993; Sampson and Laub, 1993) have likewise carried out research that examines criminal trajectories and pathways into, and out of, crime over the life course. The studies in general tend to suggest that innate characteristics, combined with the sphere of primary socialisation, are particularly important in determining delinquent and criminal behaviour in later life. In the UK, the resulting body of work that has emerged from the data set produced by the Cambridge Institute of Criminology, which began in the 1960s, has arguably led the way in the field, with the work of Professor David Farrington being most notable. Carrying out interviews with over 400 boys from predominantly white working-class families, from the 1950s till the present day, the combined data set[2] found that – like prior longitudinal studies from the US – certain internal traits and external factors often shared a strong correlation with various forms of offender typologies. The early years and primary sphere of socialisation were highlighted as being of significance. Farrington et al (2006) defined four offender categories:

1. Persisters: individuals who have been convicted both before and after their 21st birthday.
2. Desisters: individuals who have been convicted only up to age 20.
3. Late-onset offenders: individuals who have been convicted only at age 21 or older.
4. Unconvicted: individuals who have not been convicted up to age 50.

To help identify what factors influence these offenders, Farrington et al use a range of predictors. As we are focusing on persistent offenders, we shall focus on the 'persisters' category. Within this category, it was found that 7 per cent of individuals accounted for around half of all the recorded crime reported in the study. These are deemed to be 'chronic offenders' by Farrington et al. The scholars found that when compared to those of the 'unconvicted' category, the predictors 'convicted parent', 'high daring', 'delinquent sibling', 'young mother', 'low popularity', 'disrupted family' and 'large family size' all shared, to varying degrees, a strong correlation with persistent offending behaviour. In addition, it was found that those who had first offended at 10–13 years of age were most likely to have multiple convictions over time and continue to offend over the longest duration. Yet, the study, and subsequent work that has also emerged from the Cambridge Institute of Criminology data set, does not refine which persistent offenders enter into organised or organised efforts of crime, but rather includes all within the umbrella bracket of persistent offenders, ranging from petty to serious. Yet, as seen from this study, not all persistent offenders are the same, and those who enter into organised criminal networks arguably cause considerably more socio-economic damage on the whole than persistent, yet petty, offenders.

In relation to this study, I am particularly interested in the first set of predictors, which suggest that the factors of 'convicted father', 'high daring', 'delinquent sibling', 'young mother', 'low popularity', 'disrupted family' and 'large family' are consistent predictors that are evident in the lives of persistent offenders when compared with unconvicted participants. Likewise, regarding the sample group, the overwhelming majority of participants in the study had several, if not all, of these factors evident in their lives. High daring or risk taking was an evident trait found in much of the sample. Similarly, most of the sample had been raised by young mothers and had experienced disruptive or reordered families at home. Yet, while not all the participants had large immediate families (that is, siblings, mother, father), extended family networks (cousins, aunties, uncles) were usually found to be quite extensive and also prominent within the local community. In addition, Farrington et al (2006) highlight that late-onset offenders tended to reside within areas of poor housing. Yet, while much of the sample in this study were more akin to persisters than late-onset offenders, in relation to offending behaviour, poor housing, low income and low socio-economic status were nonetheless frequently mentioned as 'justifications' for engaging in organised efforts of crime and organised crime per se, as opposed to simply delinquent or petty criminal behaviour. Thus, in developing a framework that similarly seeks to identify predictors in offending types among the most persistent offenders, I extended Farrington et al's (2006) model to include persistent offenders involved in organised efforts of crime/organised crime, while simultaneously further refining the existing 'persisters' category. The expanded model is as follows:

1. Persistent offenders involved in organised efforts of crime/organised crime: individuals who have been convicted both before and after their 21st birthday and are involved in organised efforts of crime/ organised crime.
2. Petty persistent offenders: individuals who have been convicted both before and after their 21st birthday and are not involved in organised efforts of crime/organised crime.
3. Desisters: individuals who have been convicted only up to age 20.
4. Late-onset offenders: individuals who have been convicted only at age 21 or older.
5. Unconvicted: individuals who have not been convicted up to age 50.

By extending the work of Farrington et al (2006) to compare persistent petty offenders with persistent offenders involved in organised efforts of crime/organised crime, I aim to help identify those persistent offenders most likely, yet by no means exclusively, to engage in organised efforts of crime and organised crime (at least in relation to illegal drug supply). I was interested in identifying those predictors that would see some persistent offenders become involved in organised crime, while others do not. I found two key differences to be evident. These are the predictors 'access to pre-existing criminal networks' and 'high popularity'. High popularity is attributed given that participants in the study worked in social group settings. Similarly, having access to pre-existing criminal networks, the participants in the study were able to move beyond petty criminality and instead use their criminal contacts and know-how to re-engage back into mainstream society through the sale of commodities in illegal markets. Yet, given that the research method for this study is based upon a qualitative methodology, with in-depth interviews, while Farrington et al (2006) apply a primarily quantitative methodology, such insights are limited. Rather, the purpose of extending this model is merely to highlight those predictors that were evident in the research. In order to determine how significant relationships are, further research would be required. However, it should be noted that other studies by Farrington et al (1998) do identify some correlation between intergenerational criminality, access to criminal networks and progression towards more serious types of offending.

Despite limitations, the gang typology, the illustration of the Scottish drug market and the persistent offender model presented here can all be used to help provide accurate definitions and exploratory insights of gang organisation as a means for gang business for relevant law-enforcement agencies and multi-agency partnerships, including the National Crime Agency (NCA), Action for Children Scotland, the Scottish Crime and Drug Enforcement Agency (SCDEA) and the Violence Reduction Unit (VRU). Likewise, academic researchers may also benefit from such research, which provides, at least, some much-needed groundwork from which future research can be developed.

A need to combat the causes of crime and not just the consequences

However, while I have previously stressed a real need, and put forward a subsequent strategy, for law enforcement to tackle linchpin areas in detecting, deterring, disrupting and dismantling gang structures at various levels of organisation, gang organisation as a means for gang business is by no means confined to the sphere of law enforcement alone. Rather, law enforcement is effectively dealing with the consequential effects of deeply embedded causes of crime that lie at the very heart of the political, economic and social system of advanced capitalist Western democracy (see Kinsey et al, 1986). One should ask not only 'How do we halt the proliferation of gang organisation?', but also the more difficult question 'Why is gang organisation occurring in the first place?' While the first question is, in its punitive form, first and foremost relegated to the sphere of law enforcement, the second question ultimately addresses the root causes and driving forces that bring about and encourage gang organisation in the first place.

Lawler (2010), drawing upon similar variables put forward by early strain theorists, argues that advanced capitalist society inevitably perpetuates criminality, and more so when situated against the backdrop of 'risk taking' and 'consumerism' (see Beck, 1992; Bauman, 2005). Nowhere else is this truer than perhaps the US–Mexico border, where the cities of El Paso and Juarez meet. On one side (El Paso/US) is a prosperous city, epitomising prosperous capitalism, and on the other is a war-torn region plagued by Mexican cartel activity and intra-gang warfare (Juarez/ Mexico). The contrast between the cities captures the polarising and exploitative nature of advanced capitalism. With the largest distributor of drugs into the US (Mexico) and the US as the largest consumer of drugs, the stark dichotomous position of capitalism is played out perfectly, in which the economic base produces and reproduces infrastructures that support, on the one side, the illegitimate economy and, on the other, the legitimate economy. Yet, it is the exploitative nature of the legal market in the US that, in turn, creates and shapes the illegal market in Mexico. As the US increases in wealth off the back of neighbouring countries such as Mexico, the Mexican economy responds in kind by filling the void with an illegal market, in this case, the drugs economy.

While capitalism operates on a supply and demand basis, certain products and services are prohibited. Yet, this prohibiting generally comes by way of the more powerful imposing themselves or their ideology upon the less powerful (see Foucault, 1977). For example, the American 'War on Drugs' has been a continual theme in the fight against crime in the US. Despite particular products being in significant demand, their supply is nonetheless prohibited, for whatever reason.[3] Yet, regardless, the important point to note is the power relations as to who imposes what upon whom. Gootenberg (2007, 2011) details how US intervention has time and again seen once lawfully obtained substances that had no prior inherent links to criminality become prohibited as part of wider strategic policies and strategies. Ultimately, the advanced capitalist system in the North America, in which the rules of capitalism are themselves dictated by the disproportionately powerful US, has seen the resulting system act like a vacuum, whereby all goods, commodities and services deemed valuable flow out of peripheral countries and into the US, while population movement is simultaneously subjected to intense regulation. The drug trade in the region, which is also ultimately now a global trade in the contemporary era, is an inevitable consequence of the USA's dictatorial, and exploitative, relationship with neighbouring countries, all under the banner of capitalism.

This phenomenon has been extrapolated to other Westernised countries, including Britain (Bowling, 1999). As gangs in the early 1990s/2000s were a product of globalisation and US and North American influence, so too are the drug-dealing criminal gangs that we see here to some degree. Britain has followed suit in many ways. Yet, while the US plays out this relationship at a transnational level, in Britain, the same processes are also at work internally. Deindustrialisation, with inadequate replacement, training and investment, coupled with austerity, welfare cuts and the polarisation of not just wealth, but also opportunities, goods and other life chances, has meant that many marginalised populations in isolated communities have become disenfranchised from the system while their population nonetheless still adheres to neoliberal ideology within a consumerist society (see Wintour, 2015; Trussell Trust, 2016). This has ultimately led many to turn to various forms of criminality, often only to a minor degree (for example, fraudulent welfare claims), or blurring the legal and illegal spheres of activity, in order to not only makes ends meet, but also partake in the social world as social actors. It is perhaps no surprise that since the 2008 economic recession, and as the cost of living has increased at rates that outstrip income and wages (see Blyth, 2013), OCG activity has increased considerably.

To suggest that one directly leads to the other would be ridiculous, but there is undoubtedly some degree of correlation and influencing factors. Davies (2013) found similar trends during the early recession of the 20th century. The participants in this study typically came from deprived backgrounds. Likewise, they regularly spoke of wanting to 'live' as opposed to merely 'surviving' in today's materialistic society. Indeed, Bauman (2005) suggests that for such populations, the perception is that the time to act is now, there are no second chances and those who wait simply fall behind, never to recover again. Identity in Britain today is largely related to how one lives as opposed to how one earns their money. This is a theme that was evident in the participants. In Scotland, as the CIRV (2008) initiative took place to tackle youth violence, the recession had begun. While CIRV was championed by the VRU (2011) as having addressed youth violence and knife crime in the city, knife crime and violence dropped as a whole steadily across the region and not just in areas where CIRV operated (see Deuchar, 2013). Yet, coinciding with this process was the rise in OCG activity and organised criminal engagement, a process captured in subsequent years in Scottish Government (2009a, 2013, 2015) reports. The model and data presented here show the evolving nature of gangs. It is possible that many YSGs did not, in fact, 'disappear', but rather evolved – a process also found by Whittaker et al (forthcoming), who re-examined ten years of the gangs studied by Pitts (2008) in London.

To tackle gang organisation, a law-enforcement strategy alone is not enough. While it may have a significant impact in the short term,[4] in order to adequately address the wider issue as to why people join gangs and engage in organisation as a means for business, there needs to be a combined approach, whereby multi-agency partnerships work across the board (that is, the public, private and third sector spheres) to address more deep-rooted causalities. However, there ultimately needs to be greater distribution of equality, and not just wealth. The current political climate has led to a deterioration of already-deteriorating services and environment. The same conditions found in those countries such as Mexico where drugs are the largest export are being forged here in the isolated communities of Britain, such as those communities in which the gangs are predominantly arising. These pre-existing conditions are not issues such as poverty per se – along with other externally perceived social ills – but rather the structural properties that facilitate their development and sustainability (see Matthews and Young, 2003). The British government needs to do more to bring a fairer and greater distribution of equality and services to those in marginalised communities. Since the gradual reduction of the middle-class population, more individuals and families than ever in the contemporary era are again being exposed to the conditions in which criminality not only flourishes, but may to some extent be perceived as a legitimate means for one to partake in social engagement, if not of survival itself (see Young, 2007).

Reflections and limitations

As with any research, there are always limitations to be considered. This study is no different and limitations are evident. Research limitations may include issues of sampling, location, interpretation and labelling, among others. First, in relation to the study itself as a whole, a number of limitations are evident. One of these limitations that has to be acknowledged is that by merely analysing the potential for gang organisation, there is always the possibility that a number of diverse social groupings may become labelled under umbrella terms. This is because gang organisation looks at the subsequent stages that gangs may progress through as they become intrinsically criminal in their outlook. While it was necessary to create gang typologies in order to identify gang organisation, this can nonetheless bring adverse effects, such as labelling and categorisation. With regard to first identifying the gang, as discussed by contemporary Scottish gang literature as a whole, it was necessary to use an umbrella term, that is, YSGs. Only by doing so was the current research able to move beyond existing literature and identify errors. Yet, YSGs were shown to often differ in many respects from one another, as referenced throughout the findings by participants. While these differences were acknowledged, only by using an umbrella term could the participants and future readers understand that which is being discussed. While 'YSG' is arguably a more precise terminology than previous literature using the broad and loosely defined term 'gang', further investigation could nonetheless show significant differences to exist that could potentially bring about subcategorisations. Hallsworth and Young (2006) similarly point out that gang typologies can, on the one hand, prove useful conceptualisations, yet, on the other, be stigmatising and potentially contain net-widening consequences.

Similarly, umbrella terms also have the ability to convey powerful subjective images that may not always necessarily be true. These terms are often open to individual interpretation as individuals seek to identify common denominators, linked with personal experience, in order to understand and interpret their own social realities. For example, terms often bring along with them certain images that exist in the subjective. Ultimately, images, whether or not the individual recognises them to be so, are often largely stereotypical and, as such, these images are likely to be applied, at least initially, to anything that is also placed under umbrella terminology. To clarify, if I was to think of a house, for example, then certain stereotypical images based upon my own understanding of what a house is and my own experience of living within a house will be applied to the term 'house'. Personally, when I hear the term 'house', I think of a mid-terrace house with a back garden. Yet, while I know that houses come in all shapes, forms and sizes, this image is nonetheless the first my mind conjures up. Likewise, this is typically accompanied by 'good memories' given that I had an enjoyable experience with my family life. Yet, the same term, 'house', may conjure up a completely different image in the mind of another individual. Similarly, the term 'YSG', for myself, immediately relates back to an enjoyable period where I spent much time socialising with friends. Yet, the same term may be subjectively interpreted in a very different manner by another individual who may have had a negative experience with or having spent time in YSGs. Thus, there is always danger when applying umbrella terminology. Arguably, I could have gone even further in providing additional categories for YSGs, not to mention additional subcategories within YSGs, particularly given that the distinction between the core and outer layer had already laid the foundations to do so. Likewise, the same could be said to be true of other terms used throughout.

Another limitation of the data that has to be acknowledged is that concerning the measurements used to define intrinsic criminality, which, in turn, defined core and non-core members. First, given that it has been shown that persistent offenders and those who have access to criminal networks are more likely to continue offending patterns into adulthood, which may also, at times, increase in severity and intensity (see Sutherland 1939; Farrington et al, 2006; Fader, 2016), I believed that those who had been involved in gangs and organised crime would most likely have been persistent offenders, in accordance with findings by Agnew (2013), Farrington et al (2006), Moffitt (1993) and Rowe and Farrington (1997). Thus, it was deemed necessary in distinguishing between offender typologies, which meant that some form of measurement was required. Therefore, given that the research design advocated a qualitative approach, I felt that it may prove beneficial to simply ask how participants viewed their identity and whether or not they felt criminality to be intrinsic to their nature. Yet, simultaneously, I was aware that participants all too readily tell the researcher that which they believe the researcher wants to hear (see Sandberg, 2010). Thus, it was decided that an additional form of measurement should be applied in order to help support participant claims. In seeking some tangible measurement to be used in conjunction with participant subjectivity, I decided to look at offending patterns. While participants often had their claims verified by others, including voluntary workers, on other occasions, participants would provide other means of verification. Yet, at times, such claims were simply unverifiable given that offences in early childhood are not recorded with disclosure checks (Disclosure Scotland, 2016). Therefore, while all participants were able to discuss, in specific detail, incidents that they claimed to have occurred in early childhood, these were still nonetheless unverifiable in some cases by third parties. While the research was more concerned with how the participants viewed themselves, those additional tools used to measure whether claims of criminality were inherent to the participant could be developed more adequately. This is a point (outlined in policy and practice) for future research to build upon. Ultimately, limitations are inherent to any research, yet the importance is not only in acknowledging such limitations, but building upon such insights when carrying out future research. It is hoped that by pointing out these limitations, future research can avoid such potential pitfalls.

In addition, of course, the research aims as a whole influence the sampling techniques, intended interviewees and various demographics. Looking to explore gang organisation meant that I was already looking to work with those who progressed along criminal trajectories. This meant that this research largely reflects the voices of the minority, as opposed to the voices of the majority. This is even true with regard to core offenders as a significant number do not carry on to the higher echelons of the criminal underworld. Much of this is missing from the sample itself, and follow-up studies would be needed to explore those turning points that emerge, or other factors that see gang organisation halted. Furthermore, as only offending that includes more than one individual is considered organised crime by Police Scotland, this affects the sample as group offending was one of the sample criteria. This skews the research towards those who have been involved in group offending and neglects a number of offender types that may operate individually. The research may give the impression that all criminality is therefore a group activity, yet this is not the case, and such considerations of sampling, intentions, aims and so on should be taken into consideration when reading the book.

Notes

[1]   It is perhaps worthy to note that according to current definitions of organised crime in Scotland, individuals cannot technically carry out organised crime given that Police Scotland identify organised crime as largely a phenomenon carried out in a group context. A number of scholars, such as Von Lampe (2016), note similar issues in organised crime definitions, but highlight that given that organised crime requires planning, coordination and the pulling together of resources, individuals typically have a need for the efforts of others. This also makes the situating of OCGs under the gang umbrella a helpful application for some practitioner services.

[2]   While I draw upon Farrington et al (2006) as a point of reference, the data set has in fact produced countless publications from an array of collaborators (for example, Farrington et al, 2001, 2009). I merely put forward the publication by Farrington et al (2006) as it sums up well the overall findings in a general sense.

[3]   These reasons tend to differ by who is doing the arguing and from what perspective such arguments are being perceived.

[4]   This is much like zero-tolerance policing in New York in the 1980s, brought about by the 'Broken Windows' thesis.

References

Adamoli, S., Di Nicola, A., Savona, E.U. and Zoffi, P. (1998) *Organised crime around the world*. Helsinki: HEUNI.

Agnew, R. (2006) *Pressured into crime: An overview of general strain theory*. Los Angeles, CA: Roxbury Publishing Company.

Agnew, R. (2013) 'When criminal coping is likely: an extension of general strain theory'. *Deviant Behaviour*, 34: 653–70.

Agnew, R., Matthews, S., Bucher, J., Welcher, A. and Keyes, C. (2008) 'Socio-economic status, economic problems, and delinquency'. *Youth & Society*, 40(2): 159–81.

Albanese, J.S. (2014) 'Choosing a micro or macro perspective for understanding organized crime: the contributions of Ernesto Savona'. In: S. Caneppele and F. Calderoni (eds) *Organized crime, corruption and crime prevention*. New York, NY: Springer International Publishing, pp 263–8.

Aldridge, J. (2011) 'Review of reluctant gangsters: the changing face of youth crime by J. Pitts'. *Youth Justice*, 10(2): 202–4.

Aldridge, J., Medina, J. and Ralphs, R. (2008) 'Dangers and problems of doing gang research in the UK'. In: F. van Gemart, D. Peterson and I. Lien (eds) *Street gangs, migration and ethnicity*. Devon: Willan.

Aldridge, J., Medina, J. and Ralphs, R. (2011) 'Counting gangs: conceptual and validity problems with the Eurogang definition'. In: F. Esbensen and C. Maxson (eds) *Youth gangs in international perspective: Tales from the Eurogang program of research*. New York, NY: Springer.

Alexander, C. (2008) '(Re)Thinking gangs'. Available at: www.runnymedetrust.org/uploads/publications/pdfs/RethinkingGangs-2008.pdf (accessed 15 February 2010).

Alonso, A.A. (2004) 'Racialized identities and the formation of black gangs in Los Angeles'. *Urban Geography*, 25(7): 658–74.

Anderson, E. (1999) *Code of the street: Decency, violence and the moral life of the inner city*. New York, NY: W.W. Norton.

Antonopoulos, G.A. and Papanicolaou, G. (2010) 'Asterix and Obelix in drugland: an introduction to the special issue on "drug markets"'. *Trends in Organized Crime*, 13: 1–12.

Bakowski, P. (2013) 'The EU response to organised crime'. Library of European Parliament, pp 1–6.

Bannister, J., Pickering, J. and Batchelor, S. (2010) *Troublesome youth groups, gangs and knife carrying in Scotland*. Edinburgh: Social Research, Scottish Government.

Bartie, A. (2010) 'Moral panics and Glasgow gangs: exploring the new wave of Glasgow hooliganism, 1965–1970'. *Contemporary British History*, 24(3): 385–408.

Bartie, A. (2014) 'City of gangs: Glasgow and the rise of the British gangster'. *Contemporary British History*, 29(1): 139–41.

Barton, C. (2000) 'Restorative justice empowerment'. Available at: www. voma.org/docs/barton_rje.pdf (accessed 16 May 2015).

Bauman, Z. (1989) *Modernity and the Holocaust*. Ithaca, NY: Cornell University Press.

Bauman, Z. (2005) *Work, consumerism and the new poor*. Buckingham: Open University Press.

BBC (British Broadcasting Corporation) (2018) 'The downfall of Scotland's most dangerous crime gang'. BBC News, 22 January.

Beck, U. (1992) *Risk society: Towards a new modernity*. New York, NY: Sage Publications.

Beck, U. (2007) 'Beyond class and nation: reframing social inequalities in a globalizing world'. *The British Journal of Sociology*, 58(4): 679–705.

Becker, H. (1963) *Outsiders*. New York, NY: Free Press.

Bell, D. (1953) 'Crime as an American way of life'. *The Antioch Review*, 13: 131–54.

Bennett, T. and Holloway, K. (2004) 'Gang membership, drugs and crime in the UK'. *British Journal of Criminology*, 44(3): 305–23.

Berger, P.L. and Luckman, T. (1966) *The social construction of reality*. London: Random House.

Bjerregaard, B. (2010) 'Gang membership and drug involvement: untangling the complex relationship'. *Crime & Delinquency*, 56: 3–34.

Blyth, M. (2013) *Austerity: The history of a dangerous idea*. Oxford University Press: Oxford.

Bourdieu, P. (1984) *Distinction*. Abingdon, Oxon: Routledge.

Bourdieu, P. (1986) 'The forms of capital'. In: J. Richardson (ed) *Handbook of theory and research for the sociology of education*. New York, NY: Greenwood, pp 241–58.

Bourdieu, P. (1989) 'Social space and symbolic power'. *Sociological Theory*, 7(1): 14–25.

Bowling, B (1999) 'The rise and fall of New York murder: zero tolerance or crack's decline?' *British Journal of Criminology*, 39: 531–54.

Boyle, J. (1977) *A sense of freedom*. London: Pan Books.

Bradshaw, P. (2005) 'Terrors and young teams: youth gangs and delinquency in Edinburgh'. In: S.H. Decker and F.M. Weerman (eds) *European street gangs and troublesome youth groups*. Oxford: AltaMira Press.

Braithwaite, J. (1989) *Crime, shame and reintegration*. Cambridge: Cambridge University Press.

Bullock, K. and Tilley, N. (2003) *Crime reduction and problem-oriented policing*. Devon: Willan Publishing.

Campana, P. and Varese, F. (2011) 'Eavesdropping on the Mob: the functional diversification of Mafia activities across territories'. *European Journal of Criminology*, 8(3): 213–28.

Campana, P. and Varese, F. (2018) 'Organized crime in the United Kingdom: illegal governance of markets and communities'. *British Journal of Criminology*, advanced online.

Campbell, A. and Muncer, S. (1989) 'Them and us: a comparison of the cultural context of American gangs and Sundar British subcultures'. *Deviant Behavior*, 10(3): 271–88.

Canadian Justice (2018) 'A typology of profit driven crimes'. Department of Justice. Government of Canada. Available at: www.justice.gc.ca/eng/rp-pr/csj-sjc/jsp-sjp/rp02_12-dr02_12/p3.html

Carlsson, C. (2012) 'Using "turning points" to understand processes of change in offending: notes from a Swedish study on life courses and crime'. *British Journal of Criminology*, 52(1): 1–16.

Carrapico, H., Irrer, D. and Tupman, B. (2014) 'Transnational organised crime and terrorism: different peas, same pod?' *Global Crime*, 15(3/4): 213–18.

Casey, J., Hay, G., Godfrey, C. and Parrot, S. (2009) *Assessing the scale and impact of illicit drug markets in Scotland*. Edinburgh: Scottish Government.

Caulkins, J. (1992) 'Thinking about displacement in drug markets: why observing change of venue isn't enough'. *Journal of Drug Issues*, 22: 17–30.

Centre for Social Justice (2008) 'Breakthrough Glasgow: ending the costs of social breakdown'. Available at: www.centreforsocialjustice.org.uk/core/wp-content/uploads/2016/08/BreakthroughGlasgow.pdf (accessed 14 December 2016).

Centre for Social Justice (2009) 'Dying to belong: an in-depth review of street gangs in Britain'. Available at: www.centreforsocialjustice.org.uk/core/wp-content/uploads/2016/08/DyingtoBelongFullReport.pdf (accessed 14 December 2016).

Chamberlin, H.B. (1920) 'The Chicago Crime Commission – how the businessmen of Chicago are fighting crime'. *Journal of the American Institute of Criminal Law and Criminology*, 11(3): 386–97.

Chamberlin, H.B. (1921) 'Reporting of the operating director (Bulletin No.10)'. Chicago Crime Commission, pp 6–7.

Chatwin, C. and Potter, G. (2014) 'Blurred boundaries: the artificial distinction between "use" and "supply" in the U.K. cannabis market'. *Contemporary Drug Problems*, 41(4): 536–50.

CIRV (Community Initiative to Reduce Violence) (2008) *Second year report*. Glasgow: Violence Reduction Unit.

CIRV (2009) *First year report*. Glasgow: Violence Reduction Unit.

Cloward, R. and Ohlin, L. (1960) *Delinquency and opportunity: A theory of delinquent gangs*. London: Macmillan.

Cohen, A.K. (1955) *Delinquent boys: The culture of a gang*. Illinois, IL: The Free Press.

Cohen, S. (1972) *Folk devils and moral panic: The creation of the Mods and the Rockers*. Oxford: Blackwell.

Cohen, S. (1980) 'Footprints in the sand: a further report on criminology and the sociology of deviance in Britain'. In: M. Fitzgerald, G. McLennan and J. Pawson (eds) *Crime and society: Readings in history and theory*. London: Routledge and Kegan Paul, p 240.

Community Safety Glasgow (2015) 'Community Safety Glasgow – nine years on'. Report published by Community Safety Glasgow.

Coomber, R. (2006) *Pusher myths: Re-situating the drug dealer*. London: Free Association Books.

Coomber, R. and Moyle, L. (2014) 'Beyond drug dealing: developing and extending the concept of "social supply" of illicit drugs to "minimally commercial supply"'. *Drugs: Education, Prevention and Policy*, 21(2): 157–64.

Coomber, R. and Moyle, L. (2017) 'The changing shape of street-level heroin and crack supply in England: commuting, holidaying and cuckooing drug dealers across "county lines"'. *British Journal of Criminology*. Available at: https://doi.org/10.1093/bjc/azx068

Coomber, R. and Turnbull, P. (2007) 'Arenas of drug transaction: adolescent cannabis transactions in England – "social supply"'. *Journal of Drug Issues*, 37: 749–54.

Coope, S. and Bland, N. (2004) *Reducing the impact of local drug markets: A research review*. Edinburgh: Scottish Executive.

Cox, A. (2011) 'Youth gangs in the UK: myth or reality?' *Internet Journal of Criminology*, 12: 1–18.

Croall, H. (2011) *Crime and society in Britain* (2nd edn). Harlow: Longman.

Cyster, R. and Rowe, S. (2006) *Low-level heroin markets: A case study approach*. Edinburgh: Scottish Executive Social Research.

David, F. (2012) *Organised crime and trafficking in persons*. Trends and Issues in Crime and Criminal Justice, No 436. Canberra: Australian Institute of Criminology, Australian Government.

Davies, A. (1998) 'Street gangs, crime and policing in Glasgow during the 1930s: the case of the Beehive Boys'. *Social History*, 23(3): 3–4.

Davies, A. (2007) 'The Scottish Chicago? From "hooligans" to "gangsters" in inter-war Glasgow'. *Cultural and Social History*, 4(4): 511–27.

Davies, A. (2008) 'Street gangs, crime and policing in Glasgow during the 1930s: the case of the Beehive Boys'. *Social History*, 23(2): 251–67.

Davies, A. (2013) *City of gangs: Glasgow and the rise of the British gangster*. London: Hodder & Stoughton.

Decker, S.H. and Chapman, M.T. (2008) *Drug smugglers on drug smuggling: Lessons from the inside*. Philadelphia, PA: Temple University Press.

Decker, S.H. and Curry, G.D. (2002) 'Gangs, gang homicides, and gang loyalty: organized crimes or disorganized criminals'. *Journal of Criminal Justice*, 30: 343–52.

Decker, S.H. and Kempf-Leonard, K. (1991) 'Constructing gangs: the social definition of youth activities'. *Criminal Justice Policy Review*, 5(4): 271–91.

Decker, S.H. and Van Winkle, B. (1996) *Life in the gang*. Cambridge: Cambridge University Press.

Decker, S.H., Pyrooz, D. and Moule, R.K., Jr (2014) 'Disengagement from gangs as role transitions'. *Journal of Research on Adolescence*, 24(2): 268–83.

De Coster, S. and Hiemer, K. (2001) 'The relationship between law violation and depression: an interactionsist analysis'. *Criminology*, 39(4): 799–836.

Densley, J.A. (2012) 'The organisation of London's street gangs'. *Global Crime*, 13(1): 42–64.

Densley, J.A. (2013) *How gangs work: An ethnography of youth violence*. London: Palgrave Macmillan.

Densley, J.A. (2014) 'It's gang life: but not as we know it: the evolution of gang business'. *Crime & Delinquency*, 60: 517–46.

Densley, J.A., McLean, R., Deuchar, R. and Harding, S. (2018a) 'An altered state? Emergent changes to illicit drug markets and distribution networks in Scotland'. *International Journal of Drug Policy*, 58: 113–20.

Densley, J.A., McLean, R., Deuchar, R. and Harding, S. (2018b) 'Progression from cafeteria to à la carte offending: Scottish organised crime narratives'. *Howard Journal of Crime and Justice*, DOI:10.1111/hojo.12304

Denton, B. and O'Malley, P. (1999) 'Gender, trust and business: women drug dealers in the illicit economy'. *British Journal of Criminology*, 39(4): 513–30.

Deuchar, R. (2009) *Gangs, marginalised youth and social capital*. Stoke on Trent: Trentham Books Ltd.

Deuchar, R. (2011) 'People look at us, the way we dress and they think we're gangsters: bonds, bridges, gangs and refugees. A qualitative study of inter-cultural social capital in Glasgow'. *Journal of Refugee Studies*, 24(4): 672–89.

Deuchar, R. (2013) *Policing youth violence: Transatlantic connections*. London: Institute of Education Press.

Deuchar, R. and Holligan, C. (2010) 'Gangs sectarianism and social capital: a qualitative study of young people in Scotland'. *Sociology*, 44(1): 13–30.

Deuchar, R. and Sapouna, M. (2016) '"It's harder to go to court yourself because you don't really know what to expect": reducing the negative effects of court exposure on young people – findings from an evaluation in Scotland'. *Youth Justice*, 16(2): 130–46.

Deuchar, R., McLean, R., Harding, S. and Densley, J. (2018) 'Deficit or credit? A comparative, qualitative study of gender agency and female gang membership in Los Angeles and Glasgow'. *Crime and Delinquency*, DOI: 10.1177/0011128718794192

Disclosure Scotland (2016) 'Homepage'. Available at: www.disclosurescotland.co.uk (accessed 22 October 2016).

Downes, D.M. (1966) *The delinquent solution*. London: Routledge and Kegan Paul.

Eitle, D., Gunkel, S. and Van Gundy, K. (2004) 'Cumulative exposure to stressful life events and male gang membership'. *Journal of Criminal Justice*, 32: 95–111.

Esbensen, F., Peterson, D., Taylor, T. and Freng, A. (2010) *Youth violence: Sex and race differences in offending, victimization and gang membership*. Philadelphia, PA: Temple University Press.

Eysneck, H. (1947) *Dimensions of personality*. London: Transaction Publishers.

Fader, J.J. (2016) 'Criminal family networks: criminal capital and cost avoidance among urban drug sellers'. *Deviant Behavior*, 37(11): 1325–40.

Farrington, D., Lambert, S. and West, D. (1998) 'Criminal careers of two generations of family members in the Cambridge Study in Delinquent Development'. *Studies on Crime and Crime Prevention*, 7: 85–105.

Farrington, D., Joliffe, D., Loeber, R., Stouthamer-Loeber, M. and Kalb, L. (2001) 'The concentration of offenders in families and family criminality in the prediction of boys' delinquency'. *Journal of Adolescence*, 24: 579–96.

Farrington, D., Coid, J.W., Harnett, L., Jolliffe, D., Soteriou, N., Turner, R. and West, D.J. (2006) *Criminal careers and life success: New findings from the Cambridge Study in Delinquent Development*. London: Home Office.

Farrington, D., Jeremy, W., Coid, J.W. and Murray, J. (2009) 'Family factors in the intergenerational transmission of offending'. *Criminal Behaviour and Mental Health*, 19(2): 109–24.

Ferris, P. (2005) *Vendetta: Turning your back on crime can be deadly*. Edinburgh: Black and White Publishing.

Ferris, P. and McKay, R. (2001) *The Ferris conspiracy*. Edinburgh: Mainstream.

Ferris, P. and McKay, R. (2010) *Villains: It takes one to know one*. Edinburgh: Black and White Publishing.

Foucault, M. (1977) *Discipline and punish: The birth of the prison*. New York, NY: Pantheon Books.

Fraser, A. (2013) 'Street habitus; gangs, territorialism and social change in Glasgow'. *Journal of Youth Studies*, 16(8): 970–85.

Fraser, A. (2015) *Urban legends*. Oxford: Oxford University Press.

Gambetta, D. (1993) *Codes of the underworld: How criminals communicate*. Princeton, NJ: Princeton University Press.

Garot, R. (2007) *Where you from*. New York, NY: New York University Press.

Gilroy, P. (1987) *There ain't no Black in the Union Jack: The cultural politics of race and nation*. London: Routledge.

Glasgow Indicators Project (2013) 'Overview. Children's safety'. Glasgow Centre for Population Health, Scotland. Available at: www.understandingglasgow.com/indicators/poverty/overview (accessed 12 October 2015).

Glasgow Indicators Project (2015) 'Overview. Poverty'. Glasgow Centre for Population Health, Scotland. Available at: www.understandingglasgow.com/indicators/poverty/overview (accessed 12 October 2015).

Glueck, S. and Glueck, E.T. (1950) *Unravelling juvenile delinquency*. California, CA: Harvard University Press.

Gootenberg, P. (2007) 'The pre-Columbian era of drug trafficking in the Americas: cocaine 1947–1965'. *The Americas*, 64(2): 76–133.

Gootenberg, P. (2008) *Andean cocaine: The making of a global drug*. Chapel Hill, NC: University of North Carolina Press.

Gootenberg, P. (2011) 'Cocaine's blowback north: a pre-history of Mexican drug violence'. *Lasaforum*, XLII(2): 7–10.

Gordon, R. (2000) 'Criminal business organisations, street gangs and "wanna be" groups: a Vancouver perspective'. *Canadian Journal of Criminology and Criminal Justice*, 42(1): 39–60.

Gottfredson, M.R. and Hirschi, T. (1990) *A general theory of crime*. Stanford, CA: Stanford University Press.

Gray, A.M. (1989) *A history of Scotland: Modern times*. Oxford: Oxford University Press.

Hagedorn, J. (1994) 'Neighbourhoods, markets and gang drug organization'. *Journal of Research in Crime and Delinquency*, 31: 264–94.

Hagedorn, J. (1998) *People and folks: Gangs, crime and the underclass in a rustbelt city*. Chicago, IL, and Washington, DC: Lakeview Press and American Psychological Association.

Hagedorn, J. (2008) *A world of gangs: Armed young men and gangsta culture*. Minneapolis, MN: University of Minnesota Press.

Hales, G. and Hobbs, D. (2010) 'Drug markets in the community: a London borough case study'. *Trends in Organized Crime*, 13: 13–30.

Hall, S. and Jefferson, T. (1975) *Resistance through rituals: Youth subcultures in post-war Britain*. London: HarperCollins Publishers.

Hall, S., Critcher, C., Jefferson, T., Clarke, J. and Roberts, T. (1978) *Policing the crisis: Mugging, the state, and law and order*. London: Macmillan.

Hallsworth, S. (2013) *The gang and beyond: Interpreting violent street worlds*. London: Palgrave McMillan.

Hallsworth, S. (2014) 'Gang talking criminologists: a rejoinder to John Pitts'. *Youth and Policy*, 112: 35–43.

Hallsworth, S. and Brotherton, D. (2011) *Urban disorder and gangs: A critique and a warning*. London: Runnymede.

Hallsworth, S. and Young, T. (2004) 'Getting real about gangs'. *Criminal Justice Matters*, 55(1): 12–13.

Hallsworth, S. and Young, T. (2006) *Urban collectives: Gangs and other groups. Report for Operation Cruise*. London: HM Government and Metropolitan Police.

Hallsworth, S. and Young, T. (2008) 'Gang talk and gang talkers: a critique'. *Crime, Media & Culture*, 4(2): 175–95.

Harding, S. (2012) 'A reputational extravaganza? The role of the urban street gang in the riots in London'. *Criminal Justice Matters*, 87(1): 22–3.

Harding, S. (2014) *The street casino: Survival in the violent street gang*. Bristol: Policy Press.

Harding, S., Deuchar, R., Densley, J. and McLean, R. (2018) 'A typology of street robbery and gang organization: insights from qualitative research in Scotland'. *British Journal of Criminology*, doi.org/10.1093/bjc/azy064

Hazani, M. (1986) 'A path to deviance: a multi-stage process'. *Deviant Behavior*, 7: 159–74.

Hebdige, D. (1979) *Subculture: The meaning of style*. London: Methuen.

Hignett, K. (2004) 'Organised crime in East Central Europe: The Czech Republic, Hungary and Poland'. *Global Crime*, 6(1): 70–83.

Hlavka, H.R., Wheelock, D. and Cossyleon, J.E. (2015) 'Narratives of commitments: looking for work with a criminal record'. *The Sociological Quarterly*, 56: 213–36.

Hobbs, D. (2012) *Lush life: Constructing organised crime in the UK*. Oxford: Oxford University Press.

Hobbs, D. and Antonopoulos, G.A. (2013) '"Endemic to the species": ordering the "other" via organised crime'. *Global Crime*, 14(1): 27–51.

Hobbs, D. and Dunningham, C. (1998) 'Glocal organised crime: context and pretext'. In: V. Ruggerio, N. South and I. Taylor (eds) *The new European criminology: Crime and social order in Europe*. London: Routledge.

Hobbs, D., Hadfield, P., Lister, S. and Winlow, S. (2003) *Bouncers: Violence and governance in the night-time economy*. Oxford: Oxford University Press.

Holligan, C. (2013) 'Breaking the code of the street: extending Elijah Anderson's encryption of violent street governance to retaliation in Scotland'. *Journal of Youth Studies*, 18(5): 634–48.

Holligan, C. and Deuchar, R. (2010) 'Territorialities in Scotland: perceptions of young people in Scotland'. *Journal of Youth Studies*, 12(6): 727–42.

Holligan, C. and Deuchar, R. (2015) 'What does it mean to be a man? Psychosocial undercurrents in the voices of incarcerated (violent) Scottish teenage offenders'. *Criminology and Criminal Justice*, 15(3): 361–77.

Holligan, C., McLean, R. and Deuchar, R. (2016) 'Weapon-carrying among young men in Glasgow: street scripts and signals in uncertain social spaces'. *Critical Criminology*, 25(1): 137–51.

Huff, C.R. (ed) (1990) *Gangs in America*. Newbury Park, CA: Sage.

Hughes, A. (2004) 'Representations and counter-representations of domestic violence on Clydeside between the two world wars'. *Labour History Review*, 69(2): 169–84.

Humphries, S. (1981) *Hooligans or rebels: Oral history of working class childhood and youth, 1889–1939*. Oxford: Blackwell Publishers.

Hutchings, A. (2014) 'Crime from the keyboard: organised cybercrime, co-offending, initiation and knowledge transmission'. *Crime, Law and Social Change*, 62(1): 1–20.

Hutton, F. (2005) 'Risky business: gender, drug dealing, and risk'. *Addiction Research and Theory*, 13(6): 545–54.

Jeffery, R. (2003) *Glasgow's godfather: The astonishing inside story of Walter Norval, the city's first crime boss*. Edinburgh: Black and White Publishing.

Johnson, S. (2010) 'Scotland named murder capital of Britain'. *The Telegraph*, 13 December. Available at: www.telegraph.co.uk/news/uknews/scotland/8199703/Scotland-named-murder-capital-of-Britain.html (accessed 9 November 2015).

Karim, M. (1999) 'Wild life: representations and constructions of Yardies'. In: J. Ferrell and N. Websdale (eds) *Making trouble*. New York: Aldine de Gruyter, pp 179–201.

Katz, J. (1988) *Seductions of crime: Moral and sensual attractions in doing evil*. New York, NY: Basic Books.

Katz, J. and Jackson-Jacobs, J. (1997) 'The criminologists' gang'. In: C. Sumner (ed) *Blackwell companion to criminology*. London: Blackwell.

Keddie, A. (2003) 'Little boys: tomorrow's macho lads'. *Discourse: Studies in the Cultural Politics of Education*, 24(3): 289–306.

Kenney, M. (2007) *From Pablo to Osama: Trafficking and terrorist networks, government bureaucracies, and competitive adaptations*. University Park, PA: Penn State University Press.

Kinsey, R., Lea, J. and Young, J. (1986) *Losing the fight against crime*. London: Blackwell.

Kinsley, H. and McArthur, A. (1957) *No mean city*. London: Corgi Books.

Kintrea, K., Bannister, J., Pickering, J. and Reid, M. (2008) *Young people and territoriality in British cities*. York: Joseph Rowntree Foundation.

Klein, M.W. (1971) *Street gangs and street workers*. Englewood Cliffs, NJ: Prentice Hall.

Klein, M.W. (1995) *The American street gang: Its nature, prevalence and control*. New York, NY: Oxford University Press.

Klein, M.W. and Maxson, C.L. (2006) *Street gang patterns and policies*. Oxford University Press. Oxford.

Klein, M.W., Kerner, H.J., Maxson, C.L. and Weitekamp, E.G.M. (2001) *The Eurogang paradox: Street gangs and youth groups in the U.S. and Europe*. New York, NY: Springer.

Klein, M.W., Weerman, F.M. and Thornberry, T.P. (2006) 'Street gang violence in Europe'. *European Journal of Criminology*, 3: 413–37.

Lammy, D. (2018) 'Knife crime offences rise to highest since 2010'. *The Guardian*, 1 February. Available at: www.theguardian.com/uk-news/2018/dec/13/knife-crime-offences-rise-to-highest-level-since-2010-official-figures (accessed 20 May 2018).

Lashly, A.V. (1930) 'The Illinois Crime Survey'. *Journal of the American Institute of Criminal Law and Criminology*, 20(4): 588–605.

Laub, J.H. and Sampson, R.J. (1993) 'Turning points in the life course: why change matters to the study of crime'. *Criminology*, 31(3): 301–25.

Lauritsen, J.L., Heimer, K. and Lynch, J.P. (2009) 'Trends in the gender gap in violent offending: new evidence from the National Crime Victimization Survey'. *Criminology*, 47: 361–99.

Lavezzi, A.M. (2008) 'Economic structure and vulnerability to organised crime: evidence from Sicily'. *Global Crime*, 9(3): 198–220.

Lavezzi, A.M. (2014) 'Organised crime and the economy: a framework for policy prescriptions'. *Global Crime*, 15(1/2): 164–90.

Law, A., Mooney, G. and Helms, G. (2010) 'Urban "disorders", "problem places" and criminal justice in Scotland'. In: H. Croall, G. Mooney and M. Munro (eds) *Criminal justice in Scotland*. Abingdon: Routledge and Willan, pp 43–64.

Lawler, K. (2010) *The American surfer: Radical culture and capitalism.* New York, NY: Routledge.

Lawson, R. (2013) 'The construction of "tough" masculinity: negotiation, alignment and rejection'. *Gender and Language*, 7(3): 369–95.

Lea, J. and Young, J. (1984) *What is to be done about law and order? Crisis in the Eighties.* Harmondsworth, UK: Penguin.

Levi, M. (1998) 'Reflections on organised crime: patterns and control'. *The Howard Journal of Criminal Justice*, 37(4): 335–438.

Levitt, S. and Dubner, S.J. (2006) *Freakonomics: A rogue economist explores the hidden side of everything.* New York, NY: William Morrow.

Levitt, S. and Venkatesh, S. (2001) 'An economic analysis of a drug-selling gang's finances'. *The Quarterly Journal of Economics*, 115: 755–89.

Lombardo, R.M. (2010) *The black hand: Terror by letter in Chicago.* Urbana, IL: University of Illinois Press.

Lusthaus, J. (2013) 'How organised is organised cybercrime?' *Global Crime*, 14(1): 52–60.

Maitra, D., McLean, R. and Deuchar, R. (2017) '"If you want to get paid, you've got to do it": a qualitative study on the morality of crime'. *Deviant Behavior*, 39(7): 949–61

Mares, D. (1999) 'Globalization and gangs: the Manchester case'. *Focaal*, 35: 135–55.

Mares, D. (2001) 'Gangstas or lager louts?' In: M.W. Klein, H.J. Kerner, C.L. Maxson and E.G.M. Weitekamp (eds) *The Eurogang paradox: Street gangs and youth groups in the U.S. and Europe.* Dordrecht: Kluwer Academic Publishers, pp 153–64.

Marshall, B., Webb, B. and Tilley, N. (2005) *Rationalisation of current research on guns, gangs and other weapons: Phase 1.* London: University College London and Jill Dando Institute of Crime Science.

Matrix Knowledge Group (2007) *The illicit drug trade in the United Kingdom.* London: Home Office.

Matthews, R. and Young, J. (2003) *The new politics of crime and punishment.* Milton: Willan Publishing.

Matza, D. (1964) *Delinquency and drift.* New York, NY: Wiley.

Matza, D. and Sykes, G.M. (1961) 'Juvenile delinquency and subterranean values'. *American Sociological Review*, 26(5): 712–19.

May, T. and Hough, M. (2004) 'Drug markets and distribution systems'. *Addiction Research and Theory*, 12: 549–63.

McAra, L. and McVie, S. (2007) 'Youth justice? The impact of system contact on patterns of desistance from offending'. *European Journal of Criminology*, 4(3): 315–45.

McAra, L. and McVie, S. (2010) 'Youth crime and justice: key messages from the Edinburgh Study of Youth Transitions and Crime'. *Criminology and Criminal Justice*, 10(2): 1–32.

McArdle, H. (2010) 'Scotland among world's worst for drug abuse'. *Herald*, 2 August.

McCallum, F. (2011) *Knife crime*. Edinburgh: Scottish Parliament Information Centre (SPICe).

McCarron, M. (2014) 'It is in the interests of justice and health to decriminalise drug users'. *Scottish Justice Matters*, 2: 17–18.

Mceachran, J. (2003) 'The murder city – Glasgow is the Western European killing capital'. *The Daily Record*, 27 November.

McElrath, K. (2004) 'Drug use and drug markets in the context of political conflict: the case of Northern Ireland'. *Addiction, Research and Theory*, 12, 577–90.

McGrath, T. and Boyle, J. (2011) *The hard man*. Edinburgh: Fairplay Press.

McHugh, R. (2016) 'Anarchism and informal pedagogy: "gangs", difference, deference'. In: S. Springer, M. Lopes de Souza and R.J. White (eds) *The radicalisation of pedagogy: Anarchism, geography and the spirit of revolt*. Lanham, MD: Rowman and Littlefield.

McHugh, R. (2017) 'Inside out outside in: in search of "gangs", finding outside-in groups and the dual parallax of spaces and positions'. *International Journal of Zizek Studies*, 11: 1. Available at: http://zizekstudies.org/index.php/IJZS/article/view/1006

McKay, R. (2006) *The last godfather: The life and crimes of Arthur Thompson*. Edinburgh: Black and White Publishing Limited.

McLean, R. (2017) 'An evolving gang model in contemporary Scotland'. *Deviant Behavior*, 39: 309–21.

McLean, R. (2018a) 'Glasgow's urban landscape and gangs formation'. *Deviant Behavior*, 4 (5): 498-509

McLean, R. (2018b) 'Focus groups with gangsters in Scotland'. *SAGE Research Methods*. Available at: http://dx.doi.org/10.4135/9781526477460

McLean, R. (2018c) 'Making research work: negotiating grounded theory, and exploring those dilemmas involved in interviewing mid-level drug dealing crime gangs in Glasgow'. *SAGE Research Methods Cases*, doi.org/10.4135/9781526439628

McLean, R (forthcoming) (2019) *Criminal trajectories, gang activity and entrepreneurial ventures into Britain's illegal drug trade*. Policy Press: Bristol.

McLean, R., Densley, J. and Deuchar, R. (2017) 'Situating gangs within Scotland's illegal drugs market(s)'. *Trends in Organized Crime*, 21(2): 147–71.

McLean, R., Deuchar, R., Harding, S. and Densley, J. (2018a) 'Putting the "street" in gang: place and space in the organisation of Scotland's drug selling gangs'. *British Journal of Criminology*, 59, 396–415.

McLean, R., Robinson, G. and Densley, J. (2018b) 'The rise of drug dealing in the life of the North American street gang'. *Societies* [open access]. Available at: www.mdpi.com/2075-4698/8/3/90

McPhee, I. (2013) *The intentionally unseen: Illicit & illegal drug use in Scotland.* Saarbrucken, Germany: Lambert Academic Publishing.

McPhee, I., Duffy, T. and Martin, C.R. (2009) 'The perspectives of drug users within the social context of drug prohibition'. *Drugs & Alcohol Today*, 9: 2.

McSweeney, T., Turnbull, P. and Hough, M. (2008) *Tackling drug markets and distribution networks in the UK.* London: KCL.

McVeigh, J. and Begley, E. (2016) 'Anabolic steroids in the UK: an increasing issue for public health'. *Drugs: Education, Prevention and Policy*, 24: 1–8.

Merton, R. (1938) 'Social structure and anomie'. *American Sociological Review*, 3: 372–682.

Miller, J. (2015) 'In every scheme there is a team: a grounded theory of how young people grow in and out of gangs in Glasgow'. Unpublished MEd thesis, University of the West of Scotland.

Miller, W. (1958) 'Lower-class culture as a generating milieu of gang delinquency'. *Journal of Social Issues*, 14: 5–19.

Miller, W.B. (1982) *Crime by youth gangs and groups in the United States. Report to the Office of Juvenile Justice and Delinquency Prevention,* National Institute for Juvenile Justice and Delinquency Prevention, US Department of Justice: Washington, DC.

Miller, W.B. (2000) *The growth of young gang problems in the United States: 1970–98.* Washington, DC: US Department of Justice.

Moffitt, T.E. (1993) 'Adolescence-limited and life-course-persistent antisocial behavior: a developmental taxonomy'. *Psychological Review*, 100: 674–701.

Moore, J. (1991) *Going down to the barrio: Homeboys and homegirls in change.* Philadelphia, PA: Temple University Press.

Morselli, C. (2009) *Inside criminal networks.* New York, NY: Springer.

Moyle, L. and Coomber, R. (2016) 'Bourdieu on supply: utilizing the "theory of practice" to understand complexity and culpability in heroin and crack cocaine user-dealing', *European Journal of Criminology*, 14: 309–28.

Mruck, K. and Breuer, F. (2003) 'Subjectivity and reflexivity in qualitative research: the FQS issues'. *Forum: Qualitative Social Research*, 4 (2): 33.

Murray, K. (2016) 'The value of understanding organised crime business structures and processes: background paper commissioned by the EMCDDA for the 2016 EU drug markets report'. European Monitoring Centre for Drugs and Drug Addiction.

Naylor, R.T. (2009) 'Violence and illegal economy activity: a deconstruction'. *Crime, Law and Social Change*, 52(3): 231–42.

NCA (National Crime Agency) (2013) *Serious and organised crime strategy*. London: Home Office and HM Government.

NCA (2016) 'County lines gang violence, exploitation and drug supply'. National Briefing Report. Drug Threat Team, HM Government.

National Online Manufacturing Information System (NOMIS) (2015) 'Labour market profile – Glasgow City Council'. Available at: www.nomisweb.co.uk/reports/lmp/la/1946157420/report.aspx?town=glasgow#tabempunemp (accessed 9 November 2015).

Paoli, L. (2000) *Pilot project to describe and analyse local drug markets – First phase final report: Illegal drug markets in Frankfurt and Milan*. EMCDDA Scientific Report. Lisboa, Portugal: European Monitoring Centre for Drugs and Drug Addiction.

Paoli, L. (2003) *Mafia brotherhoods: Organized crime, Italian style*. Oxford: Oxford University Press.

Paoli, L. (2004) 'Italian organised crime: Mafia associations and criminal enterprises'. *Global Crime*, 6(1): 19–31.

Park, R.E. and Burgess, E.W. (1924) *The city: Suggestions for investigation of human behavior in the urban environment*. Chicago, IL: Chicago University Press.

Parker, H., Aldridge, J. and Measham, F. (1998) *Illegal leisure: The normalization of adolescent recreational drug use*. London: Routledge.

Patrick, J. (1973) *A Glasgow gang observed*. London: Methuen.

Peakin, W. (2014) 'Side by side: a focus on Bearsden and Drumchapel'. *Inside Politics*, 28 December.

Pearson, G. and Hobbs, D. (2001) *Middle market drug distribution*. Home Office Research Study No. 227. London: Home Office.

Pearson, J. (1995) *The profession of violence: The rise and fall of the Kray twins*. Glasgow: William Collins.

Pitts, J. (2008) *Reluctant gangsters: The changing shape of youth crime*. London: Willan Publishing.

Pitts, J. (2012) 'Reluctant criminologists: criminology, ideology and the violent youth gang'. *Youth Policy*, 109: 27–45.

Preble, E. and Casey, J.J. (1969) 'Taking care of business: the heroin user's life on the streets'. *International Journal of Addict*, 4: 1–24.

Presser, L. and Sandberg, S. (2015) *Narrative criminology: Understanding stories of crime*. New York, NY: NYU Press.

Quinn, J.F. (2001) 'Angels, bandidos, outlaws, and pagans: the evolution of organized crime among the big four 1% motorcycle clubs'. *Deviant Behavior* 22: 379–99.

Rafanell, I. (2013) 'Micro-situational foundations of social structure: an interactionist explanation of effective sanctioning'. *Journal for the Theory of Social Behaviour*, 43(2): 181–204.

Rafanell, I., McLean, R. and Poole, L. (2017) 'Emotions and hyper-masculine subjectivities: the role of affective sanctioning in Glasgow Gangs'. *NORMA: International Journal for Masculinity Studies*, 12 (3-4): 187–204.

Rahman, M. (2016) 'Understanding organised crime and fatal violence in Birmingham: a case study of the 2003 New Year shootings'. *British Society of Criminology*, 16: 71–89.

Ralphs, R., Medina, J. and Aldridge, J. (2009) 'Who needs enemies with friends like these? The importance of place for young people living in known gang areas'. *Journal of Youth Studies*, 12(5): 483–500.

Ratcliffe, J.H. (2008) *Intelligence-led policing*. Devon: Willan Publishing.

Reuter, P. (1983) *Disorganised crime*. Cambridge, MA: MIT Press.

Robertson, I.M.L. (1984) 'Single parent lifestyle and peripheral estate residence: a time-geographic investigation in Drumchapel, Glasgow'. *Town Planning Review*, 55(2). Available at: http://dx.doi.org/10.3828/tpr.55.2.0277j44465371071

Robinson, G., McLean, R. and Densley, J. (2018) 'Working county lines: child criminal exploitation and illicit drug dealing in Glasgow and Merseyside'. *International Journal of Offender Therapy and Comparative Criminology*, doi.org/10.1177/0306624X18806742

Roger, J.J. (2008) *Criminalising social policy: Anti-social behaviour and welfare in a de-civilized society*. Devon: Willan Publishing.

Roldán, M. (1999) 'Cocaine and the "miracle" of modernity in Medellín'. In: P. Gootenberg (ed) *Cocaine: Global histories*. London: Routledge, ch 4.

Rowe, D. and Farrington, D. (1997) 'The familial transmission of criminal convictions'. *Criminology*, 35: 177–201.

Rowe, E., Akman, T., Smith, R.G. and Tomison, A.M. (2013) *Organised crime and public sector corruption: A crime scripts analysis of tactical displacement risks*. Trends and Issues in Crime and Criminal Justice, No. 444. Canberra: Australian Institution of Criminology, Australian Government.

Sampson, R.J. and Laub, J.H. (1993) *Crime in the making: Pathways and turning points through life*. London: Harvard University Press.

Sandberg, S. (2010) 'What can "lies" tell us about life? Notes towards a framework of narrative criminology'. *Journal of Criminal Justice Education*, 21(4): 447–65.

Savona, E. and Vettori, B. (2009) 'Evaluating the cost of organised crime from a comparative perspective'. *European Journal on Criminal Policy and Research*, 15(4): 379–93.

Schelling, T. (1971) 'What is the business of organized crime?', *The Journal of Public Law*, 20: 71–84.

Schiray, M. (2001) *Introduction: Drug trafficking, organised crime, and public policy for drug control*. Oxford: Blackwell Publishers.

Scottish Government (2008) *The road to recovery: A new approach to tackling Scotland's drug problem*. Edinburgh: Scottish Government.

Scottish Government (2009a) *Letting our communities flourish: A strategy for tackling serious organised crime in Scotland*. Edinburgh: Scottish Government.

Scottish Government (2009b) *Assessing the scale and impact of illicit drug markets in Scotland*. Edinburgh: Scottish Government.

Scottish Government (2012) *Scottish Index of Multiple Deprivation*. Edinburgh: Scottish Government.

Scottish Government (2013) *Public perceptions of organised crime in Scotland*. Edinburgh: Scottish Government.

Scottish Government (2014) *Homicides in Scotland 2014*. Edinburgh: Scottish Government.

Scottish Government (2015) *Scotland serious organised crime strategy report*. Edinburgh: Scottish Government.

Scottish Government (2016) 'Scotland's serious organised crime strategy 2016 annual report'. Available at: www.gov.scot/Publications/2016/11/2111/3

Scottish Parliament (2017a) 'SPICe briefing: Drug misuse'. Edinburgh: Scottish Parliament.

Sharp, C., Aldridge, J. and Medina, J. (2006) 'Delinquent youth groups and offending behavior: findings from the 2004 Offending, Crime and Justice Survey'. Home Office Online Report 14/06.

Shaw, C.R. (1930) *The Jack-roller: A delinquent boy's own story*. Chicago, IL: University of Chicago Press.

Shaw, C.R. and McKay, H.D. (1942) *Juvenile delinquency in urban areas*. Chicago, IL: University of Chicago Press.

Sheptycki, J., Ben Jafel, H. and Bigo, D. (2011) 'International organised crime in the European Union'. Available at: www.europarl.europa.eu/document/activities/cont/201206/20120627ATT47775/20120627ATT47775EN.pdf (accessed 20 June 2015).

Short, J.F. (1968) 'Introduction: on gang delinquency and the nature of subcultures'. In: J.F. Short (ed) *Gang delinquency and delinquent subcultures*. New York, NY: Harper and Row.

Shropshire, S. and McFarquhar, M. (2002) *Developing multi-agency strategies to address the street gang culture and reduce gun violence among young people.* Briefing No. 4. Manchester: Steve Shropshire and Michael McFarquhar Consultancy Group.

Sillitoe, P., Sir (1956) *Cloak without dagger.* London: Pan.

Silverstone, D. (2011) 'From Triads to snakeheads: organised crime and illegal migration within Britain's Chinese community'. *Global Crime,* 12(2): 93–111.

Silverstone, D. and Savage, S. (2010) 'Farmers, factories and funds: organised crime and illicit drugs cultivation within the British Vietnamese community'. *Global Crime,* 11(1): 16–33.

Smith, D.J. (2006) *Social inclusion and early desistance from crime.* Edinburgh Study of Youth Transitions, no. 12. Edinburgh: Centre for Law & Society, University of Edinburgh.

SOCA (Serious Organised Crime Agency) (2009) *The UK threat assessment of serious organised crime.* London: Home Office.

Spergel, I.A. (1995) *The youth gang problem.* New York, NY: Oxford University Press.

Spergel, I.A. and Curry, G.D. (1993) 'The National Youth Gang Survey: a research and development process'. In: A. Goldstein and C.R. Huff (eds) *The gang intervention handbook.* Champaign, IL: Research Press, pp 359–400.

Sproat, P.A. (2012) 'Phoney war or appeasement? The policing of organised crime in the UK'. *Trends in Organised Crime,* 15: 313–30.

Squires, P., Silvestri, A., Grimshaw, R. and Solomon, E. (2008) *Street Weapons Commission: Guns, knives and street violence.* London: Centre for Crime and Justice Studies.

Stelfox, P. (1998) 'Policing lower levels of organised crime in England and Wales'. *The Howard Journal of Criminal Justice,* 37: 393–406.

Stevenson, C. (2008) 'Cannabis supply in Northern Ireland: perspectives from users'. In: D. Korf (ed) *Cannabis in Europe.* Lengerich, Germany: Pabst, pp 124–36.

Stryker, S. (1967) 'Symbolic interactionism as an approach to family research'. In: J.G. Manis and B.N. Meltzar (eds) *Symbolic interactionism.* Boston, MA: Allyn and Beacon, pp 371–83.

Sutherland, E.H. (1939) *The professional thief.* Chicago, IL: University of Chicago.

Sutherland, E.H. (1947) *Principles of criminology.* Philadelphia, PA: JB Lippincott.

Swartz, D. (1997) *Culture and power.* Chicago, IL: University of Chicago Press.

Sweeten, G., Pyrooz, D.C. and Piquero, A.R. (2013) 'Disengaging from gangs and desistance from crime'. *Justice Quarterly*, 30(3): 469–500. Available at: https://doi.org/10.1080/07418825.2012.723033

Symeonidou-Kastanidou, E. (2007) 'Towards a new definition of organised crime in the European Union'. *European Journal of Crime, Criminal Law and Criminal Justice*, 15(1): 83–103.

Thompson, T. (1995) *Gangland Britain: Inside Britain's most dangerous gangs*. London: Hodder and Stoughton.

Thompson, K. (2002) *Emile Durkheim*, revised edition. New York: Routledge.

Thornberry, T.P., Krohn, M.D., Lizotte, A.J., Smith, C.A. and Tobin, K. (2003) *Gangs and delinquency in developmental perspective*. Cambridge: Cambridge University Press.

Thrasher, F. (1927) *The gang: A study of 1313 gangs in Chicago*. Chicago, IL: University of Chicago Press.

Trussell Trust (2016) 'Food bank use remains at record high'. Available at: www.trusselltrust.org/2016/04/15/foodbank-use-remains-record-high/ (accessed 17 July 2016).

UNODC (United Nations Office on Drugs and Crime) (2004) 'United Nations Convention against Transnational Organized Crime and the Protocols Thereto'. Available at: www.unodc.org/documents/ middleeastandnorthafrica/organised-crime/UNITED_NATIONS_ CONVENTION_AGAINST_TRANSNATIONAL_ORGANIZED_ CRIME_AND_THE_PROTOCOLS_THERETO.pdf (accessed 1 July 2016).

UNODC (2016) *World drug report*. Vienna: UNODC.

Van der Rakt, M., Nieuwbeerta, P. and De Graaf, N.D. (2008) 'Like father, like son: the relationships between conviction trajectories of fathers and their sons'. *British Journal of Criminology*, 48(4): 538.

Varese, F. (2001) *The Russian mafia: Private protection in a new market*. Oxford: Oxford University Press.

Varese, F. (2010) 'General introduction: what is organized crime?' In: F. Varese (ed) *Organized crime, critical concepts in criminology*. New York, NY: Routledge, pp 1–33.

Varese, F. (2011) *Mafias on the move: How organised crime captures new territories*. Princeton, NJ: Princeton University Press.

Venkatesh, S. (2008) *Gang leader for a day*. London: Penguin Books.

Vigil, J.D. (1988a) *Barrio gangs: Street life and identity in Southern California*. Austin, TX: University Texas Press.

Vigil, J.D. (1988b) 'Group processes and street identity: adolescent Chicano gang members'. *Ethos*, 16(4): 421–45.

Von Lampe, K. (2016) *Organized crime*. Thousand Oaks; CA: Sage.

VRU (Violence Reduction Unit) (2011) *The violence must stop: Glasgow's community initiative to reduce violence. Second year report.* Glasgow: VRU.

Wacquant, L. (2001) 'Deadly symbiosis: when ghetto and prison meet and mesh'. *Punishment & Society*, 3(1): 95–133.

Wacquant, L. (2008) *Urban outcasts: A comparative sociology of advanced marginality*. Cambridge: Polity Press.

Wacquant, L. (2009) 'The body, the ghetto and the penal state'. *Qualitative Sociology*, 32(1): 101–29.

Wacquant, L. (2010) 'Crafting the neoliberal state: workfare, prison fare and social insecurity'. *Sociological Forum*, 25(2): 197–220.

Ward, J. and Pearson, G. (1997) 'Recreational drug use and drug dealing in London: an ethnographic study'. In: D. Korf and H. Riper (eds) *Illicit drug use in Europe*. Amsterdam: University of Amsterdam.

Weerman, F., Maxson, C., Ebensen, F., Aldridge, J., Medina, J. and Gemart, F. (2009) *Eurogang programme manual: Background, development and the use of the Eurogang instruments in multi-site, multi method comparative research*. Europe: Eurogang Network.

Whitehead, S.M. (2002) *Men and masculinities: Key themes and new directions*. Cambridge: Polity Press.

Whittaker, A., Densley, J., Cheston, L., Tyrell, T., Higgins, M., Felix-Baptiste, C. and Havard, T. (forthcoming) 'Reluctant gangsters revisited: the evolution of gangs from postcodes to profits'. *European Journal on Criminal Policy and Research*.

Whyte, W.T. (1942) *Street corner society*. Chicago, IL: University of Chicago Press.

Willis, P. (1977) *Learning to labour: How working class kids get working class jobs*. London: Ashgate.

Windle, J. (2013) 'Tuckers firm: a case study of British organised crime'. *Trends in Organised Crime*, 16: 382–96.

Windle, J. (2017) 'The impact of the Great Recession on the Irish drug market'. *Criminology & Criminal Justice*. Available at: http://dx.doi.org/10.1177/1748895817741518

Windle, J. and Briggs, D. (2015) 'Going solo: the social organisation of drug dealing within a London street gang'. *Journal of Youth Studies*, 18: 1170–85.

Wintour, P. (2015) 'Budget 2015: Osborne to slow pace of welfare cuts'. *The Guardian*, 8 July. Available at: www.theguardian.com/uk-news/2015/jul/07/george-osborne-slow-pace--12bn-welfare-budget-slash (accessed 20 August 2016).

Wirth, L. (1928) *The ghetto*. Chicago, IL: University of Chicago Press.

Wright, R. and Decker, S. (1997) *Armed robbers in action: Stickups and street culture*. Boston, MA: Northeastern University Press.

Yablonsky, L. (1959) 'The delinquent gang as a near group'. *Social Problems*, 7: 108–17.

Young, J. (2007) *The vertigo of late modernity*. California, CA: Sage Publications.

Zhang, S. and Chin, K.L. (2003) 'The declining significance of Triad societies in transnational illegal activities: a structural deficiency perspective'. *British Journal of Criminology*, 43: 469–88.

Index